WE TOOK NAMES

The Time of Vikings, Friends and Family

We learned the game as friends and became unstoppable as teammates. We were a little wild, crazy, and reckless. We were Vikings, name takers, and brothers, and football needed us. We gave it everything.

www.WeTookNames.com

WE TOOK NAMES:
The Time of Vikings, Friends and Family

Copyright © 2016 by Jeffrey G. Rooney

All rights reserved. No part of this publication may be reproduced, distributed, or transmitted in any form or by any means, including photocopying, recording, or other electronic or mechanical methods, without the prior written permission of the author, except in the case of brief quotations embodied in critical reviews and certain other noncommercial uses permitted by copyright law.

Disclaimer: Some of the events described in this book were dangerous and reckless. They are mentioned as historical facts only and are not endorsed or encouraged. They should not be replicated.

ISBN: 978-0-692-78717-5

Library of Congress Control Number: 2016917882

Editing by: Janis Hunt Johnson

Cover design © 2016 Mark Baranowski

Second Edition

Author contact information:
www.WeTookNames.com

This book is dedicated to the game of football, my former teammates, coaches, and family. You gave me much. This is my way to honor you. Thank you for those memories. They were the best of days.

You are missed, big brother. RIP.

My brother Tim and me in Texas, as judo masters.

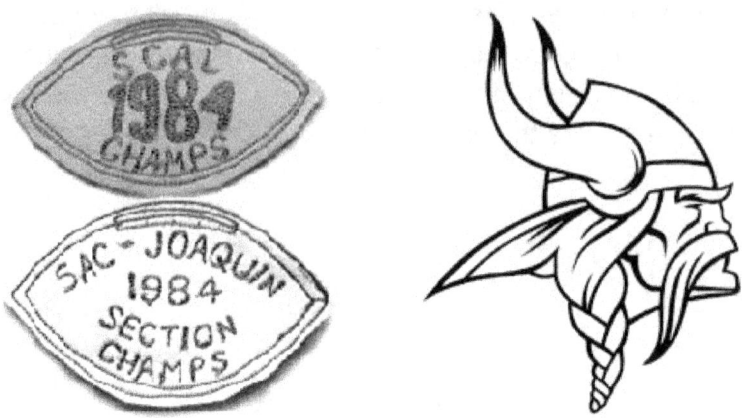

The above left photo of our championship patches was provided by Mark 'Baro' Baranowski #64 on the 1984 12-0 Vanden team. The above right image was our Viking mascot.

We Took Names: The Time of Vikings, Friends and Family follows the five-year journey of a group of friends, their love for the game of football, and their quest for the Sac-Joaquin Section title. Their story details the triumph and tragedy they faced and the wild times they shared to become one of the best football teams in California and in the country. This true story is written by one of those friends.

The below image overlooks the football locker room at Vanden High School—"48 Minutes of Football And A Lifetime To Remember"

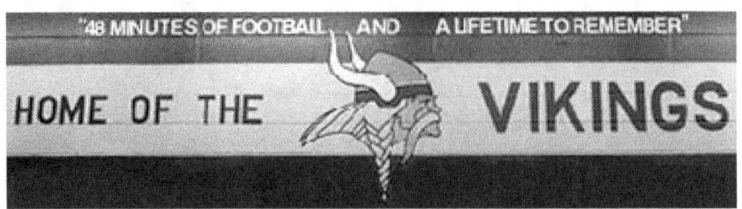

Acknowledgments—Thanks to:

Vanden High School and Travis Unified School District for allowing the use of photos from past yearbooks.

Vacaville Reporter Newspaper for allowing the use of photos and data from past archived newspapers.

Fairfield Daily Republic Newspaper for allowing the use of photos and data from past archived newspapers.

Jeff Martin, teammate #52, for providing personal game photos and archived newspaper photos and data.

David Reyes, teammate #24, for providing photos and data.

John McClellan (and wife Kris), teammate 'Murdock' #65, for providing photos and data.

Mark Baranowski, teammate 'Baro' #64, for designing the book cover and providing photos and data.

Coaches Ronald 'Bev' Beverly and Mike Kelly for providing thoughts on the teams and data.

Mike Holovach (and family), teammate, for providing personal game photos and data.

Timothy O'Donnell and Jon Martin for supplying photos and data from archived newspapers.

Anthony Poulos and Pamela Marcengill for their input.

Special Thanks

To Vanden and Coach Bev, thank you for purchasing me an air helmet so I could play football again in 1984. I can never thank you enough.

To my mom, thank you for allowing me to return to football my senior season after my head injury. I know you were worried for my safety. I'm grateful I had that final year on the gridiron to make a lifetime of memories.

To my dad, thank you for being the team doctor for the Travis Redskins in 1980. We had a lot of fun that season.

To God, thank you for keeping my friends and me injury-free during our final season together. You gave us a wonderful gift that will stay with us all during our time here.

To my coaches from 1980–1984, Coach Kelly, Coach Long, Coach Batchan, Coach Slaybaugh, Coach Hatcher, Coach Moore, Coach Cesna, Coach Conley, Coach Ordez, Coach Larry Hogue, Coach Lyent Hogue, Coach Harden, Coach Newsom, Coach Kiefer and Coach Beverly, you taught my friends and me to play as a team and trust each other. We listened and did. You made us champions. Thank you.

To Jim Wallace, thank you for introducing me to football. It changed my life. I will always owe you, Maniac. I wish you could've finished this journey with us.

Contents

32 Dive—The gridiron gives birth to "No Names"..................1

Young Vikes..52

Perfect and Scoreless—Two coaches, the best and the worst..90

Injury and Loss—The setback...................................122

That 1 Lace and 8 Stitches—Just one more time...........155

576 Minutes in 1984—A coach's time, a team's chance, and a player's return..169

"It's the story of friends, the love of football, and how the two made us the best.

This book details the true story of the 1984 12-0 Vanden Vikings SCAL and Sac-Joaquin Section championship football team, and my friends and my five-year journey from 1980–1984 on the gridiron and off. All the accounts are factual and supported by archived documentation when available. The other information was compiled from the memories of multiple teammates and other witnesses. This story is written through my eyes from what I remember, witnessed, and was a part of. I know this detailed journey is true, because I was there. This is our story."

Jeff Rooney ('Psycho') #55, co-captain of the 1984 Viking squad—Vanden's first undefeated varsity football team. Photos below (L-R): Me in 2016 and 1985.

Note: The newspaper photos and images shown in this book are in the same chronological order they were published during our playing years.

Prologue

The magic that I saw and the legends I played alongside—to say it was amazing would be an understatement. I still felt a connection thinking about that journey. Those unforgettable days long past.
Why were we so good? I had been asked many times. (As a father passed me in uniform to come see his son play) it was a simple answer: we were military brats who loved football, and the gridiron was our classroom.
Like our parents that were serving our country, we were taught unity. Work together to adapt and overcome. Work as one and win at all costs. Defeat wasn't an option. We were raised with certain values—we never saw skin color, and we learned the value of teamwork. Our parents instilled that in us and the teachers to the coaches practiced it. It became second nature in everything we did.
Early on we were taught those core values in our education. Our teachers planted those seeds and our coaches cultivated them. With their direction we flourished. We became unstoppable. We became Titans.

We were no different than a platoon or a squadron—except we wore shoulder pads. The mission's success became our goal. Our mission was to win football games and we did. A lot of them.

I was glad my friend and old teammate David Reyes had invited me to join him at the game. It was the first time in 17 years I had been back. It brought back fond memories as I looked around and emotions stirred in me. I missed those glory days. I knew I couldn't deny it. Like a shadow, they followed me. Mostly when I was alone. Those reflections never left.

Someone called David's and my name. I turned and it was Mrs. Valmore, a PE teacher, from when we were students here at Vanden. She walked over to us from the other side of the chain link fence. She looked the same, as if the years hadn't touched her.

As David and Mrs. Valmore talked my eyes were drawn back to the field. I knew it recognized me. It was an old friend. We were close once. Inseparable. The things I saw there long ago were incredible. I could hear the game whispering to me. It missed how we honored it. We made it proud. I missed how it made me feel.

Studying everything—my eyes could not get enough. The scoreboard stopped me and drew me in. I had watched the scores change on it many times during our years playing football here. It elicited excitement or dread.

I knew I was being lost in the moment. I was being drawn in, and I went willingly. I was on the field with my friends. Doing what we loved. I could feel that green grass under my feet. I was home.

32 Dive
The gridiron gives birth to "No Names"

I could still see the fury in Mr. Fritch's aged eyes. They burned a hole through me as I ran for my life. It must've looked crazy—a teacher chasing a student to the principal's office. Riveted eyes, open mouths, and dropped jaws were frozen to our fox and hound pursuit. It was a scene that would become Golden West lore.

I couldn't believe it, no phone, no television, no friends, and it was the beginning of summer. I'd been banished to my room by my parents for 14 days of isolation. Thankfully I had a window to look out.

I was 13, soon starting 8th grade, and testing my adolescent boundaries. Two gutsy episodes had landed me in the upper far corner of our home alone. Were those two incidents worth the time? I really wasn't sure.

When my teacher Mr. Fritch told me I lost the spelling contest to Tracy Wilkinson, I knew he was wrong. I spelled the word before her, and put my chalk down first. When he sternly told me to sit down I felt compelled not to move. I debated my case. As he walked towards me I kept my distance backing up. He followed me around the room as we circled my classmates. Reminiscent of an Old West showdown we both slowed; then stopped; studying each other. Mr. Fritch's steely-eyed gaze spoke his intention. It wasn't good. Twenty-nine stunned kids fixated—glued to our standoff—apprehensive for what came next.

I could tell Mr. Fritch was serious. He was a former Marine, short and stocky with gray hair. His hearing aids captured our whispers and his trained vision caught our passed notes. Like a military guard he stood watch, always on the ready. He had my best friend Jim and me in front of the classroom doing push-ups daily for talking. Our feet to the wall under the chalkboard on display: struggling. There we stayed until exhaustion prevailed.

Mr. Fritch made the first move, walking faster, then to a jog. Next the running started, with desks being shoved aside as he rambled madly towards me with an invisible net. I escaped—barely—darting out the of classroom into the open quad. I had committed myself. The frenzied chase was on. I ran towards the principal's office. Seventy-five yards in front of me was my protection. I could hear Mr. Fritch barreling after me. Looking back I could see that old 'Devil Dog' look in his eyes. He still had it. Age and years of teaching fueled it more.

I ran into the administration building and right into the principal's office and sat down. I was breathing heavily and safe for the moment. The principal was asking me what had happened as Mr. Fritch entered. I knew I was in trouble as they hovered over me. When my parents found out, I landed 7 days of exile to my room.

The last day of seventh grade was supposed to be fun. I'd just rode my bicycle to Golden West all the way from Vacaville that morning. After school, my friends Carlos and Jim were going to ride their bikes back with me. When Pat Woods and Jim told me about the plan to fill water balloons in the school bathroom and soak some of our classmates with them, I couldn't resist. I was in. Perfect plan and perfect day to drench our friends. We were going to be the talk of the school, and all the girls would think we were really cool.

We had a sink overflowing with filled water balloons when the custodian walked in. He grabbed all three of us by our collars, and off to the principal's office we went, without getting a chance to launch one balloon. It was a good plan that was foiled. I was sent home early and had to ride my bicycle back to Vacaville alone. When my parents found out about my second incident the last month of school, I was screwed. Fourteen days was the punishment and here I sat. Thirteen more days to go.

When that final day of restriction passed and I was free to enjoy what was left of the summer break, I was stoked. I could enjoy our pool, ride my bike, and visit my friends. I was ready to hang out with Jim and the others. There were girls waiting and adventures ahead. I was ready to start the journey and build a reputation.

Before I could leave the confines of our home and wander outside though, I was sat down on the couch by my parents and given a talk. Time to grow up and be responsible. No getting in trouble, talking back, or not listening to authority. My parents ran a pretty strict home. We had to answer incoming phone calls a certain way. My brothers and I were taught to say, "Rooneys' residence, (our name) speaking, how may I help you?" We were instructed to say "Yes sir" and "Yes ma'am." We had chores to do regularly. If we screwed up, we were still stood in corners of the room with our noses to the wall.

I told my parents I would try harder and not get into anymore trouble. I was given that final stern look of 'don't screw it up' and released to smell the fresh air of freedom.

I was the third of four boys. Sean was the oldest. Tim followed, then me and Craig. Only 4.5 years separated us. Sean was born on the same day as my dad and carried the same name. We were raised Catholic, were altar boys, and went to Sunday School. We had been Cub Scouts, then Boy Scouts. We were your typical middle-class home, and all our friends would say we had the perfect family. I had to agree with them. I came from a good home and had a great childhood.

My family. (Left to right) My mom, Craig, Sean, me, my dad and Tim.

I wanted to follow in my brothers' footsteps. They were great athletes. They excelled at baseball and wrestling. They had lots of friends and were well-liked. I had played baseball starting at tee-ball to majors, and I had just finished my second year of wrestling. Being older, Sean and Tim had more freedoms, and were having fun escapades. Craig and I were kept on closer reins, and not as fortunate yet.

I was only off restriction for about a month when I heard those four words that would change my life. Come out for football? Oh I wanted to. I told Jim I wanted to play badly but I wasn't sure if my parents would let me. Jim Wallace had been my best friend for almost a year. I still remembered the first day I met him. It was in PE class and Jim was kneeling, tying his sneakers, when a bully tried to kick him in the face. Jim quickly turned the tables and had the bully cornered, while I handled the bully's accomplice. After that encounter we became inseparable. We were peanut butter and jelly. We mixed well together but were messy sometimes in our adventures. Jim was going to play his second year on the Travis Redskins and wanted me to join him. It was only about 30 days earlier I had been paroled by my parents from my bedroom incarceration. I told Jim I would ask them if they would let me play. I didn't have high hopes, and told him not to, either. I sure wanted to join Jim and my other friends, though.

I was surprised with the answer I got when I asked if I could play: yes. I could play, but I had to get myself to practices after school, as my dad was working as a Physician Assistant at David Grant Hospital on Travis Air Force Base, and my mom worked nights as a registered nurse.

My mom would be sleeping when I needed to get to football after school. I told my parents I would get myself there, and I believe they thought I would quit after a few weeks. I was going to have to ride my bicycle seven miles each way, to and from practice.

Jim and I turned in our paperwork at the Youth Center to play for the Travis Redskins midget football team in the Pop Warner league. My dad decided he would be the team doctor and would go to the games. It was all coming together.

My dad was a wealth of medical knowledge, so I knew my teammates would be in good hands. He had just been offered a job to work at the White House as a PA. One recent afternoon he had returned from lunch to find the hospital brass all assembled, awaiting him. Dad's boss informed him the White House had called to speak with him. Dad thought it might be a friend of his from the Air Force Physician's Assistant program who was working there. He returned the call and spoke to his friend. The man was leaving his position and was asked to recommend someone. He'd picked my dad to replace him. My parents didn't want to move to Washington, D.C., so Dad declined the offer.

My parents had met when they were both in the Air Force. My mom was an officer, a 2nd Lieutenant, and my dad was enlisted, an E-4. He was 20 and she was 21. When my mom got pregnant with Sean, she gave up her career to be a mother and support my dad in the military. It was a selfless decision. My mom later continued her career as a RN. If my brothers and I got hurt wrestling around, we were medically covered at home.

The day came when we were issued our Redskin football uniforms. They were white helmets, one white and one red jersey, and white pants. We also received white practice jerseys that were mesh, and left our stomachs exposed. I knew the girls would like that.

As I watched my friends trying on their shoulder pads and helmets, I realized it wasn't like baseball or wrestling. When I put on my helmet for the first time and looked through the facemask, I could see the difference in the sports. I was hooked from that moment. My brother Sean had played football for a short time as a sophomore at Vanden High School. Other than that, my family didn't follow the game. I was wading into new territory.

My friends and I were Mustangs at Golden West. (It was known for its population of seagulls that would defile our lunches.) It was the junior high school for the Travis Unified School District and located directly outside the gates of Travis AFB in Northern California, between the communities of Vacaville, Fairfield, and Suisun. It was an 'Air Force' school. Most students had a parent stationed at Travis, also known as TAFB. The Travis Redskins football team, though, wasn't affiliated with Golden West, even though we were going to practice behind the school. It was sanctioned by the base.

Besides the issued parts of the uniform, I was responsible to provide some of my own things. I purchased new cleats and a mouthpiece. I was excited the night I boiled the mouthpiece in water, stuck it in my mouth, bit down, and molded it to my teeth. As I sat in front of the television wearing it, my brothers began the ritual "Va Va Voom" and the "Va Va Vee" taunts I often heard. The three of them liked to tease me because both my upper front teeth crossed, forming an inward 'V.' Like a nursery rhyme they sang it in chorus—repeatedly. It was worse than nails on a chalkboard. Withstanding their unrelenting barrage, I wore the mouthpiece for several hours.

Sitting there I felt like I was already a football player, and we hadn't even practiced yet. I wondered if wearing the mouthpiece nightly to bed would straighten my teeth. I knew, though, if my brothers saw my homemade retainer the whole school and neighborhood would know. The teasing would be merciless. I thought better of it, and took it out at bedtime.

I needed a daily plan to get to practice. Jim and I put our heads together to figure one out. After I would get home from school in Vacaville by bus, I would change quickly into my uniform. I would then ride my bicycle to his house on TAFB and we would ride our bikes to Golden West. We felt confident the plan would work.

When the school bell rang the first day of practice, I ran to the bus. I was excited and ready. I could barely contain myself. Visions of cheerleaders screaming for us to play harder filled my head.

Upon my arrival at home, I dropped my books and threw on my uniform consisting of shoulder pads, cleats and helmet as fast as I could. The shoulder pads made me feel stronger. I felt—powerful, invincible, indestructible—I felt immortal. Even though I was a Redskin, I felt like a Titan. I jumped on my olive green four-speed bicycle for the long ride to the base. I wasn't worried it didn't have brakes, I had mastered riding it without them. The 'Beast' was fast; that's why I liked it. That's what I called the bike. It was ferocious when peddled. It was so quick it seemed to devour the road—so I wrapped tape around the front bar and drew sharp red teeth on it with a marker to emphasize its speed and hunger for the roadway. I knew the Beast wouldn't fail me during the long trips.

    I rode to Vanden Road and peddled as quickly as I could. Vanden was a two-lane country road that wasn't very wide. It was curvy, wavy and remote. I needed to be careful to avoid the vehicles that would whiz by me. I kept looking over my left side, to see if a car was coming. There was no shoulder on the road, and I had seven miles to go. I was safe though, I thought. I had my football helmet and pads on, so if a car hit me I wouldn't be hurt too badly. After all, I was a Titan.

    I knew as I approached 'Black Bridge' I would have to stop and climb up the steep embankment. It was an old steel railroad bridge (which was painted black) that crossed Vanden Road. It wasn't used by trains anymore but it was a great hideout for us kids. As I came upon it I slowed my peddling and used my cleats on the ground as brakes. I carried the Beast up the embankment onto 'Farmer's Land.' It was called that because all around the railroad tracks, which sat up on a small ridge, was private farmland. It was wide open fields fenced in with barbed wire and occupied by cows, bulls, and rattlesnakes.

    Many times I had heard if a farmer caught anyone on their land they would shoot them in the rear with rock salt pellets. I was told the pellets stung a lot but they wouldn't kill me. It made me uneasy but I was willing to take the risk to play football with my friends. Plus I still had my pads on to protect me. Maybe it was an urban legend. Maybe it wasn't. I didn't know and wasn't going to take a chance, so I still kept my helmet on even though I was hot and sweating. My head was on a swivel. From a distance I must've looked nervous because I was swiveling left to right looking for farmers.

I pushed the Beast along the railroad tracks near Travis AFB. I lifted it over a waist-high chain link fence that was behind Center Elementary School. I was now on the base. I knew it well because we had lived there for several years before moving to Vacaville.

On the way to Jim's I passed 'Suicide Hill.' It was a steep road where we tested our nerves. It sloped down towards the base housing with a cross street at the bottom. All the kids I knew and many more before us would ride their bikes down it. Some attempted skateboards and roller skates. It was risky because the grade of the road would cause us to accelerate at a very high speed. Most of the time the outcome was pre-scripted. It ended with a crash, road rash, pain, bandages, and sometimes stitches or broken bones. The nickname fit perfectly. It was suicide to test the hill; but we still tried to conquer it. My friend Kelly Majerus lived at the top of it. The water treatment plant for the base was there and her grandpa ran it.

I continued to Jim's and he was waiting for me in uniform, helmet in hand. We then rode our bikes to practice. On the way I must've asked him a thousand questions about football.

There weren't enough players out there the first day. I counted them. I didn't know a lot about football because I only started watching it one year earlier because of the Dallas Cowboys cheerleaders. I did know though, there needed to be 11 players for offense and 11 for defense. It seemed to me we didn't have enough for a team.

My other two best friends, Jeff Martin and Glenn (Kelly) Barretto, were going to play for the Travis Redskins too. They had played the previous season with Jim, and they all knew what to expect. Jeff was in his fifth year of playing football and Glenn the same.

Jim and I were about the same size in height, weight and physique. Jeff was a little thinner than us though the same height. Glenn too was about the same height but stockier than the three of us. He had a rugged build like an ox. Glenn was fairly new to Golden West. He was from the Philippines and had played football there.

Looking at the three of them in uniform I had confidence in their abilities. They looked like football players. I didn't know what to expect, but I knew my friends would guide me. Though I was hooked the first time I put on the helmet, I felt like a fish out of water. I was nervous. My palms were sweaty and my stomach queasy.

The head coach, Mike Kelly, was Glenn's stepdad. By his emotion when he talked I could tell he had a love for the game. I listened intently because I wanted to learn as much as I could from him. I was going to watch all my friends closely too. I wanted to emulate how they played. I really wanted to be a good football player.

We warmed up and stretched, then did some hitting, blocking, and tackling drills. Coach Kelly was trying to get a feel for who could do what. I knew that much. He placed some of the players in positions and was going through some offensive plays. Several kids tried out for different spots. He motioned me over and told me to line up in the left side of the wishbone backfield, which had two halfbacks side by side with a fullback in front of them. Glenn was the fullback, and I had heard he was really good. Watching him that day at practice, I agreed. Coach Kelly said we were going to run a 32 Dive. He told me I was to follow Glenn between the center and the left guard, and the quarterback would turn and hand me the ball as I passed him. It was going to be my first football play. He directed me how to get into a three-point stance and how to position my hands to receive the ball. As I readied myself it felt right to be in uniform about to get the football. This was my game—I just knew it.

Coach Kelly blew his whistle, the ball was hiked by Jeff, and Glenn took off. I followed him and the quarterback turned and handed me the ball. When I got to the line of scrimmage I dove as far as I could. I let out a loud grunt as my feet left the ground. I landed hard on the football hitting me in the stomach. It knocked the wind out of me. Coach Kelly walked towards me (scratching his head) as I struggled to my feet, gasping for air. I stood proudly, because I was happy with my performance. I held onto the ball.

With a bewildered look he asked why I dove. Standing tall I responded, "I ran a 32 Dive sir." His hand pushed up the bill of his cap as he looked at me. Pausing for a moment staring, he stated the word dive was just the name of the play. "You were supposed to run upfield following Glenn. Run, not dive. You're a running back. This isn't aquatics and your pads aren't floaties!" he said shaking his head. In that moment I became the new guy with no clue how to play football. It wasn't the initial result I had hoped for to start my gridiron career. The guys teased me for the rest of the practice; and that one play, 32 Dive, followed me all season long. I was grateful it didn't become my nickname. It would've been embarrassing.

When practice ended, Jim headed home, and I left from Golden West for my long lonely ride back to Vacaville. My seven-mile trek back was much slower because my legs were tired and sore. When I arrived safely home and had dinner, my parents asked how I enjoyed my first day of football practice. I told them I liked it and shared everything—except the 32 Dive.

At dinner my mom commented it was time for a haircut. My hair was disheveled from sweating and wearing my helmet for hours at practice and riding the Beast to and from. I had the 'Helmet Head' look. I was scared as I glanced at her. Not my hair and not now. I had already been teased throughout the practice. I knew I couldn't handle another day like that tomorrow.

My mom had always cut our hair since we were little. She was a hands-on mother. She did everything for us boys—from making all our birthday cakes from scratch with the coolest designs and icing, helping design our Halloween costumes, to fixing all the repairs in our torn jeans, and trust me, we were hard on them. She had been a den mother during our time as scouts. You name it she did it. That included our haircuts. When we were small she cut the front of our hair by placing a bowl on our head. Then she went through the rubber band phase, where all of our hair was put in rubber bands and cut the same length. The personalized haircuts had ended recently, though. When Sean was on the bus sitting behind

Tim on their way to school one morning, he looked at the back of Tim's head and his hair was cut at an angle. It looked bad, he thought to himself. Sean then realized his probably looked as bad—if not worse. Begging from us four boys ended my mom's 'experiments.' We started getting our hair done by professionals.

I was worried as I sat there reliving those past experimental home cuts. Mom probably saw the terror in my eyes, so I was relieved when she said I could get it trimmed on Saturday at Supercuts.

The above photo shows my brother Tim wearing one of his homemade Halloween costumes designed with my mom's assistance.

The next day when we arrived at practice there were fifteen kids in uniform we didn't know. Coach Kelly explained they were from Fairfield and Suisun because we didn't have enough bodies to fill a squad. The Youth Center on TAFB was going to pull the team if we didn't get more players, so these new guys from different cities were brought in to join us.

We stared back and forth and neither side wanted to make the first move. We didn't trust them. They weren't from Golden West. A few "knock-it-off you knuckleheads" from Coach Kelly got the practice going. During tryouts both of our sides tried to impress the other with our skills and talent. Three of the new kids—Mike Lindsey, Anthony Gonsalves, and Kenny Herbert—were standouts. They would become an important part of our season.

I had many friends on the team besides Jim, Jeff, and Glenn. David Reyes, John McClellan, Mark Baranowski, Bryan Batchan, Mike Holovach, Pat Woods, Carlos Ponce, Darren Rysden, Greg Kling, and others were teammates. I had known most of the guys for years.

That practice I landed the starting left halfback position because Coach Kelly stated he liked how I hustled and hit. He explained I was going to be a blocking back for the right side halfback, which was going to be shared by two players, Bryan Batchan and Renard Peacock. I also made the starting right side defensive end. Jim was assigned as the middle linebacker and an offensive guard. Jeff would be the center and left side defensive end, and Glenn was the fullback and left side linebacker. David and Carlos made cornerbacks, Mark would be an offensive and defensive lineman, John would be a defensive lineman and tight end, Mike and Pat offensive and defensive lineman, Greg a defensive lineman and Darren a receiver. The team was coming together.

Coach Kelly stressed discipline, hustling, aggression, tackling hard, running through defenders, and playing from whistle to whistle. I watched Coach Kelly closely because I wanted to learn as much as I could. It was obvious to me that he enjoyed the game of football and coaching. Coach Kelly was a big man with a booming voice. I liked him. He was everything I thought a football coach should be. Bryan's dad assisted at practices along with two other men, Mr. Long and Mr. Slaybaugh.

A week later we played a scrimmage in the Sacramento area and were beaten. The next day at practice Coach Kelly sat us all down. As he looked around he called us "No Names." He said we were like the undefeated 1972 17-0 Miami Dolphins championship football team. He saw something special in us, yet no one knew who we were. Together as a squad, though, we could be unstoppable. That was the moment we began to have faith in our newfound teammates and friends.

I felt like a rock star in 8th grade. I feathered my hair and carried a big comb in my back pocket. I wore bell bottom pants, and I was playing football. I loved the game and it felt natural to me. I knew it was the sport I was born to play. I was on a high one morning when I went to my first-period class. That moment quickly burst when my teacher addressed the classroom. She had been there a long time and had a reputation. She was liked but stern. She looked around at each of us sitting there and stated, "This is my class. I am the teacher. If you screw up, your ass is grass, and I am the lawnmower!" She was upset about something. Man, I thought to myself, she is tougher than Mr. Fritch. I felt like a balloon deflating. I was no longer a running back in her class. I was just one of 30 students that had better not screw up.

Within a few days Jim, Glenn, Mark, John and I and some of my other teammates were testing Mr. Elkins' swing. Not Jeff, though. He really was the smart one in the group. He had the sense we lacked.

It was known at Golden West that it was a rite of passage for a boy to take a '10 swing' from Mr. Elkins. (The girls loved watching us get paddled.) My brothers before me had felt the thunder. If we talked in class, didn't do homework, or had some other infraction, that 10 swing from the paddle could remove detention or a leg from a F grade. Hands on the desk, all the kids watching, with Mr. Elkins playing it up by rotating his arm with practice swings. Then POW!! It hurt a lot, we would jump around in pain, but we all laughed. If it had a name—it had to be mean. The thick wooden enforcer was about three feet long. It had holes through it, so it was aerodynamic. Mr. Elkins kept that well-used intimidator on display next to his desk for all to see. From our seats it looked menacing; but it silently dared us—"try me." (I did a few times.)

We won our first game and the team played well. We trusted each other and realized then we could do anything on the gridiron, as long as we followed Coach Kelly's advice. We won our second and third games too. Our home games were played on Saturdays at Vanden High School on the George Gammon Field, which was down the road from Golden West. The first time I stepped on the grass there, I was in awe. I felt like I was in the Texas Stadium where the Dallas Cowboys played. The Vanden Vikings had a reputation of their own. They were winners. Though a small school, some of their players were the best in the area.

Jim and I would ponder what it was like to play at Vanden. We would walk the field and track, and sit in the stands before Redskin games. We would entertain each other with talk of great things we would do on the gridiron as Vikings. In our stories we always won the big game and the championship. We loved football and we couldn't help ourselves but share fantasized tales of glory. Each new story got bigger and better.

I was learning the game but kept watching my friends and teammates closely. Each had something I could learn that would make me a better player. Glenn was the star on our team. We all knew it. He would power over and crush opponents as he bulled up the field carrying the ball. Renard and Bryan were fun to watch. Both had amazing speed and finesse. Bryan, though, ran with more. He ran fearlessly. I admired his style. My job was simple as a running back. Block for Renard and Bryan, and hit our opponents hard. I liked the assignment and relished knocking down my targets.

My new friends and teammates—Mike, Anthony, and Kenny—became starters on our squad. They brought big hits and big personalities. They were fun to be around and we blended well together. I was glad they were part of our Redskin team. We were better because of them. Long after our season would end their friendships would remain. Years later we would cross paths on the gridiron.

When my dad brought home the Morse Electrophonic Stereo System from the BX on TAFB, all four of us boys were stoked. We were lucky because it was the only one they had in stock. The blinking of the colored lights to each beat of a song was like a jukebox and strobe light combined. It was the talk of our friends; and Craig, Tim, Sean, and I had parties in our upstairs family room in the dark with the colored lights flashing. Our 'party machine' came with four options to play music—records, cassettes, 8-track tapes, or the radio. We used them all, and all the time. Music was always on in our family room because the lights entertained us, probably more than the music itself. All our friends and kids in the neighborhood knew of the infamous party machine. It was the ultimate boom box. Jim and I would blare the theme from 'Rocky' and leave the upstairs windows open while we lifted weights in the backyard at night. Besides entertaining us, my dad's gift helped keep us in shape for football. It became our workout partner, and was responsible for helping me gain 10 lbs. of muscle in six months.

The above photo shows our infamous Morse party machine and workout partner.

Our team the Redskins was earning a reputation, and so were we. Our classmates knew who the players on the squad were, because on the Friday before a game we would wear our jerseys to school. Girls flocked to us.

While we prepared for our future opponents behind Golden West, we could see and hear the Vanden High School junior varsity and varsity squads practicing. They were in direct eyeshot from us across a large open field about one-third of a mile away.

Our Redskin cheerleaders were also classmates. They practiced behind Golden West near us. All the bouncing around, giggling and laughter was distracting at times. It was hard not to watch them; but if Coach Kelly caught us looking we were running laps as punishment.

The open field behind Golden West School is shown in the above photo. Vanden High School is at the center top. Golden West Junior High is shown in the below photo. Both photos provided by teammate David Reyes #24.

When not playing football together or at school, we were always hanging out as friends. Every Saturday evening Jim would stay the night at my home or I would stay at his. It became a regular thing every week.

I had a crush on our head Redskin cheerleader, Cathy Price. I wanted to go visit her one warm Friday evening, so Glenn, Jim, and I walked to her house. It was dusk when we arrived, and she didn't know we were coming by to talk. Instead of going to the front door I walked around to the back of her home where I knew her window was located. It was as if Mother Nature was in on our plan: we were being quiet and the night was still. I knocked on Cathy's window. Nothing. I knocked again, and nothing. The third time as I knocked, I spoke, telling her it was me. I was too late in my announcement.

It was one of those moments where something just doesn't feel right. I could feel the hair on the back of my neck stand up. (It was just a weird feeling.) I asked Jim to go to the corner of the home and keep an eye out to see if anyone was coming. As Jim approached it, he turned abruptly and began running in the opposite direction behind me. He looked like a world-class sprinter. He was gone in a flash. Right then, I saw a light on the ground. Cathy's dad, who was a large man, came around the corner of the house and pointed a flashlight directly at me. He ran the Security Police on TAFB. As the light glared in my face—blinding my eyes—he yelled, "Freeze or I'll crack my flashlight over your head!" I was terrified. All I could see was Mr. Fritch's flaming red eyes. My reaction was to follow Jim and run. I took off, letting my halfback feet fly as fast as they could move. I must've left a dust trail because I bolted like the Road Runner. Glenn followed our lead and ran like his own cartoon character.

We darted across open yards behind homes on the air base, with Cathy's dad in hot pursuit. Jim and I were on the right and Glenn was to our left. As we ran I could see the flashlight just a few feet behind Glenn. I screamed, "Run faster!" My voice squealed like a cheerleader encouraging him. We crossed onto a street with Jim and I still on the right and Glenn to the left of us. The flashlight followed one step behind him. As we ran for our lives not knowing why, Jim and I continued to yell, "Run faster Glenn! He'll crack that flashlight over your head!" I could see the whites of Glenn's eyes. They were as big as the moon and filled with fear.

We ran about a mile before we finally lost Cathy's dad. He was determined to catch us but we were more determined to avoid capture. Jim and I ended up laying on the ground in the dugouts at the baseball fields across from the Youth Center. We were only about 100 yards from Jim's home, but we were frozen in place. Glenn eventually found us and we all hid there for about two hours—hiding from roving patrol cars with flashing lights—as police dogs barked in the distance. Eventually we made it back to Jim's house, exhausted and dirty.

The following Monday at school I asked Cathy why her dad chased us. She was embarrassed and apologetic for him pursuing us across the base. Someone had been harassing her family nightly, and she thought it was the same person knocking on her window. She said she knew it wasn't us because I lived in Vacaville—seven miles away. I joked asking how much was the reward on the wanted posters for the three stooges that got away. I knew Cathy's dad must've been furious we had slipped the noose (since he ran the security police) and we escaped his clutches.

    Every week the team played better together. We had our timing down on offense, and we were aggressive to the ball on defense. Our offensive machine was explosive. We primarily ran the football. We were a ground team, and Glenn was the engine of it. He was a powerful fullback who barreled over defenders like a steamroller. Most of the running was up the gut, displacing linebackers or leveling them. The outside yardage was gained by Bryan or Renard. Both were jets when given room. I rarely ran the football, maybe four times a game.

    The offensive line opened wide holes and kept the defense at bay while the ball was moved upfield. The line was anchored by Jeff at center, and even though he was smaller, he was an excellent blocker. He used his experience of five years in the trenches to move larger defensive linemen around. The rest of the offensive line—Jim, Mark, Pat and Mike—were crushing the opponents across from them. They dominated each week.

    John and Darren had great hands. They were catching balls most other receivers would drop. David and Carlos on the opposite side stopped receivers from doing their jobs. They worked well, shutting down passing games. Coach Kelly beamed from the sidelines. We were making him proud.

    It hurt the team when we lost Darren to a broken leg at practice. He missed the rest of the season, yet he still attended the games to support the squad.

Our next game, we faced Richmond at their field. It was mainly dirt. I looked around for a blade of grass and couldn't find one. We were playing in the dust bowl. The yardage lines were getting destroyed with each tackle. One offensive play I was given the opportunity to run the ball up the gut. I barreled about 25 yards when one of the Richmond cornerbacks hit me on the left hip with his helmet. He struck me hard. The impact jarred me, causing my feet to flip above my head, and I came down on my facemask still holding the football. When I got up from the ground my face was covered in dirt and my mouth was full of it. I took my helmet off to shake it out and clear my mouth by spitting. I was dazed. As I went to the huddle I kept asking my teammates if they saw what happened. That hit caused my feet to go straight up in the air, I kept repeating—like a broken record.

Though I got hammered that one play, we showed Richmond we were the hitters. We shut them down and left the field with another win. We were on a roll as Redskins. In our little world of Pop Warner midget football, we were making names for ourselves. We were becoming the team to beat in our league.

On defense, Jim and Glenn proved to be vicious hitters who put fear in running backs. John and Mike kept quarterbacks scrambling, while the rest of the team was a dam against offensives trying to gain yardage. I didn't have to look far to see talent on our squad. I just had to turn my head right or left, and it was there. The guys hustled non-stop. Opposing running backs were hit by 5 or more of my teammates each and every play. A run play by our opponents always ended the same way: a huge pile-up of Redskins laying on top of their ball carrier. Our team song became Queen's 'Another One Bites the Dust.' It blared from a boom box after each victory.

    Our first introduction was meaningful and it became a special place for me. Out of the 100 it was my favorite. It's where the line in the sand was drawn. Snort, growl, and prepare. The one-yard line was everything; paydirt or stopped short. The fifty-yard line had nothing on it—not even close. It was the hardest challenge and the most rewarding during those 48 minutes. It brought out the most in me, so I enjoyed our visits.

    My dad was attentive to any injured player. He was a very good Physician's Assistant and an encyclopedia of medical knowledge. Our Redskin team was in great hands. He was the very first PA at TAFB, and one of the first in the Air Force. He had worked hard to get where he was in the medical field. Dad was a go-getter.

    At one point he had written the Air Force Times to complain that the PA's were performing the same tasks as some of the doctors in the Air Force, yet they were enlisted and not officers. Upon joining the PA program all the candidates were told they would be commissioned as officers. Upon completion of the program, though, they remain enlisted. After Dad's letter was published in the magazine, the Air Force made all the PA's officers. One week my dad left work on Friday as a E-8 and returned on Monday as a Captain. Not sure if my dad's letter was the reason for the change but it was coincidental. We were proud of him for taking a stand.

    My dad had wanted to obtain his Master's Degree at UC Davis College, but it was only open to Nurse

Practitioners, not PA's. He wrote the school requesting to join their program. UC Davis honored his request and opened their Master's program to PA's. Dad went on to complete their program and earn his Master's degree, becoming a PA/NP.

Mom in her own right had a degree in nursing and was building an amazing resume. She, like Dad, worked hard on her career. She made sacrifices for us boys and our family. There was no doubt she loved us. My friends were probably right—we came from the perfect home.

After Tim received his learner's permit to drive, he would beg daily to shuttle us around. So when given the opportunity to get behind the wheel of our new custom van one day, he couldn't resist. He drove well, until he was instructed to park in the driveway. Instead of hitting the brake—he stepped on the gas. Our closed garage door split in two, and our bikes were smashed, except for the Beast. Tim escaped punishment because it was an accident, but he cemented himself with the reputation of being a poor driver.

Jim accompanied us to church one Sunday, and I knew I had an opportunity I couldn't pass up. He had never received communion, so he wasn't sure what to do. He asked me for instruction. As I stood behind him in line I couldn't help but snicker as he belted out—"Hallelujah! Glory to God in the Highest! God is Great!"—instead of the proper response 'Amen.' The priest's face was priceless. Needless to say, my parent's weren't too happy with me. And neither was Jim.

Another time I got the upper hand on him was when I had mentioned, "Let's see who's the better escape artist." He jumped at the chance. No knots were the rules, we both agreed. He tied me to a dinner chair in our kitchen with rope. He was proud of his work when he finished securing me in place. When given clearance, I struggled and struggled. With grunts and slow movements I freed myself. It wasn't easy and took me ten minutes. Jim bragged he could beat my time. I had other plans for him.

When he sat down boasting he was going to slip out easily, I chuckled to myself. I tied him to the chair in knots on top of knots. There was no way he was going to beat my time frame. At the sound of "Go" Jim struggled. He twisted and twisted. He saw me trying to contain my laughter. He knew I cheated. Then I initiated part 'B' of my plan. I took out all the thick, gooey liquids from the refrigerator and cupboards. I took out everything from peanut butter, syrup, mustard, and ketchup to chocolate syrup. I took out flour. I took out marshmallows, olives, and anything else I could find.

Jim's eyes got big as his struggles got more intense. There was no saving him. I spent the next ten minutes turning him into a sloppy mess. His hair, ears and nostrils were filled with the kitchen goodies. I was laughing so hard I almost threw up. Jim, though, was fuming. He wanted to pummel me. That only made me laugh harder. After seeing his situation was futile, Jim swore not to touch, hurt, or pound me. Jim's word was gold. I knew it was but I still untied him carefully, making sure I had a route to evade him. Jim, unlike me, lived up to his word when released from his messy confinement. He never retaliated. Even after showering and thinking about it more, he never sought retribution. My taunts had no effect. I went unpunished. I grinned like a Cheshire cat, but I knew Jim would get me again at some point.

The Midget Pop Warner league had a 140-pound limit we all had to make, and Jim struggled to keep his weight under that limit before games. If he got close, Coach Kelly had him running laps at practice to ensure he would be able to play, or sitting in the sauna at the base gym. Jim's problem was he liked to eat too much. I could have told Coach Kelly how to keep his weight down—let me eat Jim's lunch daily.

Prior to practice one afternoon I arrived at Jim's house hungry. I asked for something to eat. Jim said they had leftover meatloaf from the night before. "It tastes like crap!" he said trying to dissuade me. It looked good so I cut a piece for our ride to Golden West. One bite was all it took. Jim was right. I didn't want to throw it on the ground for some poor dog to eat, so I shoved it up the tailpipe of a nearby car. As we peddled away Jim said, "I don't think their car will be running well now." We both laughed imagining the look on the mechanic's face when he found the cause. (What the hell?)

Each week our offensive calls had surprises in them for the opponents. One play, the Slaybaugh Shuffle, involved the center, Jeff, hiking the ball and setting it on the ground for the left or right guard to pick up and run with. Glenn and I would lead the charge and the guard would follow us upfield. It was quite inventive, and worked when we used it. We were the football version of the 'Bad News Bears.'

Coach Kelly taught us the aggressive team would be the winning team. His theory was working for our squad because we continued to dominate on the field and win on the scoreboard. I saw many big hits by my friends as they ran through players and drove them into the turf. All the guys were hitters. They liked hard hits. Sticks—as we called them—were important to us as players. We liked seeing the colored collision marks on our helmets. The more you had, the more bragging rights you received. They became our individual notches of glory.

During school hours the teachers and students would ask us questions about our exploits. It was as if we were being interviewed by reporters for newspaper articles. In our little world we were 13- and 14-year-old celebrities. It was kind of cool. The girls liked associating with us. We enjoyed that too, because we had groupies. We were living new lives. Football had given birth to us.

One of our games Jim arrived in uniform wearing bright pink pants. His mom had washed his full uniform in one load and the red dye from the jersey bled. Here was our middle linebacker looking like a flamingo. Coach Kelly was not amused. He told Jim to roll in the dirt to mask the ridiculous color. "Hey Pink Lady!" one of the guys yelled mocking Jim. (referencing the girl gang from the movie 'Grease') As we lined up for our next defensive play, Jim whined, "I'm not a Pink Lady!" From our stances all ten of us turned our heads and belted, "Yes, you are!" The refs and our opponents snickered at our back-and-forth. The only person who didn't find it humorous was Jim. We made him wear that embarrassing label for the game enjoying plenty of laughs at his expense. And we had many.

Each week the teams we faced in games continued to fall short on the scoreboard. We went through the entire season undefeated. We beat Hillsdale, Martinez, Pinole, Berkley, Richmond, Fairfield, Vacaville, Woodland, West Sacramento, and Napa. It was an exciting time for us. The hard practices had paid off, and we were headed to the playoffs.

Playoff selections were picked, and Compton was chosen to be our opponent. They came up north by bus to face us. We didn't know what to expect because they were from a larger area in Southern California. I wasn't a mind reader, but I think the team was excited, nervous, and a little intimidated because of the unknown factor facing a squad from the 'big city.'

The above photo shows the Compton Pop Warner team arriving by bus. Photo provided by teammate Mike 'Spartacus' Holovach.

Prior to their arrival, we were informed that each of us Redskins had to take one Compton player home to stay with us the night before the game. The player that was selected to come to my house was a nice guy. In the short time I knew him I liked him. I also knew at the game the following day I was going to try and knock his head off. After all, it was football and losing was never an option. Friendships with opponents ceased for those 48 minutes of play.

The morning of the game I shared breakfast with the Compton player; after a handshake, that was it. The line was drawn. I was a Redskin—he wasn't.

Game day against Compton seemed different from the other contests we played. It was more serious. Glenn looked like he was made of granite. Jim reminded me of a young Dick Butkus and Jeff didn't crack a smile. The other guys looked like they were ready for battle. We were playing a team from the southern part of the state for the playoffs. We all knew it was a big deal.

From the first play on, it wasn't close. Bryan and Renard ran circles around Compton's defensive unit while Glenn crushed them like Styrofoam. Four quarters later when the clock ticked down, we won. Our run game, blocking, and hustling to the ball overwhelmed them. The Compton players took the defeat well. I was glad I wasn't them. It was a long ride home reliving that loss to 'Air Force brats.' We shook hands, as we had with all the other teams we faced, and parted ways.

That evening was cause for celebration. Jim's parents were gone, so I stayed the night at his home. Glenn, John, Greg, and Pete were coming by to visit. We awaited their arrival on the roof above the front door with eggs. When they stepped up to knock on the door, our eggs hit their targets dead center. We laughed so hard we almost fell off the roof.

Greg had brought an adult magazine he had gotten somewhere. As we stood in Jim's kitchen, Greg told us according to ads at the back we could call a woman and she would speak sexy to us. All the guys were egging Greg on to make the call. As he reached for Jim's phone hanging on the kitchen wall, Jim yelled, "Not from my house!" He was worried it would show up on the bill and his dad would be furious. (He was probably right.)

All six of us put our heads together. Where could we call that it wouldn't end up on a phone bill and none of our parents would know? One of the guys brought up the payphone outside of the principal's office at Vanden. We all agreed that sounded like a good idea and that's where we should give it a try. We left Jim's, walking to Vanden. We crossed behind Center Elementary School onto Farmer's Land. It was dark outside so we felt we were safe from a rock salt attack. Once arriving at the high school, Greg wasted no time going for the payphone. He dialed a number and a woman's voice could be heard talking sultry. We listened closely trying to talk to her. She didn't respond—it was a recording. Our trip was a bust.

We headed back to Jim's. Walking in the dark the guys kept teasing me, "Run! Mr. Fritch is coming to get you!" Then they'd laugh. I'd respond back, "Yuk it up." As we walked behind Center and into the playground area, lights hit us from the front of the school. Dogs were barking and base police were screaming at us to stop. Had Cathy's dad finally caught up with us? Screams of "FREEZE!" had us frozen. "What do we do?" someone blurted. Jim darted like last time. He headed up the stairs to the upper grass area. The other guys followed with me, trailing. I wasn't going to get caught and go down by myself. I ran, knowing we were once again innocent and had done nothing wrong for them to chase us.

It was dark out and we had no flashlights. The grass field was huge. We had hundreds of yards to cross. "Where do we go?" Glenn was screaming. We all followed Jim. He ran to the barbed wire fence that separated the field and farmland behind the base. He climbed over with all of us right behind him. Glenn's pants got stuck on the fence. A barb had his leg hooked, and he was frantic. Jim and I came to his rescue. We dragged him over the fence in the process ripping his brand new tan corduroy pants from his groin to his knee. We all ran up a hill blocking our view from our pursuers.

Glenn was whimpering or crying. I wasn't sure which, because it was dark and I couldn't see his face. All I could hear was him repeatedly saying he was in trouble with his stepdad, Coach Kelly, for ripping his new pants. Jim muffled Glenn with a hand over his mouth. We stayed there, too afraid to move or look to see what was going on. When we heard a helicopter in the distance coming our way we moved quickly along the Farmer's Land to some brush, then back on base. We slowly and carefully made our way back to Jim's house. We all stayed there for the night, too afraid to split up. Our imaginations got the best of us. We just knew Cathy's dad was going to plaster 'Wanted' posters all over the place looking for us. He was like a bloodhound. He wasn't going to forget about us or give up the chase.

The base police thought they were chasing dangerous people infiltrating Travis. Instead they were chasing 13- and 14-year-old Redskins and Mustangs. The only danger we posed to them might be to their daughters at a school dance. (Where I would wear my rainbow Mork suspenders.) We were good kids, but we just kept stepping into trouble with our little adventures involving girls.

It was only fitting my parents had a Doughboy inground pool installed in our backyard because we had been beach babies. My brothers and I were raised on the beaches in Florida. We enjoyed the sand and ocean most days, and they became our playground. Under the lining of our Doughboy pool was sand. When my feet touched that liner it reminded me of those white beaches that helped raise us. We loved the water, and were tan all the time. It would've been hard for anyone to see our Irish ancestry. We couldn't get enough of the ocean—until that fateful night my dad wanted to take us to the movies.

He came home from work one evening, excited. "Wake the boys up, Sue, we're going to the movies." It was almost ten, and he wanted to take us to see the new shark film 'Jaws.' We went, and it had a lasting effect. The scenes scared us boys. Overnight, Sean, Tim, and I went from diving into the ocean to dipping our toes. It never affected Craig. He was fearless. That movie stayed with us, because we never swam in the ocean again. We loved our pool, though, because it was a shark-free zone.

In class, all we could talk about was football and being one game away from the state championship. It was an exciting time. The teachers, students, and the Air Force security police guarding the side base gate by the school, would all talk to us about the upcoming championship. The guard there never knew we were TAFB's most wanted. The Travis AFB newspaper, the Tailwind, was covering our season, so all the Air Force personnel on base knew we were undefeated and about to play for the state title.

The plan was decided for our team, parents, and fans to drive together by caravan, so we could face our opponent for the state title. My dad decided to take our new family van, the one Tim crashed through our garage door, and drive some of the players, including Jim.

We were going to depart on Friday morning, as the game would be the following day on Saturday afternoon. The administration at Golden West cleared all the players to miss school that Friday that we were leaving.

The morning of our departure, all the players, coaches, families, and fans met. We were all packed and ready to go. It was nice to see all the support we had for our squad. Many dads were going. Brian's, Jeff's, and Mike's fathers were there to support their sons. My dad was going as the team doctor, and of course Glenn's stepdad was the head coach. That morning as we started on our long journey it was like we were one big family.

The trip seemed to go very fast, as we talked the whole time. When we arrived, we were met by the coaches and players we were facing and by the league officials. It was obvious we were from two different worlds. We were Air Force brats from a small community, and our opponents were big-city kids. Some of my Redskin teammates were assigned to stay the night with the opposing players and officials. John and Carlos stayed with the league president. Jim and Darren stayed in the same household of an opponent. Darren asked the family if they bought the type of hot dogs that already came in buns. The family looked at him in disbelief, like he was mentally challenged. When hearing of Darren's hot dog question, I wondered if it would work to our advantage. Maybe our opponents would think they could outsmart us because we weren't very bright.

I stayed with my dad in a motel, and so did some of the other players and their parents. We went out to eat that night, and though the food was just from a diner, it tasted incredible. It was championship football food.

The next morning we all met at the field where we were scheduled to play for the state title. It was at a high school. We were all weighed, and we all were under limit, including Jim, barely. We suited as usual, taped up, and heard Coach Kelly lay out the game plan. We had beat 11 teams to be in that locker room. Though we were nervous, we also felt seasoned. In our minds we could defeat anyone we faced. We said our prayers and hit the field for stretching and warm-ups. Our cheerleaders were there in uniform. Parents, families, and friends were filling the small bleachers we were provided. It was our Super Bowl, and we wanted those rings and Disneyland trip. We were undefeated and ready for our 12th victory.

Like clockwork, we did what Coach Kelly laid out, and we were winning. Our opponent was no better than any we had faced all season. Glenn punished them up the gut, Bryan and Renard owned the outside, and we tormented their offense. It was a hard-hitting game. We went into the locker room at halftime with several touchdowns on the scoreboard. Our opponent had no points. The first 24 minutes were one-sided.

During the halftime break, Coach Kelly was approached and asked if the other team could field some players that couldn't make the 140-pound weight limit. Confident we would still win, Coach Kelly agreed. When we came out after halftime, we faced a team that was different than in the first half. Some of their players were taller, heavier, and had facial hair. We didn't recognize them from the first two quarters of play.

    We were in for a game. These new players were faster and hit harder. Renard got hurt. We dug in to give them a fight. We weren't going to roll over for anyone. We played harder than we had all season. On defense Jim, Glenn, and Jeff had the new quarterback near the sidelines as he scrambled. They grabbed him, and he spun around and threw a touchdown for 60 yards. It looked like the ball flew 40 of them in the air. We were frustrated. We tackled hard, ran fast, and never quit.

    When the clock ticked down to the end of the 4th quarter, we lost by one touchdown. We were defeated on the scoreboard but not in our hearts. We knew we should have won the game. We weren't happy with the outcome and the addition of the players outside the weight limit.

    There was controversy and anger from our coaches and parents. It was justified. An investigation was immediately launched, and our opponents were suspected of using older players that couldn't legally play in the midget league. The game was declared an exhibition. There would be no official winner, and we had made the long trip to play a game that wouldn't be recognized.

    It was an eye-opening experience for us 13- and 14-year-olds. Football was supposed to be a fun game and the innocence of it was taken from us. We learned a valuable lesson that day.

After the game, we all went to a pizza place. I took an interest in the opposing head cheerleader. She was a cute Hispanic gal. As we ate, I fed the jukebox quarters. I kept pushing the song 'Celebration' by Kool and the Gang. All the cheerleaders from both teams got up on the tables and began dancing. David was dancing with our head cheerleader, Cathy. I got up and started dancing with the cute opposing head cheerleader I had had my eye on. Some of my teammates joined the other opposing cheerleaders on top of the tables.

John and Carlos had two of their cheerleaders by the payphones next to the bathrooms, flirting with them and getting their telephone numbers. Our advances were upsetting the team we had just played. I didn't care, and neither did my teammates. It was our retribution. As Redskins we wanted payback (for the swapped players). Girls were always getting us into trouble, so there was no reason to change our behavior that afternoon.

While our revenge was playing out, Jim and Darren, or "Red" as Jim called him, left with the opposing player who took them in the night before. He had asked them if they wanted to go for a ride. Jim and Darren were interested. He took them to a bar next to the pizza place where his dad was drinking, and got the car keys. That player was a little guy, and could barely see over the steering wheel. Jim, Darren, that player, and one of his teammates then went cruising through the surrounding city. They were only fourteen years old. Fortunately, their time sightseeing went unnoticed by the police.

The next day our team planned to go to Disneyland. We didn't receive the Super Bowl rings, but we were getting the trip anyway. We got up early, ate breakfast, and drove to the world-famous park. Jim and I spent twenty dollars on sour cherry balls, and struck out on our own. We were lucky when we arrived at the 'Space Mountain' ride. There were very few people waiting to enjoy it. Jim and I rode it over and over again. Our time in between rides was how fast it took us to get off, run down, and back up through the line to sit down again. We probably enjoyed it twenty-five times in a three-hour period. Our fun-filled day at Disneyland came to an end too quickly. Before we knew it, it was time to leave.

Our ride back home was much slower than our trip down. We were all tired and disappointed. Talk was minimal. We weren't state champions but at least we were in the books as playing in it. We were still undefeated; but our egos were bruised. Football was a tough sport in more ways than one. Our arrival home ended our season, and our time as Travis Redskins. It was hard because we all liked playing together. Not only were we the best of teammates, we were the best of friends.

There would be no more rushed Beast trips down Vanden Road. I was going to miss those trips but my cleats wouldn't. The Beast was limping too, from a few hard crashes into Jim's carport when I was running late.

That season on the Travis Redskins in 1980, Glenn rushed for 2458 yards and 33 touchdowns. Bryan and Renard both rushed for over a 1000 yards each. The offense averaged 493 yards a game, with most of it on the ground. The offensive line made that happen with only two holding calls all year.

Jim, Jeff, Glenn, David, John, the other guys, and

I still hung out. I was on the wrestling team that year with Jeff, Mike, and Carlos. The team went undefeated.

Every Friday and Saturday night, Jim was still at my house for the weekend, or I was at his. Like football, if we wanted to hang out together we had to make it happen. Making it happen meant me going to his house after school on Friday and staying the night, or Jim and me walking from TAFB to my home in Vacaville. Seven miles along the railroad tracks to Black Bridge, across Vanden Road, then trekking through miles of farmland climbing over or through barbed wire fences, while trying to avoid the bulls mixed in with cattle, cow patties, and rattlesnakes in the tall grass. Some of those trips we made in the dark, with no flashlights. Dozens of trips back and forth. We became the Lewis and Clark of Golden West.

The above photo depicts the view from Vanden Road, the barbed wire fence, and the farmland Jim and I would pass through during our trips between TAFB and Vacaville. Black Bridge has since been removed. Photo provided by teammate Mark 'Baro' Baranowski #64.

Summer came quickly and most of us teammates continued to hang out regularly. Every day we were doing things together. We would go to the 'T' pool on TAFB to swim, or next door to the bowling alley for french fries, ice cream, and video games. The movies on base by the library were always a great Saturday afternoon spot.

I was quiet when my parents sat us four boys down and told us they were divorcing. It caught me off guard—because they both seemed happy—and we did many things together. As I sat there in silence I realized there would be no more fun activities and travels as a family. Our perfect home wasn't perfect after all. As I wiped away tears, I remembered the trip we made in our converted milk truck motor home. It had a screened-in porch, folding-down beds and a hole cut in the dash so one of us boys could sit up front with our parents while driving. We took our recreational vehicle all through Mexico and slept on the beaches along the Baja coast. Our beloved dog, 'Cyclone,' made the trip with us and stayed in the screened porch while we were away.

I also remembered in third grade, we drove from California to Florida in our 19-foot Tioga motor home so Dad could attend a medical program for the Air Force. All six of us and Cyclone lived in it for five months on Homestead AFB's RV park, which sat next to a large pond. From our back steps it was 75 ft. to the water. After school my brothers and I would fish for brim. Once catching the fish we would string them through the gills with our fishing line and cast them out to an alligator that lived in the pond. Usually he would take the bait, and we would reel him in and up on land. A neighbor saw what we were doing and told our folks. We were in trouble. We had no idea the 12 foot predator could reach a speed of 25 mph and bring down a horse. A week earlier on a dare we had convinced Tim to swim past the area where the carnivore lived. (Crazy—but true.) The base didn't know the gator was in the pond, so they quickly removed it for our safety.

Our family outings stuck in my mind as our parents explained why they were divorcing. I was heartbroken. I loved them both very much and didn't want to see our family torn apart. When I was in second grade I was a poor reader. My mom worked with me each day for months. By the end of that school year I was one of the best. I could clearly see my mom patiently working with me to read better as I listened to them both talk. When I ran away from home in the first grade and stayed out past dark, my dad came and found me. He wasn't mad but worried. He held my hand as I tried to pull away and walked me around the block four times, telling me how much I was loved. How was I going to make it without both my parents? I didn't know.

I think Sean and Craig took it the hardest when Dad moved out. Sean was angered and Craig was hurt. I think they both felt lost. One thing is for sure: With Dad gone, we had little supervision with Mom working full-time. I never got mad at Dad for leaving. I think I believed he was going through a mid-life crisis and lost his way.

After Dad left, he never attended any of our sporting events or games again. Because Mom worked all the time, she quit attending them, too.

A few weeks after Dad moved out I was home alone with Mom. I heard her weeping in her room. Her door was open so I walked in and asked if she was okay. Through her tears and sadness she asked what was she going to do now. I felt sad for her and didn't know what to say. I hugged her closely.

After a few minutes I went up to my room. I missed Dad too and our family. I remembered when we came home from church one day and there was a wild parakeet sitting on the telephone line outside our home. My dad was able to get it to fly to his finger. We named him Peter and he became part of our family. Every night he would ride on the wash cloth when Mom wiped the table after dinner. Peter would also take a bath under the dripping faucet as Mom did dishes. He loved sitting on our shoulders. I loved that bird. When I accidentally left the door open, and Peter escaped and was killed by a cat, I cried. As I sat there remembering all the times we had as 'the perfect family,' as my friends would say, I cried alone in my room.

Peter is shown with Craig in the above photo. Craig was 3 years old.

The above photo shows our converted milk truck motor home. We are pictured on a beach along the Baja coast with our traveling companions and best friends, 'The Roney's.' They also had a son named Craig. We enjoyed the closeness between our last names.

Preparing for football became our main focus. After our season on the Redskins we were hooked. I quickly forgot about baseball, and was losing interest in wrestling. The lure of the gridiron was addictive to me. It was all I thought about—except for girls.

My mom continued working nights and slept during the day. It gave us boys more unsupervised time. We abused it but we were still good kids. We weren't doing drugs or causing too much trouble. We were just restless and had pent-up adrenalin. My parents divorcing may have had some effect on our behavior.

That summer we were introduced to the life of stuntmen. A life we continued until I graduated high school. It consisted of dark nights on Vanden Road when vehicle traffic was light or non-existent. My older brothers introduced us to body surfing on the roof of a car. It consisted of laying on the roof of a vehicle and holding on from the left and right sides. The front driver and passenger windows were rolled down allowing us to get a good grip. The goal was to ride on top of the roof with the car driving at the fastest speed we could handle. We regularly went close to or over 95 mph. It was stupid and dangerous; but it was all us. The gridiron was closed, so we needed to fill that void.

Like football, body surfing on the roof of a speeding vehicle was addictive. From the first moment I laid down on that metal surface and gripped each side of the roof I felt a rush. Laying there holding on as the car took off and picked up speed my heart rate would increase. It felt like a drum in my chest pounding away. The wind pushed against my face, making it hard to breathe. I wanted to keep my mouth shut so a bug wouldn't find its way inside. My eyes watered but I didn't want to close them. Insects would hit me in the face. In the dark, whizzing by the open Farmer's Land I could see the barbed wire and cattle. The stench of manure on a warm night was overwhelming.

As the car accelerated I would want them to go faster, so I could record the top speed. Yet fear would tug at me to tell them to slow down. My legs would sway with the curves of Vanden Road. The small slopes throughout would cause my body to bounce off the hood. If I wanted the car to slow, I would lightly kick the rear windshield with my foot, or hit the roof hard with my hand. Like a disapproving parent I'm sure the moon was gazing down in disbelief.

Body surfing on the roof was like flying. I felt like a bird or a superhero but I didn't have a cape. Sometimes as the car whizzed down Vanden Road I wondered if that was how Superman might've felt if he existed outside of comic books and movies. It was an exhilarating feeling that made me feel alive and unbeatable. Each ride made me feel renewed and stronger. The green apple flavored Jolly Rancher stix in my back pocket would survive unbroken. (I always had one with me.) It helped ease the cottonmouth after the adrenaline-filled trip.

That few-mile trek playing a stuntman was the most exciting time I had enjoyed, and it was the most dangerous. Fear and stupidity rode shotgun. Most weekends my teammates from the Redskins, my brothers, and I were all tempting fate on Vanden Road. Thankfully, fate was kind to us. We weren't unbreakable like Superman.

That summer, we met Pete Watts, when his dad was transferred to Travis. They lived close to 'Snob Hill' on base—where all the top officers and base commander resided. All of us liked Pete the first time we met him. He was a smaller guy, not really built like a football player. We were told his older brother had been a standout running back for Folsom High School, rushing over 1000 yards the previous season. He quickly became a member of our roof surfing clique. We continued our adventures daily and were always up to something. Jim and I built a nice wooden backboard for our house, and we played basketball in our court often. Our custom-built backboard was the rave of our friends, and most days someone was out there shooting baskets.

Summer was coming to an end, and that meant one thing to us: football. We had waited impatiently for our good friend to arrive. We had been apart too long.

With little supervision Sean and Tim would stay out most nights, riding their bicycles across Vacaville to Pena Adobe with their friend Dave Seymour. They would then ride them onto interstate 80 down towards Fairfield. (Yes, on the freeway. Imagine coming around a turn and seeing kids riding their bikes in the center lanes.) All three would peddle in the middle lanes when no cars were present. They would race their bikes to the next exit, hoping not to get caught. One night they almost did, when a truck saw them and gave chase. They took an exit and ran down the embankment, hiding, leaving their bicycles off the road. When the truck occupants stopped to take their bikes, the three charged up the hill yelling, and their pursuers left. Without Dad around, and Mom working nights, we took liberties we wouldn't have when our parents were married. We were teen boys learning our way.

Craig and his friends weren't any better. They were always off doing something my mom probably would not have approved of. Though he was white, Craig started dressing in all black and acting as if he were Hispanic. He started a 'wannabe' gang. In reality it was more like a club without the dues, and it didn't last long. Sean, Tim, and I had enough sense to tell him to knock it off.

Craig had always been athletic. In fact, he probably was the best athlete out of the four of us boys. When he was three, and we lived in Florida, he would climb palm trees two to three stories high to throw down coconuts to us. He would also walk on clothes lines—barefoot, like a high-wire trapeze artist. Yeah, Craig was quite the athlete. With his natural abilities he could've been a great football player. The game never drew him in, though.

The above photo shows the Travis Redskins in 1980 as we played one of our opponents. We are in the lighter-colored jerseys on defense swarming towards a sole offensive receiver, and the pass was intercepted. Photo provided by teammate Mike 'Spartacus' Holovach.

Coach Mike Kelly's thoughts on the 1980 Travis Redskins team - Jan. 4th, 2014:

"Football I.Q. for this team was light-years ahead of your age, or at least your ability to understand what we wanted you kids to do. The last thing was, you became friends, and it has lasted a lifetime. I was and am very proud to have been your coach."

Photo shown to the right, of Coach Kelly, taken from a yearbook courtesy of Vanden High School and Travis Unified School District.

[1980 Travis Redskins Head Coach]

(Coach Spotlight) - Mike Kelly

Coach Kelly was the architect of our undefeated winning season in 1980. That year we went 11-0. His love for the game of football was evident. He called us "No Names." Coach Kelly had an inventive mind to design unique offensive plays. He stressed discipline, dedication, never quitting, and playing as a team. I liked him the first time I met him, and in my first year of football he was what I thought a football coach should be. Coach Kelly built the foundation for my teammates and me that carried us for the next four years. He taught us how to block skillfully, hit aggressively, and tackle properly, driving an opposing player into the turf. I never played for Coach Kelly again. Thanks for the memories, Coach. You took names.

The above and below photos show the front and back of our house in Vacaville, CA. The wooden backboard Jim and I made is visible.

The above photo shows Jim during one of our evening weightlifting sessions in our backyard.

The above photos show us four boys when we were young and in our teens. Left to right: Craig, me, Tim, and Sean.

Young Vikes

I was counting the days until football. We were going to be in the 9th grade and trying out for the Vanden JV team. Our time of being Redskins had passed. Our reputations as being the best Pop Warner midget team in the state of California didn't matter anymore. We now had to prove ourselves worthy as Vikings.

I'm sure my mom was ready for us to go back to school, because our house and pool were overflowing daily with our friends. A lot of my football teammates and friends from school lived in Village East or in the next housing community just down the road, Country Village. My teammates Carlos and Mark lived only a few streets away from me. I could walk to their homes in minutes.

The town of Vacaville was rapidly growing, and the orchards were disappearing to housing and business. It was still a country town at least on the side where we lived. Vacaville was known for its smell of onions. The onion plant's aroma was strong, and it saturated the entire community. Drivers on I-80 were sure to get a whiff passing through on their way to San Francisco. Our town was also known for CMF, otherwise known as California Medical Facility. It was a prison run by the Department of Corrections. Famous prisoners were housed there, and sometimes the emergency horn from the prison could be heard blaring. The landmark 'Nut Tree' road stop also put Vacaville on the map. It was a great place families would visit on the weekends for food and entertainment.

There were two high schools, Vacaville High, and Vanden, which kids from Vacaville attended. Most, though, went to Vaca High. We were the new kids in town. Air Force families with kids in the Travis Unified School District had recently started moving into Vacaville. In years past, the families with kids that attended Golden West and Vanden lived on TAFB, or closer to it.

As incoming freshmen we were starting at another school still considered 'Air Force' but that was much smaller than Vaca High. It was about one-fourth the size: Vanden had about 600 students.

I purchased new cleats and another mouthpiece for the upcoming football season. That evening I boiled my new mouthpiece and molded it to my teeth. I again wore it for several hours watching television. I wanted to get into my football mode.

The sport was fast becoming everything to me. It was all I thought and talked about. Jim and I had spent the summer working out and preparing for it. We knew football on the junior varsity squad wasn't going to be like Pop Warner. It was a step up with no weight limit, so we needed to be bigger, stronger, and faster.

Suiting up for practice the first day of Hell Week was intimidating. I was nervous sitting there in the locker room. I knew we were looking at five days of two-a-day practices. There were many faces I didn't know. Most of the varsity players, and half the JV squad, were new to me. My former Redskin teammates and I were quiet as we dressed. I wondered if they were as edgy as me.

"Hit the field" was called and sixty-plus pairs of cleats quickly hustled out of the locker room. The varsity and junior varsity squads practiced side by side behind the Shubin Sports Building in open grass fields. The same grass fields I could see in the distance when we practiced as Redskins behind Golden West.

We ran to the junior varsity field, and the varsity squad went to theirs. We were told to line up on the 20-yard line. Our new head coach, Gerald Hatcher, introduced himself and his assistants, Coach Lou Moore and Coach Len Cesna. I knew coaches Hatcher and Moore. They were my PE teachers at Golden West for three years. I liked and respected them. They had guided us during our time as Mustangs.

Coach Hatcher was about 5'7" but he was built like a little bull. He had played football in high school, and I was told he was a great running back in college. He looked like an athlete. He had a better physique than most of the players.

For the next 10 minutes Coach Hatcher explained what he expected from us and what we could expect from him. He said it with authority in a commanding tone. He was animated when he spoke, walking back and forth. He told us our moms weren't there to save us, and this was not Pop Warner football. He made an impact with me as he spoke. I was more nervous than before.

We then broke off into stretching and warm-ups. Afterwards we went into groups for those trying out for different positions. I went with the running backs. Bryan Batchan and Glenn, my teammates from the Redskins, were there. Bryan's older brother Broyce was also there and a few other players I didn't know.

They put us through drills for about thirty minutes. Bryan was faster than I remembered and his brother Broyce was even faster than Bryan. The team was going to run the wishbone backfield, the same we used on the Redskins. Glenn looked like a shoo-in as the starting fullback, but I wasn't sure I would make the first-string lineup. I didn't have speed even close to Bryan or Broyce. Some of the other players trying out also seemed a little faster than I was. I could see the writing on the wall.

We next split into defensive groups. I went with the linebackers and defensive ends. We again went through many drills so the coaches could see how we could hit, get around a defender, and tackle.

The practice was organized and nonstop. We went from one thing to the next for three hours, and it was only the morning session. We still had an afternoon session to go. I was already getting tired.

Next came wind sprints of 40- and 100-yard dashes. We ran many. My side was hurting, and I was gasping for air. I wasn't the only one, as I looked around. We were told not to bend over at the waist between sprints but to take a knee. It was hard not to bend over. I thought I was going to throw up. It was hot, and my head was baking inside my helmet. It felt like a potato in a microwave, and I thought it was going to explode. I wanted to take my helmet off for air but knew I couldn't. That fateful move would lead to more dashes.

A whistle was blown and "bring it in" was called. The players all ran to Coach Hatcher and took a knee. He told us how he thought the practice went, and we broke for lunch and rest. We had a few hours before our afternoon session.

My old teammates and I took lunch together. We were all tired. I told Jim I wasn't sure I could be a running back on the squad. I didn't have the speed (some of the guys had) and I didn't want to ride the bench as second string. I wanted to start and play both ways, like I had on the Redskins. Competing against Bryan and Broyce put that in doubt.

As we rested before the next practice, we talked about the first session. Our nerves seemed to calm. We knew we could play at this level. No doubt about it. The hitting wasn't any harder than I remembered from last season. It was the speed we would have to get used to. And we would. I knew my friends would make the JV squad proud, because the guys were studs. I saw them kick ass and play for the state title. The title that should've been ours—but was taken from us.

We were no longer a red-and-white-colored team though. Vanden was green and gold. Our helmets were yellow with a green horn. We were Vikings now and no longer Redskins. I had to keep reminding myself that. We were young Vikes—fresh, getting our horns. Our game uniforms were gold pants with a forest-green-and-gold numbered jersey for home games, and a white jersey with forest-green numbers for away. Our practice uniforms, though, were all white, except for the helmet.

The break ended too soon, and we were back to the practice fields for more stretching and warm-ups. We next went through hitting and tackling drills. Jim, Glenn, Jeff, and the guys all looked like they had something to prove. They were exploding into hits and driving through on tackles. They were playing seasoned their first day.

I think coaches Hatcher, Moore, and Cesna were impressed with the tackling by the former Redskins. My friends were doing exactly what Coach Kelly had taught us. Watch the hips to see where the feet will go. Put your facemask in the numbers. Wrap and drive into the turf. There was a lot of good basic fundamental football shown in practice that day. I thought to myself, Coach Kelly would be proud. We were still following his direction.

I took pride in hard-hitting, and I wasn't afraid to have my 'bell rung.' I knew being 'out of it' and feeling wobbly came with crushing hits. It was part of the game I loved, and I wanted to earn a reputation on the gridiron.

I studied the older players on the team to learn from their style. There was Broyce Batchan, who could be all over the field and in the mix. He was fast, very fast, and hit like a train. The other player I watched was Frank Reyes. He was David's older brother, and he was bigger, hit harder and was very aggressive. I could tell he liked hitting. He was a punisher. I knew I could learn things from Erwin Hardy and Robert Kulinski.

As we practiced, the varsity squad was doing the same about 50 yards from us. Periodically, I would look over at them. They looked so big, fast, and aggressive. I could hear their coaches, Ed Serpas, Ronald Beverly, and Ron Harden giving directions. I wondered if I would be playing for them in a few years.

When "bring it in" was called, and practice ended, I was exhausted. My friends and I dragged ourselves into the locker room. We gave it our all the first day, and left everything on the field. In the locker room I could hear John's laugh as he changed. How he had energy to laugh I didn't know. I could barely open my mouth to breathe. John was zany, though. That was his style on the Redskins and it appeared he was going to stay with that. I liked that in him, because he made the game fun.

John and Mark were our jokesters. They were always up to something mischievous. I needed to keep an eye on them at all times so I didn't fall victim to one of their pranks. I knew they had plans in the works, and I didn't want to be their next target.

I slept well that night but awoke a little sore. I missed that feeling. I was glad it was back after a year of absence. There was nothing like gridiron bruises, aches, and pain to make you appreciate football. It was a violent sport and I liked that. I liked the contact involved with it and so did Jim. When he tackled someone he tried to punish them for being on the field with him. He was a fierce competitor and because of that I was glad he was my friend and on my squad.

When we hit the practice field that day and broke off into our groups I was pulled aside by Coach Moore. I wasn't going to be a running back. They wanted to put me on the line, because they liked how I blocked and hit. I was told I didn't have Bryan's and Broyce's speed but I had other skills. I knew (in my heart) something like that was coming after that first practice. Bryan and Broyce were too explosive for me to try and compete with. My one-day 28 jersey number was taken away and I was given number 60. I was now a lineman and would battle in the trenches. That was fine with me. I just wanted to play football with my friends. I wanted to show the coaches they wouldn't be disappointed in the change. I could contribute. I pushed myself as hard as I could throughout the morning and afternoon sessions. Each block, each tackle I gave everything. I held nothing back. I knew I had to be different to be noticed, so I tried to make a lasting statement. In one day as a Viking I had lost my running back position, which I had worked so hard for on the Redskins. That hit me hard.

In the afternoon session during contact drills Coach Hatcher called me over to where he was standing. I was worried. Where were they going to put me now? I wondered. He put his hand on my shoulder pad and told me I played like a psycho out there. He said I was crazed in my play, but in a good way. He told me 'Psycho' was my nickname from now on. That label stuck with the team, and when I was on the gridiron I became that character. I didn't know it then, but that name would follow me during the rest of my football years at Vanden. I wasn't going to be replaced again by a better athlete so my mindset became simple as a football player—never back down, relish the pain, be ruthless, win. I made a promise to myself: become the most aggressive name taker on the gridiron, because I wouldn't be the best athlete.

The rest of the week Jeff solidified the fact that he would be the center on the line. David worked hard as a smaller player to set the tone that he was a hitter. Glenn was the same bulldozer he was on the Redskins. Jim was letting the team and coaches know he would leave a large footprint against our opponents. Mark, John, Pat, Mike, and Greg were tearing it up in the trenches. Bryan was starting to show why his lethalness on the field would never be forgotten.

The sophomores on the team were the perfect mentors for us. We watched and learned from them. Frank and Broyce were leaders and captains. You could go to them and ask questions. Sophomore Erwin Hardy became a friend. He loved football and wanted to contribute. I liked talking with him. Robert Kulinski was a bruiser as a tackle. He was the biggest lineman we had.

John continued with his zany behavior in practices. One of the guys said he was like that 'Murdock' character on the television show 'The A-Team.' The nickname stuck, and John relished it. One day he wore a tee shirt to practice under his pads that read "I am not crazy, I just act it." That tee shirt became a good luck charm for John and the team, so he continued to wear it under his shoulder pads for every game during his time at Vanden.

Mark had this look he created where he would tilt his head and glare. He became his own character. It was unique. I wondered what opponents would think when they were lined up against him. I wished I could emulate it, I told myself many times. Mark made his own statement with his patented tilt and glare. He looked cool with his own style.

Hell Week ended with a practice game on Saturday called 'The Watermelon Scrimmage.' We played against a local team, Armijo, at Vanden on the practice field. The varsity squad did the same. Afterwards we all ate as much watermelon as we could devour. We ate our fill. Dozens of watermelons met their fate that day behind the Shubin Sports Building. It was a great way to hydrate the players and end the torturous two-a-days.

Jim stayed at my home that evening. While my mom made us dinner we entertained her with Hell Week tales. We relived each hit, each tackle and the exhausting dashes. Jim told her about my nickname. He said he wanted one, too. Something that defined him. My mom began saying various names he could use. She went through Lunatic, Crazy, and Maniac. Jim stopped her at Maniac. He liked that one. It resonated with him. He had the name—it was time to develop its character.

The above photo shows the practice fields. The Shubin Sports Building is shown top center. Photo provided by Timothy O'Donnell #69 co-captain of the 1984 undefeated Vanden JV 9-0 team.

The next morning on Sunday my oldest brother Sean dropped Jim and me off at the Solano Mall in Fairfield. We went upstairs to a sports clothing store that did imprinting. We picked out two gray hooded zip-up sweatshirt jackets. We took them to the counter and asked the attendant if we could have names added to them. He told us we could, and asked what we wanted. I told him "Psycho" and Jim told him "Maniac." He gave us a double take and said, "What?" I told him again. His look told me that was a first for him. So it was unusual, I thought. We were unusual guys trying to build identities for ourselves.

He had us spell out the names as we wanted them and a short time later we picked them up. We put on our custom jackets and wore them home. Those sweatshirts became a part of us. When school started a few weeks later we wore our Psycho and Maniac sweatshirt jackets to Vanden as freshmen.

The starting offense and defense positions were picked. Bryan and Broyce would be in the backfield with Glenn as the fullback. The starting offensive line was Jeff, Jim, Frank, Robert Kulinski, and me. On defense Glenn, Jim, and Frank were linebackers; Jeff, Erwin, and I were defensive ends. Mark, John, Pat, Mike, and Robert were on the defensive line. Broyce was our safety, and Bryan, David, and others shared the cornerback positions.

We worked hard developing our timing on offense, and on defense we practiced stopping different types of schemes we might see. We were introduced to the dreaded 'cages,' metal contraptions we had to go through on all fours, like a bear crawl, within a certain time frame. We had to do those over and over again.

As I went through one time I stood up too early as I exited, causing a fairly deep laceration in my middle back. Some soap and water along with triple antibiotic ointment, and I was fine. Football was a painful sport. I was used to it and that's why I enjoyed the game.

Not sure what I expected the first day of school, but it was not a Hostess pie in the face. I wasn't sure who did it, but it was my brother Sean or one of his friends. I knew Sean had a reputation at Vanden. He was the wrestling team captain and was dating the varsity head cheerleader. I looked up to him. At our small school he was a leader and a standout.

The attack couldn't stand, though. There had to be payback. Jim, Pete, John, and I decided to retaliate. We gathered our stockpile. We launched a stealth attack of pies—squashed on heads and in faces. Sean and his friends were all hit almost simultaneously. We then ran for our lives. We were pursued through the school, cornered, and punished. Jim was at the top of the tennis court chain link fence when he was caught by Sean and pulled down. I was scaling the automotive class fence when Wes Cleveland and Lee Stanton caught me. Lee was the starting varsity quarterback for Vanden. The wallops were no worse than Mr. Elkins' paddle, and we would live another day. The food battle continued daily for a few weeks, with attacks coming from both sides. We were building our own reputations as freshmen. We weren't pushovers.

When I first saw her, I loved her smile. She had beautiful blue eyes and the combination drew me in. She was short, maybe 5'1", and petite. She was one of our cheerleaders and I couldn't quit looking at her. To me she looked perfect, except Tami was my head coach Jerry Hatcher's daughter. I knew I had a problem. I wanted to meet her, but I wasn't sure. I had to confer with Jim about the positives and negatives. I already knew one negative. He was 5'7" and looked like a little bull. He could also bench me physically and bench me on our squad. I had to be careful in my courtship. Football was too important to me; but Tami seemed worth the risk.

The day of our first game I couldn't wait to get into the locker room and get suited. We put on our pads and cleats. We were given last-minute instructions by Coaches Hatcher, Moore, and Cesna. We were ready to face the Winters Warriors. We played at our George Gammon Field at Vanden and won 35-6. We were young Vikings with our first win under our belt.

That weekend we lost our dog Cyclone to cancer. He had been our loyal companion for years. We buried him in the far corner of our yard by a newly planted tree. I knew I was going to miss him. He had been a member of our family and protected us and our home. He was our friend and now he was gone. I knew it would take time to get used to him not sleeping on our beds.

Monday at practice after our win against Winters, the coaches had us do cages for every point that was scored against us during our first game, 6. Some of the sophomore players weren't happy but we were used to that from our time on the Redskins. We knew winning and being champions came with hard work and conditioning.

After weeks of talking, Tami laid it on the line with me. If I wanted to date her I had to beat her in a 40-yard dash, she said. Tami was competitive like her dad, our head coach. Both were great athletes. I wasn't worried though. I had been a Redskin running back. I might be wearing the number of a lineman, but that was deceptive. I knew Tami bit off more than she could chew with her challenge. After school and before football practice we squared off by the Shubin Sports Building. When Jim said "Go" it wasn't close. Tami had a good view of the rear of my sneakers. I won the race and Tami and I became a couple. When Coach Hatcher found out, I still started on offense and defense. He didn't bench me on the squad or physically. Things were looking up for me.

    Jim and I decided to take Home Economics as an elective that first semester. It was a baking class full of girls, and we did the math: We could eat extra food at school, put on weight for football, and talk with all the females. It definitely was a win-win for us. The class went by fast every day, and I didn't mind homework from it. One homework assignment involved baking a cake. I chose to make a gingerbread one.

    I just knew it was an easy 'A.' How hard could it be? I asked myself. I decided to make my cake in the morning before school so it was fresh. Mom and I purchased the ingredients the night before and I laid them out in the kitchen before I went to bed. I got up early the next day and began to bake. I had followed all the instructions closely before with other assignments so I was confident my cake would be good. I couldn't wait to taste it and all the other goodies in class that day. I took the course for a reason—I liked to eat.

    When I took my cake out of the oven it didn't look right. Something was wrong. I had my mom look at it, and she told me it didn't rise properly. It wasn't the size it should've been. My mom's boyfriend Andre was a chef, and once worked for John Wayne on his yacht for a year, making meals for him. He told me to fill a turkey baster with water and gently squeeze it into the base of the cake, and it would rise more by the time I got to school. I trusted Andre, but I didn't know he was pulling my leg. I had been known to pull pranks on him, and he saw his opportunity to get me back. It was too good to pass up.

When I got to school and took my cake out of the Tupperware container it looked worse. Oh, no! What had I done? I worried. Jim couldn't quit laughing at my mound of gingerbread. I couldn't help laughing, too. I had been suckered by Andre. When our teacher Ms. Kubiak cut into my assignment, it was mush. It was very soggy and needed a spoon instead of a fork. She asked me what happened and I told her. She laughed along with the class and gave me a 'C' for trying. Jim's cake assignment fared much better. He got an 'A.'

Jim and I were always trying to impress the girls in that class any way we could. When Ms. Kubiak went to the office one morning, we saw an opportunity we couldn't pass up. When she returned she struggled to open the door to the classroom. She couldn't open it because Jim and I were holding the handle from inside. Ms. Kubiak twisted and twisted the handle trying to force the door open. She looked through the side Plexiglas windows (on either side of the door) and called out to Jim and me by name. She couldn't see us behind the door. We continued to hold the handle out of view while the girls giggled. We were the entertainers, and they were our audience.

We were smiling ear to ear and looking back at the girls for their approval. I added in a few winks with my grin. Ms. Kubiak became frustrated and left. Jim and I rushed to our seats, not knowing what to expect next. We had committed ourselves with our act of defiance. We were facing an unknown response. As we sat there grinning and proud, the loudspeaker came on in our classroom, startling us. It was Ms. Kubiak. She said she was in the office and would come back with the principal if needed. Jim and I were worried. We hadn't thought ahead to the consequences we might face. We begged the girls not to tell on us. We hoped they could keep our secret. When Ms. Kubiak returned she asked who had locked her out. You could tell she was upset. She was red in the face and her hands were shaking. She went down the line and asked each student. Everyone said they didn't know. Luckily, Jim and I escaped punishment for our little prank. We felt bulletproof. In our little school at Vanden, Maniac and Psycho were making names for themselves. Probably not in the best ways, either.

    Where Vanden sat in relation to TAFB made for an interesting trek to and from school for some students. Kids that lived on the left side of base housing took a different route than kids that lived on the right side. Kids on the right side walked through the side gate by Golden West for their journey to Vanden. Kids on the left side crossed over the waist-high chain link fence behind Center Elementary School. They walked along Farmer's Land until they climbed through the barbed wire fence near the high school. Each day hundreds of students braved that barbed wire and the threat of farmers with rock salt.

I'm not sure how often students ripped their clothing climbing through the fence, but I bet it happened often. During the winter kids wore long coats or overstuffed jackets, and many female students wore dresses and heels throughout the year. Books in hand they looked like an ant trail each morning. It was a common visual to see the masses going back and forth. I wondered what the Air Force or the school administration thought about the makeshift path that was created years earlier.

Some students that lived on the right of base housing had to travel through the infamous 'Secret Sidewalk.' It weaved between the homes. It had a spooky allure—which added to its mystique. It was a cement path that had six-foot chain link fences on either side. There was little light to illuminate it at nighttime. When my family lived on TAFB I was hesitant to use the path at dark.

Eighteen years after the football program began at Vanden it was in good hands, as the varsity head football coach, Ed Serpas, was a legend at our school and in our league. He was the first and only skipper to lead the Viking program. Coach Serpas knew the gridiron well. He had once been a football player himself. He had been the MVP and co-captain of the 1954 squad at Solano Community College. During that season he had earned All-Conference, All-State, and All-American honors. He was joined by his assistant coaches Ron Beverly, known as 'Bev,' Ron Harden, and Tom Newsom. Bev had played for Coach Serpas on the very first Vanden football team in 1964, and he caught the first touchdown for the program. Bev had also been a successful JV head coach at Vanden, recording three undefeated seasons.

Harden had been a longtime assistant coach to Serpas and later became the school principal. Newsom had had a successful college career as a tight end, but injured his back. Both Bev and Harden mentored troubled students at Vanden's continuation school known as 'Con' which was located near Black Bridge on Vanden Road.

Above Coach Bev #87 on Vanden's first football team in 1964.

Coach Hatcher began opening the gym daily in the Shubin Sports Building before school started, so players could lift weights. Jim and I were there most mornings, along with Jeff Martin. Glenn was a natural athlete and his build was perfect for football, so he rarely lifted.

Coaches Hatcher and Moore, along with Bev, had us follow a circuit training regimen. It was pretty scripted, and we each moved from one exercise to the next. On the wall by the leg machine was a poster of a sculpted athlete and it read, 'Bigger, Stronger, Faster.' I would stare at that poster because I wanted to be that athlete. It gave me motivation. Jim, Jeff, and I weren't big guys, so we had to push ourselves hard when we lifted weights.

Victories mostly continued for our squad. The week before the Homecoming Game, some of our JV teammates had a rift with our coaches about doing the dreaded cages on that Monday after our latest win. They felt it was wrong to be punished for any points scored against us, because we had notched another victory. Instead of following instructions like my old Redskins teammates and me, some players threatened to quit. Coach Hatcher wasn't one to be challenged. He told them to leave if they wanted. Half the team walked away, except my former Pop Warner teammates, Broyce, Frank, Robert, Erwin, and a couple others. We were left with half a squad. The coaches said we would play Friday night without those who had abandoned us. A few choice words were used to describe them. I couldn't blame the coaches for how they felt.

On that Homecoming Night, we fielded half a squad against our toughest opponent, Benicia. Erwin, Jim, and I were picked as game captains. With fourteen players, we battled the game to a tie. We were expected to be crushed against a good squad that was fully staffed, and we weren't. The coaches were happy with our performance—so were we. It was our second tie of the season.

At halftime of the varsity game I was supposed to escort my good friend Lesly Barnard as the Homecoming freshman attendant. Jim and I jogged to his house to shower and change. I was sure we had time to make it back for the halftime event. When we returned to Vanden, I missed it by five minutes. I dropped the ball. I searched for Lesly and apologized. She took it well and said it was okay, but I'm sure she was disappointed with me.

That following Monday after our game against Benicia the players that left in protest came to practice. They asked Coach Hatcher if they could rejoin the team. He allowed them to come back.

I didn't think his authority would be challenged again. The returned players learned one important lesson: follow direction without questioning why. They also discovered conditioning would make us a better team. It was as if that disagreement did something to the squad. We became closer and better as a unit. Many crushing hits and big plays accompanied our next few contests. We won every game for the rest of the year and our season ended with a 7-0-2 record. We won 7 and tied 2.

On the JV level we learned much under Coach Hatcher's guidance. He knew the game well and taught us to never quit. We listened.

The above photo show the 1981 7-0-2 Vanden Vikings JV team. Photo courtesy of Travis Unified School District and Vanden High School.

The above photo shows the 1981 Vanden Vikings on offense playing one of our opponents at Vanden on the George Gammon Field. Photo provided by teammate Mike 'Spartacus' Holovach.

The above photo shows 1981 teammate Mike 'Spartacus' Holovach heading to the sidelines during a game. Photo provided by teammate Mike Holovach.

[1981 Vanden JV Head Coach]

(Coach Spotlight) - Gerald Hatcher

Coach Hatcher had roots in football, being a former player himself. By 1981, I had known him for four years. He had been my PE teacher at Golden West. I liked him as a teacher and coach, and I respected him as a mentor. He was a firecracker as our skipper on the JV squad. Coach Hatcher enjoyed teaching the fundamentals of football. He expected a lot but gave a lot back in return. His dedication to the football program was paramount. He wanted it to be the best; and under his direction it became one of the elite programs in California. Coach Hatcher wasn't only my football coach; he was my friend. I never played for Coach Hatcher again. Thanks for the memories, Coach. You took names. Photo courtesy of Travis Unified School District and Vanden High School.

[Guard and Linebacker]

(Player Spotlight) - Jim Wallace #76
Guard, Linebacker, and Specialty Teams
Nickname 'Maniac'

Jim played with us for two seasons in 1980 on the 11-0 undefeated Travis Redskins and the 1981 7-0-2 JV team at Vanden. Jim played middle linebacker and guard. In all the years I played football, I never met a more fearless hitter, who would play with such reckless abandon. Jim was a spine-rattling type of football player. He came to knock your head off and intimidate on the gridiron. He did both. If Jim got banged up, he got mad. If he got beat on a play, he got even. The game of football was made for players like him. I never played football with Jim again after the 1981 season. Thanks for the memories, Maniac. You took names. Photo courtesy of Travis Unified School District and Vanden High School.

[Tackle]

(Player Spotlight) - Robert Kulinski #68
Offense Tackle, Defense Tackle, and Specialty Teams

I played football with Robert for one season in 1981 on the 7-0-2 JV team at Vanden. He was the biggest and strongest offensive and defensive lineman we had. He was a moose on the line. On offense he powered over his opponents, usually easily. On defense he was an anvil and hard to move. Robert was a big part of our winning season that year. I liked Robert back then, and I learned much playing alongside him as the guard. I watched and learned from Robert's style. He was quiet in those days, but when his cleats stepped on the gridiron it was evident he loved the game of football. I never played football with Robert again after the 1981 season. Thanks for the memories, Robert. You took names. Photo courtesy of Travis Unified School District and Vanden High School.

[Tight End]

(Player Spotlight) - Erwin Hardy #34
Tight End, Defensive End, and Specialty Teams

I played football with Erwin for one season in 1981 on the 7-0-2 JV team at Vanden. Erwin was our tight end and had great hands. He was tall and aggressive, which made it difficult for linebackers and cornerbacks to take him on. He probably gave opponents nightmares after playing us. Erwin was a major asset on defense. He kept coming. He never gave up or let up. Erwin was not an animated player. He just performed well. He never complained, and did what the team needed to beat an opponent. Erwin understood football was a team sport, and he never let us down. I never played football with Erwin again after the 1981 season. Thanks for the memories, Erwin. You took names. Photo courtesy of Travis Unified School District and Vanden High School.

[Lineman]

(Player Spotlight) - Rob Alexander #77
Offense Tackle, Defense Tackle, and Specialty Teams

I played football with Rob for one season in 1981 on the 7-0-2 JV team at Vanden. Rob was a martial artist, so he had good balance and coordination to maneuver opponents around, and he made games miserable for them. We could always count on Rob when he stepped on the gridiron to battle against anyone in the trenches. Rob smiled a lot, but his smile cloaked his aggression. He would go 110% for all 48 minutes in a game. Those are the types of players I appreciated. Rob would play from whistle to whistle. It was players like him who helped us to our 7-0-2 record. I never played football with Rob again after the 1981 season. Thanks for the memories, Rob. You took names. Photo courtesy of Travis Unified School District and Vanden High School.

After the football season ended, Jim, Jeff, and I tried out for track. They needed bodies, and it sounded like fun. Bev was the head coach for the team. He had also been on the first track squad at Vanden as a student. His assistant coach was a big heavyset man named Tom Newsom. Both coaches were knowledgeable, jovial, and interacted well with the kids.

We were on the team to throw the shot put, and the discus, and to do the pole vault. After watching a pole break in two as a varsity member went up in the air, we quit the vault. That was all we needed to see, so we stayed with the shot put and discus, where our feet remained on the ground. We weren't very good at those two events, but we tried our best.

Coach Newsom joked daily with us at practice. We built a friendship, and he confided in me he was trying to lose weight. He asked if I would start jogging with him after school around the track and sometimes on the weekends. I agreed. Jogging with him was very slow, almost a walk, because coach Newsom was 6'2" and about 450 pounds at the time. He was very big but dedicated to losing the extra weight. Over the next four years I jogged with him on and off, after school and on the weekends. Our trust in each other grew.

When the movie 'Porky's' came out it received great reviews from my older brothers as a 'must-see.' As 15-year-olds it peaked our interest. Jim, Glenn, Pete, John, David, and I wanted to see it at the four-plex movie theater on Marshall Road in Vacaville. We walked there one Friday evening even though it was R-rated and we couldn't get in without an adult accompanying us. We felt that was just a minor obstacle. We hoped to encourage someone to buy us tickets with our money. When we arrived, the movie theater was busy (with long lines) and everyone we asked declined. It was a wasted trip.

On our way back home we stopped at the top of 'Cemetery Hill' on Marshall Road. Across the street an old graveyard sat watching and waiting. As we stood under a light post the burial ground taunted us with its presence. "You're not brave enough to enter," it muttered faintly. Our teenage spirit was being summoned, "Courage or cowardice, pick one." The night was warm, quiet, and shadowy—an eerie setting for a foolhardy venture.

Standing there for several minutes staring at the resting place and how ominous it appeared, dares were thrown for someone to crawl under the chain link gate and go inside. Jim stepped up to the challenge. Glenn and I followed. Sliding under the weathered entrance we left our fingerprints behind. Pete, John and David were witnesses if we didn't return. Slowly following the road, peering in mausoleums, we became characters in every scary movie we'd watched. The further we went, the more on guard we became. I was nervous and more than hesitant. "Be brave," was whispered.

One hundred yards in front of us, headlights turned on, and a car engine roared to life. Our hearts stopped and we took off running. Glenn screamed, "Grave robbers!" Our feet couldn't move fast enough. We didn't know where we were going except away from the supposed danger.

We darted between graves blindly, the three of us within a few feet of each other. Without warning, Glenn flipped through the air, landing on his back. He looked like a gymnast with a poor landing. He screamed out in pain. We didn't know what happened. As Jim and I tried to quiet him and see if he was injured, we determined Glenn's knee had hit a water faucet at a full sprint. If we weren't so scared—we would've been laughing.

We laid there for a few minutes, with Glenn crying (in pain) and Jim and me expecting to be caught. The grass I was laying on was wet. When Glenn could stand on his leg we helped him out of the graveyard. The other guys were bug-eyed as we crossed the street towards them. None of us could explain what had just happened. I thought to myself too bad no one had videotaped it.

While breathlessly discussing the event, John pointed at me and said I was so scared I wet my pants. I looked down, and I was soaked. I told them I hadn't, but I was wet from the grass. I think they believed me, but teasing was too much fun for them to quit their taunts. Glenn went from crying to laughing. At least there was one good thing that came at my expense. Glenn was distracted from his pain. I needed diapers, John kept saying, and the laughs continued. One of the guys queried, "Was it Mr. Fritch chasing you?" They all laughed harder.

David, John, and Pete were staying the night together so we parted ways. Glenn, Jim, and I had a long walk to my house. We headed home slowly, with Glenn limping and moaning every step. As we walked, a police car pulled up behind us and the officer got out. He asked what had happened to Glenn. We concocted a story that he fell down and hurt his knee. The truth sounded too unbelievable. And we had trespassed at the cemetery.

The officer offered to give us a ride home. Glenn jumped at the opportunity, so we got in the patrol vehicle. Glenn was in the front seat, and Jim and I sat in back. As he drove the officer kept looking in the rear view mirror at me. I was squirming in the back seat. I didn't like the feeling of my wet pants, and I was trying to stay off the seat to not soak it. He asked if I was okay and continued watching my movements.

Finally he pulled onto my street and in front of my house. We exited the vehicle and thanked him. The officer then noticed my wet pants and looked upset. He asked if I had urinated on his back seat. I told him I fell in a puddle earlier, and it was just water. His look said he didn't believe me. As he drove away he shook his head. I think he regretted his ride offer.

We went in the house and put ice on Glenn's knee, and I changed out my clothes for a quick shower. As we went to bed, our cemetery excursion was replayed over and over in conversation. Not sure any of us slept well that night. We just wanted to see the movie Porky's, and instead we made a scene that could've been in it.

Each trip to a sporting goods store was a search for new types of football equipment. Jim and I wanted the best and newest stuff available. We found the black padded gloves that all the top varsity players were wearing. They were fairly new on the market. They looked cool and felt good on my hands. I had to have them, so I did my chores daily and saved my allowance. One Saturday I bought those black hand pads. I was going to look intimidating next year, I thought. The gloves were lightweight, contoured, and ready for action.

That weekend I wore those gloves nonstop. Jim asked if they could handle a rip against a facemask. I thought they could but wasn't sure myself. They were untested, and I couldn't risk a broken hand during football. Contemplating their protection I jabbed the stucco wall on the outside of my house. My hands didn't hurt. Jim tried it, too. The gloves passed phase one.

Jim and I always tested each other. It was just our style. I asked him if he thought he could take a punch while I wore the gloves. He said he could. I offered we should go in the backyard and see who could take the hardest hit. He agreed, and we went in back. I put on the gloves, and we set the rules. No hitting the nose. We would bend with our hands on our knees so our punches came downward towards the eye. If we got knocked down we would fall on the soft grass.

It wasn't the brightest idea. Our machismo overtook common sense. We both threw our best and took the best. Four or five shots each. The gloves were tested. They passed phase two. Our hands were fine but our eyes weren't. They were sore and swelling. We looked like Rocky and Apollo Creed at the end of their fight. By that Monday at school we both sported big black eyes.

Jim was my best friend but we both had an unusual reaction around each other. It was like mixing chemicals in a lab. We could be explosive. We were good kids, didn't do drugs, drink, commit crimes, or bully people. We respected authority and adults. We both just had a wild side that came out from time to time.

Instead, I needed to hang around more with Jeff, because he kept me grounded. He came from a good family and home, and he was more reserved. When Jeff was at my house the messy episodes Jim and I got into were absent. Jeff had more sense than to engage in the behavior Jim and I stepped into often.

Glenn, Jeff, Jim, David, John, Carlos, Pete, and Mark were regulars at my home. They could be found swimming in our pool or shooting baskets in our driveway. Mark ruled the court over us. He played on the basketball team at Vanden so he had an edge that we didn't. Playing against David was the easiest because his small frame didn't allow him to block high passes and shots. John had skills. Jim, Jeff, and Glenn were average. Pete could talk a good basketball game but not much more. In truth I was no better. We had many other friends that showed their skills in our driveway.

The tasty lunch-meat-and-cheese sandwiches we warmed in our microwave were consumed by the hundreds, if not thousands, by our friends. They became legendary in our household and a must-have when they came over. There was nothing better or easier to make. Our home became a cafeteria for growing hungry boys and girls. Our food bill must've been enormous.

On weekend nights we were back on Vanden Road playing stuntmen and tempting fate. Getting the fastest time on top of the roof was bragging rights we all wanted. It was our secret that few were allowed to know. Disclosure meant stopping our high-speed stuntmen treks. We knew that. We never did those trips in the rain or high winds, though. We knew the dangers, so the weather had to be right or we didn't ride. We were reckless but still knew what boundaries shouldn't be crossed.

Hanging a mannequin clothed from the school radio tower was a feat. It was even a bigger feat that it was so convincing, the administration called the sheriff's department, and the coroner responded, because the deputies thought someone had committed suicide. How Sean and his friends pulled that off was something Jim and I pondered. We were in awe. Jim and I told ourselves we needed to work on our pranks to keep up with Sean and his pals. Lowering the flag pole every weekend and painting the ball on top a different color was pretty inventive, too. Sean and his friends were always scheming. It didn't take Sean long to corrupt Blair Smith. He was a foreign exchange student from New Zealand who was innocent upon his arrival at our home. Within a few short weeks Sean introduced Blair to roof surfing on Vanden Road, joined him in handcuffs for being out after curfew, and had him drunk often. Blair came to America to take part in our educational system. He was educated by the time he returned home—not in the way his family had hoped.

I never saw it coming when Tami broke up with me. I was stunned. She didn't give me a reason, and I was crazy about her. For the first time I was being distracted from my first love, football. Tami was my second love and my first heartbreak, and I wanted to win her back. This was no football game, I told myself. It would be much harder to prevail than facing eleven guys who wanted to rip my head off.

I had to confer with Jim. He knew Tami well. We were like the three musketeers. Jim had been the third wheel in our relationship because he and I were like conjoined twins. We put our heads together, but we were stuck. Romance her, I thought; and Jim agreed. The first step was to write 'Jeff loves Tami' on every school locker in pencil. We did. It had no effect—and luckily no punishment from the school for defacing lockers. Every other thing I tried fell short.

As I sat at home and the rain poured from the sky, the thunder cracked and lightning flashed, it hit me just like a light bulb turning on. Take her flowers—now. Right now. I looked outside at the storm. But how would I get there? The Beast was out of commission. Then the second light bulb flipped on. Walk the three miles in the rain braving the lightning and thunder to bring her flowers. Who would do that? I knew the answer: someone who really cared.

I put on a jacket and off I went. No hat and no umbrella, just a 15-year-old broken heart that was determined. I walked through our housing community, crossing the street to Raley's. I bought a bouquet of beautiful flowers and began my trek. Three miles. Three long wet miles. When I rang the doorbell at Coach Hatcher's home I was soaking wet. My heart had swelled like a sponge. This was it, I knew. Mrs. Hatcher opened the door and I asked for Tami. When Tami came to the door I handed her the flowers and said, "I miss you." I couldn't muster anything else. The rain dripping off my hair into my eyes said it all. As Tami began to speak I just turned around and walked away. That was it, I told myself. If that won't work, nothing will.

I had my answer the next day when my phone rang. I had my second love back. I was elated. I knew those eleven guys who were going to line up against me were in for a battle. I was whole again.

Tim had a paper route in our housing community. He would get up early, roll the papers and bind them with rubber bands, then hop on his bike and deliver to his customers. Us four brothers were very competitive in sports and at home. When Tim lost the bet of who was singing the song on television as we watched MTV we had to make his loss memorable. Deliver your newspapers on your bike in your underwear and sneakers only, we told him. "No way," Tim said in return. If he could guess the next group on MTV we would have to join him, Tim countered, "But in the nude!" Tim guessed correctly, so Jim, Pete, Craig, and I had to streak naked in our tennis shoes down an adjacent street. Tim laughed as he said we would look like the friends in 'Porky's.' We didn't find it funny because we hadn't seen the movie yet.

We always lived up to our losses, so early the next morning Tim prepared for his route in his underwear and sneakers only. It was cold and foggy out. We joined him outside in the nude wearing only our sneakers. Off Tim peddled, with us jogging behind him. Once we arrived at the starting point Tim had picked for our streaking adventure, we took off running full speed home. I still had some of my old Travis Redskin dash in me. As we were nearing the front of the street a car appeared, like it was pre-planned to catch us. We passed right by and its headlights illuminated our naked run. We laughed as we passed the vehicle. I wondered what they thought. "Those were no deer in the headlights!" I mused. We made it home and Tim finished his route. That morning we also ended our time in Village East as nudists.

Then the bad news came. Jim's dad was getting transferred to Altus, Oklahoma, and he would be moving within a few months. I couldn't believe it. I asked Jim to stay with us and he was interested. I didn't want to lose my best friend. I asked my mom and she agreed. He could live with us until he graduated high school. Jim's parents also agreed but hoped he would go with them.

The week before Jim's family was to move, he decided to join them. I was crushed. I was losing my twin, half of Lewis and Clark, Rocky and Apollo, and my sidekick. Jim introduced me to football. Psycho was losing Maniac. It would never be the same again and I knew it. Those seven days came fast and Jim moved away. Our escapades ended. We never again shared a football field together. The time of 'Maniac' came to an end. Jeff, Glenn, and I were on our own to finish our gridiron journey. In Jim's memory I wanted to make it a grand one.

When Coach Hatcher approached me and asked if I wanted a summer job I was interested. He wanted to landscape his front and back yards completely and redo many things outside. I was to be his helper, and I could see Tami every day. Sounded like a great job to me. I spent that whole summer at their home working. The time kept me distracted from Jim having moved away.

Each morning I would jog to their home and jog back to my house at the end of the day. The three miles each way kept me in shape for the coming football season. Sprinkler systems, sod grass, flowerbeds, and much more were completed that summer. Coach Hatcher loved Pepsi, and he could easily drink a 2-liter a day while we worked. I grew to have an appreciation for him away from football and school. He was not only my coach, teacher, mentor, and girlfriend's father, but he became my friend.

    I knew we were a little wild but I didn't think we were that out of control. Marty Welch, our neighbor from across the court, felt differently. He came over one Saturday afternoon and said my mom was at his house crying. She was going to have a nervous breakdown, he said. I needed to send some of my friends home. He told me to come outside with him. The microwave sandwiches Jeff and I were making had to wait.

    We went out back with Marty. Mark and John were on the roof of our two-story house trying to make a rope slide down to the pool; Carlos and David were trying to take our corded phone into the water to call girls; and Pete had been depantsed and was running around the backyard naked while Greg threw eggs at him. Pete's swim shorts were on the roof. Jeff and I were the only ones not doing something wrong. We were just trying to eat. As Marty stood there pointing out the behavior, I couldn't deny it. I could see what he was talking about. I told the guys to pack it in and sent them home, except Jeff. He was my normal friend.

    I could feel it in my bones when I awoke in the mornings. Football season was coming. It was better than Christmas and all the other holidays combined. The coming season would be the first time in my football career that Jim wouldn't be there. I was going to miss his crushing hits. He had a Dick Butkus style that many opponents were unfortunate to meet. It wouldn't be the same, but the guys and I would be okay. Pete was going to play the season with us, and we had hope he would be a great addition to the team. If his talent was like his personality—he would be a star on the squad.

Bryan and I didn't associate with each other outside of school but he was one of my favorite football players. He was an incredible running back. I admired his style and respected his play. He was super-fast and a crushing hitter. When he carried the ball he became the hunter, and the eleven players on defense were the hunted. Two years on the gridiron together taught me one thing, Bryan was destined to be a legend at Vanden. I wanted to be there to see the glory he captured.

My 'V' shaped "Va Va Voom" and "Va Va Vee" front teeth marks were present in my mouthpiece after molding it. My teeth were crossed because my tongue pushed against them. I was tongue-tied and it could affect my speech and other issues. I had to have it clipped.

When I was taken to the dentist on TAFB for the procedure, Tim and Craig went along with Mom and me. Tim and Craig were told they too had to be clipped. They weren't expecting that. The tissue that held the bottom of our tongues to the floor of our mouths had to be cut back.

Our three mouths overflowed with blood and the gauze was saturated in it as we drove home. We ran into the house to spit out the mess. Craig and I ran to the bathroom as Tim ran to the kitchen. Sean yelled out in horror as Tim's blood-filled gauze clump hit the sink, "Mom! They cut out Tim's tongue!" Sean almost fainted. Though he escaped being clipped he had to deal with the aftermath and it wasn't pretty. We were always competitive, and would tease and taunt each other, but Sean's bloody visual kept him from making fun of us that day.

Perfect and Scoreless
Two coaches, the best and the worst

It was monumental. I stood looking over its landscape. So many memories, so many stories were created there. I felt a fondness as a drop of sweat found my temple. It was already getting warm. The sun gazed down like a proud parent. The football field was green and lush; freshly mowed and ready. It was waiting on us. Onlookers would see uniformed kids doing maneuvers like military drills—with one goal in mind—win football games and become champions. Respect, honor, and courage were taught. It was everything that was good; hot dogs, apple pie, and the girl next door. Connections were made there that would last forever. It was Viking country.

I wore my Psycho sweatshirt to the locker room that first day of Hell Week out of remembrance and respect for Jim. I knew it was time to play that character once again. I had to for 'Maniac' and me.

Darren Rysden was back after a year's absence. It was good to see him. Dave Haupt was playing. He had skills, and his older brother was a good quarterback on the varsity team. I was sure Dave would make a good quarterback himself. My friend Kenny Tarver was going to play. He was one of the nicest guys I had ever known, and we had been friends for many years. Other friends, Kye Purnell Jones and David Smith, were there also. I knew we'd have a good team with them.

As I looked around the locker room a few new faces looked like great additions. Ronnie Beverly, Jr., the son of varsity coach Ronald Beverly, who had just been promoted to head coach, was trying out for quarterback. Ronnie was a clone of his dad, and he was eager to prove himself. I had heard Ronnie was a great athlete. His dad carried himself like he was when he was younger, so I figured what I heard about Ronnie was probably true. Chris Stiltner was another new member. He was big for a freshman and he was friendly as I talked to him. I already like the guy, I thought.

I heard Mike telling people he wanted to kick and punt. Mike was still a weightlifter and had the most muscular physique on the team, and with the addition of his hair, he had been nicknamed 'Spartacus.'

I wondered what pranks John—our 'Murdock'—and Mark—or 'Baro' the nickname I started calling him—would pull. Baro was short for his last name Baranowski. Both of those guys needed flashing lights on their heads so you could monitor them. I had been their prank victim in the past and figured that would continue. It made our time together on the gridiron memorable.

"Hit the field" was called and sixty-plus pairs of cleats between the JV and varsity squads began to trot en masse on the tile and then the asphalt outside. I loved that sound. Anytime I heard that noise it triggered a reaction of hunger, like Pavlov's dogs salivating—but in place of food—I was craving football.

Our head coach was Lou Moore. I liked him. He had been my wrestling coach for three years at Golden West. He had also been my 6th-grade history teacher. He was the assistant coach last year, and I knew what to expect from him. Coach Moore was very athletic. He jogged every single day and lifted weights. He had a muscular build and looked like a football player himself.

His assistant coaches were Len Cesna and Mr. Ordez. Coach Cesna was an assistant the previous year and a long-time football coach at Vanden. I liked him, too, I thought, and I knew what to expect from him. Coach Ordez was new. He was a shorter plug of a man. Looked like a lineman. I was looking forward to learning from him. Be a sponge, soak it all in and modify what works best for you, I would tell myself. That was something we were taught on the Redskins and I still followed it.

We took a knee, and Coach Moore laid out his vision, what we were to expect and what he wanted from us. He was comfortable in his speech and firm in his words. He looked and talked like a head coach. Coach Cesna spoke a little, then we heard from our new coach Ordez. He spoke like he had a love for football. I was feeling good about his addition.

Stretching and warm-ups ensued. Afterwards, we broke off into our groups. I went with the linemen. I had grown fond of my number 60 and had no desire to be a running back again. We did some hitting and blocking drills. Next, to defense. I went with the linebackers. Glenn, of course, was there. He was going to dominate the left side of the field, no doubt. I was going to be the middle linebacker. Jim was gone, so I was put there to stop the run up the gut.

By the end of the second practice that day it was evident Ronnie was going to be our starting quarterback, and Dave Haupt would be his backup and a defensive end. Bryan was our ace in the hole as our tailback, and Glenn would barrel up the gut as the fullback. Jeff was our center and defensive end; Pat would be a guard on offense and a defensive tackle; Mike a guard and defensive tackle; Darren our wide receiver; John tight end and defensive line; and David a cornerback and backup running back. I was going to be the right tackle along with plugging the center on defense as the middle linebacker.

The second day of Hell Week went well with no problems. We were coming together as a team. Our timing was already improving and on defense we swarmed. We were injury-free, and that was important. We needed healthy bodies to have a good season.

During hitting drills on day three I slammed into my friend Kenny Tarver. His shoulder was injured. Practice was stopped and Kenny checked. He needed to go to the hospital. I felt bad. He was my friend for so many years and a good kid. Just darn, I thought. The rest of the day was dampened for me. I was mad at myself.

Waking up sore and bruised was becoming something I expected and looked forward to during Hell Week. I actually felt better that way when on the gridiron. It awakened my senses. It made things more realistic for me, and it was why I chose to play the game of football. It was a dangerous sport that caused injuries. Be the aggressive one, I would tell myself. Most of the time the dominant players would stay injury-free. It was the players who hesitated that got hurt. That wasn't always the case, though. There were no guarantees in the game. Anyone could be hurt at any time. When 22 bodies in helmets and pads all scramble for one football and collisions occur, injuries will happen. I always knew that. It came with this game we all shared.

As Hell Week continued I wanted to look for Jim in the locker room. It would never be the same without him; I knew that. I relived every adventure we had, and I heard every conversation we shared. We were like Butch Cassidy and the Sundance Kid. I had never trusted anyone more and nor I had I ever laughed harder at someone's antics. He had brought out the best and sometimes the worst in me. I knew I was going to miss our food binges at his house—the endless supplies of Cheez-It, Ritz crackers, and Honeycomb cereal. We were always elbow deep in them. We ate truckloads worth.

Kenny wasn't going to play again, the coaches said at practice. He was injured, but he would help the team with equipment when he came back. I wished I could've taken back that hit. It was my fault for hurting him. I couldn't deny it.

Mike did make the kicker and punter positions. He had quite the leg when his foot touched the pigskin. The football looked like an orbiting satellite when he launched it into the air. As a field goal kicker his accuracy was spot on. Who said weightlifters could not kick like soccer players? I thought as I watched him kicking.

Some of the guys were quite the characters. Of course Murdock and Baro were in a class of their own. You couldn't remake their molds if you tried. Dave Haupt was a thrasher. He loved his skateboarding. On four little wheels and a board he could do amazing things. David had become a lowrider. Low and slow was the way to go, he would say. Our team was full of 'A-Z' personalities. That made it memorable playing together.

Chris was making his mark as a freshman. A natural tackle on both sides of the line. In the short time I had played with him and watched his style he impressed me. He had talent.

Ronnie was fast and agile as a quarterback and had a strong arm. He ran a great option and could throw accurately on the run. If he kept the ball and ran with it, look out. He had moves. I was learning quickly it was much better to have him as a Viking than an opponent. His and Chris's additions to the team were notable.

Hell Week ended with the annual Watermelon Scrimmage. We played against Armijo again at Vanden. Good contact, hard hits, great tackling and blocking—with no injuries. The watermelon tasted phenomenal. Jeff's, Bryan's, and Chris's dads were there, cutting the melon for us to enjoy. Soon we were going to be playing games, and after only one week together our team had bonded.

School was right around the corner. My brother Sean and his friends had graduated in 1982, but my brother Tim was a senior this year. Tim was well-liked and popular, like Sean was. Tim also was a great wrestler, like Sean had been. I did not plan on starting any feuds this year with Tim and his senior classmates. I was going to plead with my friends not to start another battle.

The first day of school I wore my Psycho sweatshirt jacket again, and I continued wearing it every single day until school ended that year. And yes—I washed it regularly. I wanted to remember those times with Maniac, and it was my way of honoring our friendship. Jim introduced me to football and it was changing the course of my life. I owed him my gratitude, and the least I could do was wear that sweatshirt out of respect for him.

Behind the facemasks and under the shoulder pads we were learning as 'one.' Trust stronger than steel was being shaped with each practice. It was artistry. The creation of an unstoppable squad began on the grass behind the Shubin Sports Building at the direction of coaches Moore, Cesna, and Ordez.

Each huddle, block, and tackle our strength grew. Our eyes said it. The glances and head nods spoke volumes. We learned each facet of the game like chess moves. Helmet slaps and coaches barking orders refined our skills. We became better; more disciplined. What was planted as Redskins was starting to flourish as Vikings.

The tied shoelaces; the socks that slumped; the grass stains, dirt, and blood on uniforms; the adjustment of pads after a play; the hustling down the field or off the ground; the swearing and sweating; all told our story and what was coming.

What would a writer put in his column if he sat and watched us? Would he write about all the little nuances? Would he see what I saw as each minute passed? A lot of kids put on shoulder pads and played football. Not many of them would accomplish what we would on the gridiron.

Coach Bev was only the second skipper to lead the varsity program, and in his first season at the helm he was working hard. Since the varsity and JV squads practiced in close proximity, I could hear the expertise he and his coaches, Harden and Newsom were putting into their team. Tim's best friend, Bill Green, was the punter and a receiver on the squad. He sported the same red hair as Darren Rysden and was a great athlete. I liked Bill. He was always positive and had a never quit attitude.

Coach Moore, like Coach Hatcher, liked to use cages to develop us as better scramblers, so we did many of them. He also favored wind sprints at the end of practices and stressed that the most-conditioned team would win. At the end of each practice we ran until we cramped and felt like vomiting. It was excruciating.

Bryan's dad would come to Vanden sometimes to see him and Broyce practice. Since the practice fields were side by side, he could watch them both play. It was evident he was proud of his sons. He should've been. They were both great football players with lightning speed, and huge-impact players on the squads.

Viking alumni were proud of our school, and many over the years gave back. Former football player Lyent Hogue, the older brother of Larry Hogue—a Vanden legend on the gridiron who went on to play in the Canadian Football League—joined the coaching staff as an assistant. Like Larry Hogue was doing himself for the varsity squad that season, he came to mentor, guide, and help mold us into better Viking football players. He accomplished that goal. I instantly liked Lyent, and he earned my respect. He took great pride in the program.

When our first game finally arrived, we had to travel to face the Winters Warriors. Our contest started at 5:45 p.m. We planned to make an example out of our initial opponent and set the tone for the season. We wanted to be the best. Bryan and Ronnie both scored a touchdown, and Mike kicked a 40-yard field goal. We won 17-0. We followed Coach Moore's game plan, playing together as one and putting trust in each other. Ronnie and Bryan both showed their skills by creating some of the magic that would make them legendary at Vanden.

I was your typical teenage boy—except for my need for football. I had worn frayed cutoff shorts, bell bottom pants, and now 501 jeans. I could be found upstairs in the family room planted in our bean bag chair watching television, while chewing a mouthful of Bubble Yum gum with 'Shadow' (a mangy poodle mix mutt my mom found digging in our outside trash) by my side. I wasn't a deep thinking kid. Football, girls, and working out. Those were my hobbies and I was good at them.

> Lou Moore won his first game as coach of the Vanden junior varsity, 17-0. Mike Holovach kicked a 40-yard field goal, and Ron Beverly and Bryan Batchan both scored touchdowns. Jeff Rooney and Chris Stiltner led the local line and defensive play, respectively.

Above article is from the Daily Republic written by Rick Jensen. Courtesy of the Daily Republic. Used with permission. Submitted by teammate Mike 'Spartacus' Holovach.

I think I was in shock when my mom told me the news—my second-grade teacher Mrs. Gifford and her family had been murdered. I couldn't believe the words Mom was saying as I sat there. Mrs. Gifford had been my favorite teacher during my school years. She was kind, loving and grandmotherly. Who could do that to her? Tears filled my eyes. I was devastated. My friend Stephen Carpenter and I had stayed in contact with Mrs. Gifford, and we'd been to her home many times to swim and barbecue since graduating from her class at Center Elementary School. She had been very important to us.

Mom told me what happened. The night before, she was the night nurse in charge of the emergency room at Fairfield Community Hospital. She received a radio call, "At your backdoor with four patients with gunshots to the head." As they wheeled them in, Mom knew the victims. Mrs. Gifford, her husband, son, and daughter. All four died. The police quickly determined who committed the murders. Mrs. Gifford's son had brought a new acquaintance home from college and as they all slept he burglarized the home. It was believed that during the burglary he found the gun he used. He then shot all four family members.

I couldn't get thoughts of Mrs. Gifford out of my head. She had been a great teacher and taught so many young students. What a tragedy and a loss. Memories of her stayed with me for a long time. I missed her a lot.

That Monday after the game we didn't have any cages to do because we held the Warriors scoreless. Coach Moore and his assistants began to prepare our squad to face our next opponent. We practiced hard all week working on our offensive plays and defensive schemes we would use. Fun school events were scheduled throughout the week to entertain the students and elevate school spirit. We were fortunate the Vanden football program had strong support from the Travis Unified School District, administration, teachers, students, cheerleaders, band, stat girls, Booster Club, fans, and parents.

That Friday night we won again and shut out our opponent. We were 2-0. That following Monday we were able to once again escape cages at practice. Coach Moore increased our wind sprints, though, so we would be in better shape than our opponents in the second half and, most importantly, the fourth quarter. When the teams we faced would be running out of steam, we would still have something left in the tank, he would say. Escaping cages only meant more wind sprints.

I just couldn't get enough of them. When a play was in motion it was like flipping a switch and igniting craziness. Anything could happen. And would. A single football play was like watching a variety of sports combined: one serving of sumo wrestling; mixed with hockey; tossed with rugby; and covered in track. It was explosive and encompassed so much movement the naked eye couldn't see it all. It would be easier watching a hummingbird's wings flutter. Being in the middle of it all was like dancing with a tornado. It only lasted a few seconds but exerted so much energy. It was exhausting and exhilarating. It was a whirlwind. A fun amusement ride that kept bringing me back for more. I would rather have a stack of unused plays in my wallet than money. I was always ready for the next down—I had a desire for them that was hard to fill.

My girlfriend Tami was heavily involved in her church and religion so I started joining her on Sundays in Vacaville. I grew up Catholic going to services on TAFB, like many of our friends, but Tami was a Baptist. That didn't matter much to me. I joined her anyway.

When we had to dissect a pig fetus in biology I had a tough time. The smell of the formaldehyde was overwhelming. I almost threw up. Since my assignment partner was a cute girl—I swallowed my regurgitated lunch without her noticing. I barely made it through the class without passing out. There was a reason I preferred history as my favorite class: no dissecting animals.

Unfortunately Pete wasn't getting much playing time on the gridiron. Nothing like he had hoped. I think he mainly joined the team to support our friendships. He was a good baseball and soccer player, and his heart was with those sports. I was still glad he was on our squad.

The coming weeks saw more victories and shutouts, with Bryan continuing his streak of rushing over a hundred yards per game. Hard-hitting was accompanying our play on the gridiron. Almost every game one or more opponents were injured, some with possible broken bones. My teammates were hitters. Mike and I broke a quarterback's collarbone as he kept the ball on a run off-tackle. Seeing limping players leave the field was commonplace; some left on stretchers.

One of our opponents was John Swett of Crockett. Anytime we played them it was an adventure—and not a good one. They were known at the time for not being a very good squad, hard hitters though, and their fans were prone to violence. We had to travel to face them. It was the only team we played where we wore our uniforms, including shoulder pads and helmets, as we arrived at the school. With other teams we stored our equipment in compartments under the bus.

Coach Moore instructed us to wear our uniforms because the John Swett fans were notorious for throwing beer bottles at arriving buses and players from a hill that overlooked the parking. When we arrived at their school we crossed at the 50-yard line, heading directly to the locker room to avoid being hit by thrown objects.

I had high hopes our winning streak would continue. It was John Swett after all. The coaches, though, didn't want us to underestimate them. Coach Moore stressed we could lose the game. Never give up and be the aggressor, he repeated over and over. Anyone can be beat, he continued.

We took the field and crossed at the 50-yard line again to avoid the thrown debris. No players were injured by incoming bottles. That part of our game plan worked flawlessly. From the kickoff to the whistle at halftime we played hard, but so did they. There was good sticking on the field by both teams. The collisions were earth-shattering. Those smashing sounds narrated our gridiron clash. (Bighorn rams would've shied away from our contact.) We were winning, but by only one touchdown. John Swett was scoreless.

As we jogged into the locker room from the 50-yard line, safe from incoming bottles, Coach Moore caught up with me. He asked me what was going on out there on the field. I made the mistake to say they were hitting hard. It was the first time in my years of football I upset a coach. Coach Moore was angered by my response, and I understood why. I should've chosen better words. Three seasons of hard-nosed football taught me to fear no one on the field, so making a comment like I had was sure to draw ire from him. That was the last thing a captain should say to his coach in a close-fought game. It was also the last thing a coach wanted to hear.

When we entered the locker room, one of the players left his helmet sitting in the middle of the walkway. So he wouldn't trip over it (and out of frustration), Coach Moore kicked the helmet, and it sailed across the room like a soccer ball bouncing off a wall.

Adjustments were made for Bryan to join Glenn, John, and me as linebackers. He would be beside me in the middle. Together we were like the dynamic duo—but not Batman and Robin—more like Batman and Batman. It gave me assurance knowing he was by my side, because he was the fastest guy on the team. If I couldn't catch someone he would. He hit harder than most of the guys in our league; however, he was our most valuable asset so we had to be careful he wasn't injured.

The second half of the game was one-sided. We dominated and gave them a beating they wouldn't soon forget. When the last second ticked off the clock we had a convincing shutout. The team had stepped up and performed well. I knew the coaches must've been proud. David Reyes had his first interception that game.

When we were on the bus ready to leave, our windows were shot out by a pellet gun. Coach Moore told all the players, cheerleaders, and support staff to put our heads down. We left there with our heads in our laps, but with a victory. We were still undefeated and unscored-upon. Coach Moore was unable to jog for weeks after kicking that helmet at John Swett.

He was nicknamed after a television character, and he was struggling with his school grades: John was a great tight end and linebacker. He chewed tobacco at practices, and it had to end. The coaches didn't care about his habit, but it was getting old tackling in his spittle. John was our 'Murdock' for sure. His presence had consequences for all of us on our squad. He made an impact, and we couldn't afford to lose him. So he had to hit the books harder. I needed the fun he was bringing to the game. He was a multi-dimensional character.

As we continued with victories and shutouts it was evident the play by my teammates was the reason why. They really honored the game with their effort. Individually, we probably had only two great athletes—Bryan and Ronnie—but as a team we were unstoppable. Our friendships, trust in each other, aggressiveness, and desire to be the best were carrying us towards greatness. Our season was mirroring our success as Travis Redskins.

Homecoming was right around the corner. It was the time of the year at school when the spirit was very high, and many events were planned for the students and players. Enthusiasm was off the charts.

On Homecoming Day we were excited as we loaded onto the flatbed trucks with rails for the football parade. The varsity players were on one truck and we had our own for the junior varsity squad. All the players, coaches, cheerleaders, and band members were there. The parade route was to take us around TAFB, so the

Air Force personnel and families could enjoy the event. Vanden and TAFB had strong ties. Military kids for decades had filled the Viking teams.

As we drove slowly around the base, thousands came out to wave, clap, and cheer. It was the closest thing to being a movie star. I knew Pat Woods felt at home being cheered, because he was quite the performer with his electric guitar in front of crowds. The parade lasted several hours and everyone had a great time. The annual event for the football program was a success.

We had prepared all week to face our Homecoming opponent at Vanden. We were as ready as we could be for the game. Kickoff was just a few minutes away when my contact lens fell out of my right eye. I felt it slipping and caught it with my hand. I ran to Coach Moore in a panic. I told him I needed to put it back in, and he asked me if I was able to do it quickly. I said I could, and I took off running from the field towards the locker room, which was about 125 yards away. I was breathing heavily as I struggled to put the contact back in using water as a lubricant. My hands were shaking because I was panicked. I stood in the locker room alone in front of the mirror knowing my coaches and teammates were waiting on me. I felt the pressure.

A lens falling out had never happened before, and I had been wearing them all through my freshman season and this one. With all the hard hits, the blocking, and the tackling there was never an issue. Fortunately, I was able to put it in and rushed back to the field. I found Coach Moore and told him I was ready to go. I was already exhausted from running back and forth in uniform.

Kickoff was still a few minutes away. As I went to the sidelines (as if fate was playing a cruel joke) my other contact fell out. I was able to catch it too with my hand. I was in a real panic now. I again told Coach Moore. There was no time now to put this one back in. I was on the kickoff and receiving teams and needed to go out for the coin toss. I knew what I had to do. I scrambled to find a clean cup. After what seemed an eternity, I found one. I placed the contact in the cup and took out the other one and put it in there too.

I had seen every issue happen with my contacts over the last few years and knew they could dry out and still be hydrated later with saline solution. I gave the cup to my teammate David Smith. I asked him to safeguard them. They were expensive, and I needed them to see, I told him. David said he would protect my contacts. They were in good hands.

I played the game struggling with my vision. Everything was blurry. I followed the movement of the play, and my teammates would yell where they thought the ball was going. On offense it was not a major problem because I knew who I had to block. Kickoffs, kickoff returns, and defense were another matter, though. Especially defense. If I squinted I could follow the ball, but barely.

We won the game with another shutout. I was relieved the game was over because I had a headache from the strain to my eyes. I went to David Smith to retrieve my contacts. He started to hand them to me, then giggled and shook the cup. I knew the end result before looking. I yelled for him to stop—it was too late. David didn't know dried contacts were brittle. He gave me the cup, and I looked inside. Yep, they had shattered. David apologized. I wasn't mad at him because he didn't understand what would happen with his little 'joke.'

The squad knew we were a few short games away from a perfect season. We wanted to finish the way we started. We knew we couldn't let up, or overlook any of our remaining opponents. Coach Moore stressed how important it was to continue playing as a team for every play. Hustle from whistle to whistle, he reminded us.

Coach Moore was looking at a season that most coaches would never see. An undefeated record, and one where no points were scored against us. It was something no Vanden squad before us has accomplished. Our JV team was good. It was every bit as good as the Travis Redskins two seasons earlier. Coach Moore and his assistants trained, developed, and conditioned us. Our season was a reflection on them.

In his initial season as the varsity skipper, Coach Bev was looking at a different outcome than Coach Moore's. Almost a 180-degree difference. It was apparent Coach Bev was frustrated. It had to be humbling. I wondered if he questioned himself or the capabilities of his assistants. It wasn't his fault or theirs, from where I stood. I watched them practice and watched every minute of the varsity games. They had a talented squad yet kept falling short. Injuries and important yardage never developed when they needed it.

The 1982 Vanden football program was a tale of two coaches: one looking at the best record, and one possibly the worst the school had ever seen. That season was a good and bad year in Viking football history.

We played hard and won those remaining games. We finished our season 9-0 undefeated and unscored-upon. Bryan easily rushed for over 1000 yards. He last accomplished that feat when we went undefeated on the Travis Redskins. There were many parallels between our Viking squad and that team. The running styles of Bryan and Glenn made both teams champions.

Coaches Moore, Cesna, Ordez, and Hogue developed us into the team we became. Our new coach Ordez directed the offensive and defensive lines into controlling the trenches. Coach Moore laid out winning offensive plays and all we had to do was follow his direction, perform, play with heart, and never quit. They lived up to their responsibilities to the squad and we did too.

Coach Bev and his team didn't fare well in their remaining games. They finished their season at 1-5-3. One win, five losses, and three ties. It was the worst record a Vanden varsity squad had seen in the 19 years since the inception of the program.

Turning in our equipment that year was tough because I really liked our team. We knew we had accomplished something special together as friends. We had two more years left in our football journey and we had had three winning seasons together. We had won 27 games and tied 2. Not a bad record for some Air Force brats. When we played together we were hard to beat because we played as 1 and not 11. We didn't have egos; we knew that the team winning was more important than personal glory. We were headed to the varsity level next. Were we ready for that test? I wondered. I knew dedication, guts and hard hits would decide our outcome.

The above photo shows the undefeated and unscored-upon 1982 9-0 Vanden Vikings Junior Varsity team. Photo courtesy of Travis Unified School District and Vanden High School.

I had known some of these guys since the first grade. We grew up together and shared life experiences: first girlfriends; class projects; school trips; ate meals at each other's homes and knew each other's families; and we won games as 'one.' We had struggled through physical exertion at practices, grew from kids to teenagers—and at the cusp of becoming men. I saw them go through embarrassing moments, awkward haircuts, acne, and world events. We were in school together when President Reagan was shot. We shared jokes, serious moments, and bonded. I had seen them laugh, cry, and get mad. I had a connection with these guys. That connection made us difficult to beat. These were good guys, great football players, and better friends.

[1982 Vanden JV Head Coach]

(Coach Spotlight) - Lou Moore

By 1982, I had known Coach Moore for five years. He had been my PE and History teacher, and wrestling coach at Golden West going back to 1978. Jeff and I would cut firewood with him from time to time. In those settings I liked and respected him as much as I did as my coach and teacher. In 1982, he was perfect as our skipper, directing our undefeated and unscored-upon season. Not many coaches can claim such a record but he can. That season was a direct result of his guidance. He made us champions. He wasn't only my teacher and coach, he was my friend. I never played for Coach Moore again. Thanks for the memories, Coach. You took names. Photo courtesy of Travis Unified School District and Vanden High School.

[1982 Vanden JV Coach]

(Coach Spotlight) - Mr. Cesna - (RIP)

Coach Cesna was a long-time fixture in the football program on the JV level at Vanden. I could tell he enjoyed teaching the fundamentals of football to young players. He helped mold us into a team that was undefeated and unscored-upon in 1982. Coach Cesna had a mild temperament, but he was able to instill his vision of what he wanted us to do and how to perform. We followed his winning direction. I respected him and liked him. I never played for Coach Cesna again. Thanks for the memories, Coach. You took names. Photo courtesy of Travis Unified School District and Vanden High School.

[1982 Vanden JV Coach]

(Coach Spotlight) - Mr. Ordez - (RIP)

In 1982, Coach Ordez was new to Vanden's JV football program. He fit right in, and took over duties of the offensive and defensive lines. I played for him as the right tackle, and interacted with him daily at practice. He had a strong grasp on how to develop trenchers. Our winning season that year was a direct result of Coach Ordez's input and assistance. In the one season I played for him, I liked him, and he earned my respect. He was a great addition to Vanden's football program. I never played for Coach Ordez again. Thanks for the memories, Coach. You took names. Photo courtesy of Travis Unified School District and Vanden High School.

[Guard and Defensive Tackle]

Player Spotlight) - Pat Woods #75
Guard, Defensive Tackle, and Specialty Teams

Pat played with us for three seasons in 1980 on the 11-0 undefeated Travis Redskins, the 1981 7-2, and the 1982 9-0 JV teams at Vanden. Pat played in the trenches on offense and defense during those three years, and he was a rock. Pat was very aggressive. He was able to shut down the run. He was the 'rocker' on our squad. He loved music and played the electric guitar. Pat liked to joke around, so in our team photo for the yearbook he intentionally made himself look small. I never played football with Pat again after the 1982 season. Thanks for the memories, Pat. You took names. Photo courtesy of Travis Unified School District and Vanden High School.

[Multi-Position]

(Player Spotlight) - Pete Watts #34
Multi-position and Specialty Teams

Pete was new to Vanden in 1981. In 1982, Pete played his first and only season of football with us. When Pete arrived as a new student, everyone liked him. He was very personable. In sports, Pete was a great athlete. He excelled at baseball and soccer. I think he joined us for football because he wanted to have fun and make memories with his friends. He did have fun and we did make memories that will last a lifetime. Pete performed well on the gridiron, and he could make you laugh when you needed it. I never played football with Pete again after the 1982 season. Thanks for the memories, Pete. You took names. Photo courtesy of Travis Unified School District and Vanden High School.

[Manager]

(Manager Spotlight) - Kenny Tarver #64

By 1982, I had known Kenny for many years. We went to school growing up at Golden West, and on Travis AFB at the elementary schools there. Kenny was my friend and one of the nicest guys I played football alongside. During our season in 1982, I injured Kenny during Hell Week. He hurt his shoulder and never played football again. That bothered me a lot. In the five seasons I was blessed to play football, that is my only regret. After the injury, Kenny stayed with the program and became the team equipment manager. He did that job extremely well. I never played football with Kenny again after the 1982 season. Thanks for the memories, Kenny. You took names. Photo courtesy of Travis Unified School District and Vanden High School.

After the football season ended, Jeff and I again went out for the track program. We were there to give our best efforts at throwing the shot put and discus. During one track practice, Jeff threw his shot put inside the ring and went to recover it. While he was bent over and just starting to stand up, a teammate threw his shot and caught Jeff between the shoulder blades, knocking him down. I rushed to him, expecting the worst. Jeff was injured but not seriously. A few more inches on the throw, or if he had been a few more inches closer, it would've caught Jeff in the back of the head and seriously injured or killed him. He recovered from the hit and was able to finish the track season. His years on the gridiron made Jeff a tough kid. Pain was just an obstacle for him to overcome, and he did often.

Like Sean, my brother Tim wanted to make his mark on a wrestling mat. At almost 6 foot Tim was the tallest of us four boys, yet he wrestled at only 128 pounds. Tim was thin and had a different build than mine. However, on a mat he was very good. Tim became the captain for the wrestling team. He also was dedicated to his education and graduated later that year as his class Salutatorian. He was offered and accepted a full scholarship to USC for Aeronautical Engineering.

My mom had her hands full with us four brothers, and we worked together to make sure she didn't know everything. Our home was a magnet for females, and Sean held parties often while Mom was working. I came home from the gym one weekend evening to discover Tim's right-hand index finger bandaged. The tip of it had been cut off when he and Sean had fought over a female classmate. Tim's hand had been slammed in a door, causing the injury. Fortunately for him, we didn't live far from the hospital, and they sewed the tip back on.

Did she have a premonition? I don't know; but that last kiss was different. It was intense and lasting. As I stood there by the side of her car, Tami stared up at me and said, "Now don't go fall in love with another girl." I thought that was silly when she said it. At 16, Tami was everything to me except football. I was in love with her—or thought I was—and I only had eyes for her. Then she gave me that last kiss. It made an impression.

Tami was supposed to join her mom and me on a 10-day mission to Mexico to help the poor. The trip was sponsored by her church. The day before we were to leave, Tami had to cancel and couldn't go with us. So there we stood saying our goodbye. Mine was a 'I will see you in ten days,' but Tami's was different. Hers was like a foretelling of impending doom.

Standing in that church I was sweating. It was hot and dusty in the small poor town we had stopped. We had been there for four days and it had been a memorable trip, but a hard one. I drank water from a faucet after playing soccer and had gotten sick. Now, I was singing, and scanning the room with my eyes. Where was she? I found her. She was looking back at me. I met Julie Leopold the first day of the trip. She was the most angelic girl I had ever known. She was a pastor's daughter from Pinole, California, and she always smiled.

After everyone left the church, there we both stood alone. Julie took my hand, and for a moment everything seemed right. I kissed her softly on the lips. Just a small kiss but with huge implications. I had a problem. A serious problem to face now. Why did I kiss her? Why was I falling for her? I didn't know. Maybe it was the combination of doing something good for the poor; the thickness of spirituality surrounding the trip; being in a foreign country at a young age without my family; and the way Julie looked at me.

    The ride home from Mexico reminded me of that trip home after playing for the California State Championship as a Redskin. It was a quiet ride for me, deep in thought. Tami was my second Musketeer. My second love. I didn't know what to do but I couldn't get Julie out of my mind. By the time we arrived back in Vacaville I was physically and emotionally exhausted. I knew what I had to do—I wasn't looking forward to it.

    Tami picked me up in the same spot when I left, and we drove to her home and sat in front. She began to cry. Did she know before I even told her? Something bad had happened while we were away and she was devastated. Tami wouldn't tell me what it was but she was broken, and tears poured down the side of her face. My guilt was overwhelming. I had to be honest. I owed Tami that much. When she was able to control her crying, I told her I had bad news. I had fallen for another girl and was leaving. Tami never saw my intentions coming, and began to cry harder. Why did I tell her then, when she was already heartbroken? I don't know. It was callous and mean, and the wrong timing. At 16, though, we make mistakes. I knew I made one as I watched her sob.

    I got out of her car and walked home, carrying my bags. Three miles alone, feeling small. That Monday at school I made the situation worse. I was walking to the school library when Tami stopped me. I was wearing the shirt she bought me for my last birthday. As Tami stared at me she reached for my breast pocket and removed the photo I had there. It was a picture of Julie. Tami looked at it and asked, "Is that her?" I told her yes. She put the photo back in my pocket and walked away without saying another word. I felt even smaller. We never got back together, and I began to date Julie. When I would see Tami in school or at sporting events, I was always reminded I had hurt a good decent girl who cared about me. Coach Hatcher never treated me any different for hurting his daughter. I think he understood young love.

It was presented like a scene from the movie 'Chariots of Fire.' A great race of Olympic proportions. It was one that would be remembered, he said. "I can beat him," Gem kept repeating. No matter how hard I tried to dissuade Gem, he wouldn't listen. There is no doubt he had the heart of a lion but Bryan had the speed of a cheetah. I knew he couldn't beat Bryan in a 40-yard dash; but Gem wouldn't let it go. Yes, they had similar builds and were about the same size, but I had played football with Bryan for 3 years. I had witnessed his speed. I knew his capabilities. Bryan was a beast, and not to be reckoned with in a foot race. Gem was proud, though. He was Turkish, and a running back from Michigan, and my age. He was an Air Force brat too, and had amassed 1000-plus yards rushing season the year before. I saw the newspaper clippings. He was my friend, and Bryan was too.

I met Gem Nalkiran at the base gym the prior summer, and he made a lasting impression with me. He was an entertainer at heart. He wore a gold chain, and his personality was much bigger than his frame. It was the second summer in a row he came to Travis AFB to spend time with his mom and stepdad. I had told him the stories of Bryan, so when he met him that day at the gym, Gem had to challenge the legend.

Gem billed it as the Great Race as he asked all the airmen to come outside. He wanted witnesses, so about 30 of us were there. Sidewalk to sidewalk on the grass area behind the gym was the scene. I wanted no part of it, so I wouldn't do the countdown and say "Go." An airman gave the green light and it was over in a few seconds. Gem was very fast but it wasn't that close. Bryan just seemed to get faster each time I saw him. His legend grew. Did it humble Gem? No. I don't think anything could dampen his belief in himself. I liked Gem, though, because he wasn't arrogant, just proud.

Gem and I spent a lot of time together that summer. In a way he replaced Jim for those few months. Gem became Jeff's and my weightlifting partner there at the base gym. All three of us spent those months pushing ourselves to gain strength and size. Gem returned home to Michigan in 1983 and I never saw him again. When I thought of Gem, I knew my Turkish friend was taking names in Michigan and becoming a legend of his own. I wished I could've shared the gridiron with him.

The summer break came and went quickly. It was ending soon and that meant the good news I wanted to hear. Football season was near. It had been too long since we last stepped on the gridiron. The upcoming season was going to be on the varsity level. The collisions would be more intense. I couldn't wait for those 'stingers.' They were addictive.

The above two photos show Gem Nalkiran (Bertone) during his gridiron years as a running back. Photos supplied by Gem. The below photo shows (left to right front to back) my brother Sean, Gem, me, and David Smith cleaning our pool in 1983.

Injury and Loss
The setback

They had prepared for us. The pads were on the sleds; cones were configured; blocking and tackling bags were laid out and ready. There were plays on the chalkboard written in X's and O's. The coaches were wearing their whistles and shorts. We were suited, quiet, and awaiting direction. I was chewing on my mouthpiece.

Sitting in the locker room I was tapping my feet. I was usually calm—this morning I wasn't. I felt nervous, uneasy. Looking around I saw most of my friends except David Reyes and Pat Woods. Neither wanted to play this season. I wished they were here. We could use their help. A few deep breaths didn't ease my nerves.

I understood why I was nervous. We would finally find out how good we were as a team and as individual players. The varsity level was a lot different from JV and Pop Warner. Some of the opponents we would face would be much bigger, stronger, and faster than most of us. I wasn't afraid or worried but an ominous feeling lingered. I tried to shake it off.

"Hit the field" was finally called. 60-plus pairs of cleats hit the tile almost in sequence and scrambled towards the door. Once they hit the asphalt outside, it sounded like a herd. Head Coach Ronald Beverly, known as 'Bev,' called us all over to the center of the varsity field. The JV squad went to theirs. Their head coach was Gerald Hatcher. Our other coaches, Ron Harden and Tom Newsom, stood near Bev.

Last season, Bev had struggled in his first year as head coach, but he seemed confident as he talked. I believe he had something to prove to himself, to the school and to our fans. He wasn't a 1-5-3 coach. He was better than that, and the next few months would mold the casting for his time as Vanden's varsity skipper. He laid out his vision for Hell Week, what he wanted to accomplish and what he expected. He looked around as he talked to us. He made eye contact with me a few times. Coach Bev had a Fu Manchu mustache, and he was in good shape. His shorts couldn't hide the surgical scars on both his repaired knees.

Next, Coach Harden spoke. He looked rough and grizzled. He was seasoned, and had a mustache, too. He snapped his words out. His speech was firm and direct.

Finally, Coach Newsom spoke. He had lost a lot of weight from when I first met him as a freshman. He looked almost 150 pounds lighter. The jogging was paying off for him.

Coach Bev instructed us to break off for stretching and warm-ups. After about fifteen minutes of prepping we were ready to go.

We split into groups. I went with the linemen. It was already getting hot out. I was sweating and my hair was damp inside my helmet. I looked around at the other linemen. Jeff, Chris, Mark, John, Mike, and Frank (David's older brother from my freshman season) were there, along with Bob Weber, Gary Jennings, and a new guy named Joe. We started with basic drills and bag hitting. We were on display for Coach Harden. He was sizing us up to see who could do what. Drill after drill. The drills started slow but began picking up in speed and intensity. This wasn't junior varsity football, I told myself.

Frank was quick and aggressive. He had talent. Bob, who was a senior like Frank, was much bigger but a little slower. Jeff had put on weight from lifting and he seemed quicker. Mark and Mike seemed faster and taller. Chris too was bigger. He was only a sophomore but I was sure he would be starting. John was always quick off the ball and was already playing his 'Murdock' character. Gary was showing he had skills and wanted to play. The new guy, Joe Leonard, was tall. He had recently moved down from Alaska. He was quiet as we drilled.

The call was made to break off into defensive groups. I went with the linemen but was switched back and forth from there to work with the linebackers. That is where I wanted to play. I enjoyed hunting running backs with Glenn. Frank was a linebacker and a good one. There was a new transfer student named Darrick Peterkin. He was big and fast. I heard he wanted to be our tight end. I could tell we were going to have some hitters on the team.

There was some speed and big playmakers on

our small squad: Broyce Batchan, Bryan Batchan and Alvin Baldwin. I never played with Alvin but he had been an impact player for the varsity football program for the last two seasons. He started on the squad as a sophomore. With Broyce, Bryan, and Alvin in the backfield, we had three quarters of the fastest 220-and 440-yard relay track team in the state. Ronnie Beverly was back as our starting quarterback. He was bigger and faster and his arm had matured. It was a rocket. Ronnie was only a sophomore like Chris; but both would be vital to the squad.

The team had tons of potential provided we stayed healthy. I almost didn't want that thought to cross my mind because I worried about jinxing us. I believed in jinxes. Yeah, I know it's stupid; but I did. I would 'knock on wood' if someone said something I thought might cause a bad omen. That was just me. I wanted to have a good season without it being affected by bad thoughts.

Late in the practice we broke off into specialty teams. One of our kickoff returnees was a senior named Doug Chong. He was athletic, quick, and a great addition to our squad. Punts were being launched into the air by my friend David Smith, and Doug and others were to field them. As one of the punts fell from the sky Doug went to catch it. It should've been an easy one to move upfield, but he dropped it and yelled out in pain. Practice stopped. Everyone looked over. I was not far from Doug, so I jogged towards him. He had a severely broken finger. It was twisted and looked very painful. Doug left the field for medical attention and never returned that season. We had lost a big impact player our very first practice. It was not a good start to our 1983 season.

"Line up on the 40" was called. I knew what that meant. The dreaded wind sprints. I always disliked those but knew they were necessary to get conditioned to last four quarters in a football game. Since we were a small school some of us played both ways and rarely had any rest during a contest.

The whistle blew and we sprinted. Twenty 40-yard dashes later I was sucking wind and so was everyone else. Without giving us a chance to recover Coach Bev told us to line up on the goal line for "Gassers": 200-yard timed sprints. We did ten of them. My legs felt like noodles. I thought I was going to throw up, and my head was baking in my helmet. It was hot outside and dripping sweat burned my eyes. I struggled not to bend over to catch my breath.

Thankfully "bring it in" was finally called, and we jogged to Coach Bev and took a knee. He commended us on a good practice, and we broke for lunch and rest. We would be back in a few hours for the afternoon session. Water was the main course for most of us as we rested.

The afternoon practice went about the same: seeing who could do what, blocking, hitting, running, and catching drills. Darrick did have great hands. He could run a nice route and catch well. Darren was going to be in a battle with several players for a wide receiver position.

It was obvious Mike would be kicking field goals and extra points. He had accuracy and power for distance. The previous season he kicked a 47-yard field goal and made several others in the 40 range.

The conditioning part of the practices always seemed to come too fast. It was gut check time. We struggled through our wind sprints and gassers again and finished our first day without another injury. We didn't have many players on the squad, so we couldn't afford to lose anyone else. Losing Doug was bad enough, and it would be noticeable. We played with the personnel we had and there was no deep bench to draw from. With Vanden being an Air Force school we could lose players at any time to a parent being transferred.

I didn't fear much when I played. I knew I would face better athletes, so I expected that. I knew pain and stingers from hard collisions were in the forecast, so I was prepared for them. I knew I would get beat on a play sometimes, so I would get even on the next one. I knew we would fall behind in games and comeback. That was football, so I could handle those things. The only thing that truly worried me was the unknown factor—an unwelcome surprise that could affect the outcome of a game.

Many drills, offensive and defensive plays, sled pushing and conditioning all followed throughout the week. No more injuries occurred. The starting offense and defense units were being solidified. The coaches needed to form somewhat of a team for our coming Saturday Watermelon Scrimmage against Armijo.

Ronnie was our quarterback, with Broyce, Alvin, and Bryan as our running backs. Our fullback was going to be a player named Mike Brown. We had another new player that season named Maurice Gwinn who was showing promise as a fullback. Glenn wasn't going to play offense. His days of running up the gut and over linebackers was coming to an end. If we needed him, though, there was no doubt in my mind Glenn could still be a devastating blocker and ball carrier up the middle.

Our tight end was going to be Darrick Peterkin, with Michael Farace and Eric Barnes, Ronnie's stepbrother, backing him up. The split end position was wide open with several players vying for it. Darren was in the mix.

The offensive line consisted of Jeff at center. It was his ninth year in the trenches. Frank was right guard, with Bob right tackle. Chris was left tackle, with me as the left guard. Since Frank wore the number 54, I changed to the number 55, which Mike had worn for two years on the JV squad. The new number quickly eclipsed my old numbers (28 and 60) as my favorite.

Defense consisted of Jeff and Dave Haupt as defensive ends, and Chris, Bob, Mark, John, Mike, Gary, and me as defensive tackles. John and I could play nose guard. The linebackers were Glenn, Frank, Darrick, and me. Broyce and Paul Wilkerson were safeties, while Ronnie and Alvin were cornerbacks.

As Hell Week ended successfully we had our team. The Watermelon Scrimmage (at Vanden) against Armijo went well. My former Redskin teammate—Mike Lindsey—was a standout on the Armijo squad. Though we were on either sides of the ball, our friendship remained. That 1980 season bonded us forever.

A pre-season Quadraplay known as the 'Benicia Jamboree' was set. It was an exhibition night game scheduled in Benicia. We were to face three other teams, each of us getting offensive and defensive series against the other squads. It was a feeling-out period for coaches to see how their teams were developing. It was an annual event for the squads to test each other.

The Quadraplay was going well with our team showing promise against the Benicia, Dixon, and Hogan teams. Broyce was having a big scrimmage with two interceptions. In the fourth quarter, he leapt into the air to successfully knock down a potential touchdown pass in the end zone.

As Broyce went up, a stress fracture in his shin snapped the bone. The fracture had occurred during the basketball season a year earlier yet he had been cleared medically to play football. Broyce was taken off the field on a stretcher and gone for the season. It was a huge loss to the team because he was a starting two-way impact player. He was one of our biggest weapons, and he was gone. Just like that we had lost a captain with a speed of 4.2 seconds in the 40-yard dash.

Broyce's loss meant Alvin and Bryan would share the halfback positions in our wishbone offense. Paul Wilkerson was moved to safety and Alvin would share safety and cornerback positions. In a matter of a few weeks we lost two players that could make the difference between wins and losses. I wondered if our season was cursed before it began.

School started, and as I walked around the campus that first day, I met Mr. Kiefer, a history teacher. He was a large man with a short flat-top haircut. A former football player in college, he had been a teacher at Vanden since it opened in 1964. Mr. Kiefer was a friendly man who laughed loud and liked to joke with the students.

One student Mr. Kiefer liked to joke with was Theresa Bellew. He could be heard calling her "Buck" loudly in front of other students. He nicknamed her Buck because there was a great quarterback who had played at the University of Georgia with the same-sounding last name as her, but spelled differently, Buck Belue.

My brother Tim had graduated the year before, so that left my younger brother Craig and me at Vanden. Craig was a freshman but was quickly carrying on the Rooney name in reputation. Of the four of us boys, Dad leaving appeared to affect Craig the most, and it became more apparent when he became a Viking. He in his own way began to rebel. I didn't notice it at first because I was so busy with football.

Our first scheduled game was against Galt, and we had to travel to face them. It was a non-league contest in the outlying area of Sacramento. Galt was ranked #2 in small schools in Superior California, so we knew it would be a tough battle. They had a good solid football program. They were a good match as our first opponent.

When the whistle blew ending the contest, our offense had compiled a total of 343 yards with 181 yards coming on the ground. Our sophomore quarterback, Ronnie Beverly, threw for 162 yards. Alvin Baldwin scored two touchdowns rushing. We won 20-7 against a very good team.

That Monday when we watched game film, Coach Bev stressed we would have to step it up against our next opponent, Hogan. They were in the MEL league, and Hogan had four times as many students as Vanden.

Our practice that day involved extra wind sprints and gassers to prepare us to play four quarters that Friday night. Coach Bev knew he didn't have many players and even fewer with big bodies. He knew he had to train and develop us well. He wasn't going to have another losing season no matter what obstacles we had to face.

Coach Bev stressed the importance of conditioning. He knew the difference between a good and a great team was conditioning. It made champions. He would tell us conditioning would matter in the second half and especially the fourth quarter. The team with the better-conditioned players would have the energy needed to prevail. As we struggled with those side-cramping runs, Bev would bark at us that no opponent would be more physically or mentally prepared. He was determined to never see a 1-5-3 season again.

That Friday, we played Hogan at Corbus Field in Vallejo. Their players were big and fast and they had more suited than we did. It was a hard-fought contest. Jarring hits and crushing tackles were plenty. It was action-packed. Ronnie threw for 130 yards and three touchdowns. We were still outplayed and lost 27-18. It was a tough bruising game that battered our team.

Mark pulled ligaments in his right thumb and would miss the next month. Bob jammed a thumb, and I had to be helped off the field on a stretcher when a helmet hit me in the right shin, flipping me over as I blitzed in. I thought I broke my leg but thankfully the x-ray said otherwise. Our 1-1 record was starting to reflect the damage the team had suffered in players lost for the season and the building injuries we were facing. Two games into the season our squad was hampered.

Just like military ribbons or medals, stickers decorating an opponent's helmet displayed their resume as a football player. Each sticker signified something they had done in a game. The stickers were given out for big hits or big plays. The amount of stickers were like earned chevrons of a corporal, sergeant, or lieutenant. The players with the most stickers were the true leaders on a team. Those were the ones we liked to battle and test ourselves against.

That week during practices we were hobbled. We couldn't practice full speed on offense or defense, as three of us linemen were injured. Half-speed drills were used so we could still go through our game plan to face our coming opponent that Friday night, Dixon. For the third week in a row, we were going to be on the road traveling to face an opponent.

She had never been to any of my games since I started playing football. I think she was worried for my safety and thought the game was dangerous. She saw my bruises and limps often, and knew how much I loved it all. When my mom told me midweek that she and Andre were coming to our game Friday night in Dixon, I was excited. I wanted to make them proud. I planned on making an impression they both would remember. I didn't know it would be the first and last game my mom would ever attend.

When we arrived in Dixon that Friday night it was like all the other games I played over the past four years. I was looking forward to facing the Rams, and ready to notch another victory in our column. The game against Hogan was the first my friends and I had lost in four seasons. We were 28-1-2 as teammates.

We suited, listened to the plan Coach Bev had

developed, and went over the offensive and defensive schemes. We got down on our knees and prayed. I prayed for a victory and everyone's safety. When we exited the locker room and jogged onto the field to warm up, I looked towards the stands. I wondered where in the stadium my mom was sitting.

From the kickoff, the first half didn't go as we hoped. Dixon was ready for us. We were down at halftime, held scoreless, while Dixon had two touchdowns on the scoreboard. It was not the impression I wanted to make with my mom and Andre, or with the Rams. I also didn't want a second loss two weeks in a row, and the second of my career. We had to turn the tide.

During the halftime break, adjustments were made by our coaches as to what we would do in the second half. We had to step things up, play harder, and take chances, with more blitzing. We had to take the fight to the Rams. I told myself—play like 'Psycho' would.

We finally got on the scoreboard early in the third quarter, when Ronnie threw a 28-yard pass to Darrick for a touchdown. We were coming back.

On defense I was playing middle linebacker with Frank. Glenn and Darrick were the outside linebackers. We had plans to blitz repeatedly, to throw off their offensive timing, disrupt plays, and shut down their running and passing game. We needed to stop their offense. As the defensive calls came in, all four of us linebackers took turns blitzing or all together. We were having some success in stopping Dixon's forward progress, making tackles and shutting them down.

Another blitz was sent in for the next play. I was

ready to go. I had my knees bent. My eyes watched the quarterback closely. I was glued to his every move. Explode hard and fast, and go for the ball, I repeated to myself. It seemed like forever before I saw movement. The ball was hiked and I went flying into the backfield. The quarterback swung back and to the left, with me pursuing him. I was on his heels. My head turned to the right and then it happened. For a split second I saw it coming—a facemask. I didn't have time to react to the impact.

    I went down hard, landing on my face. I was knocked unconscious and the play stopped. Coaches, teammates, and referees along with medical staff rushed to where I lay. After assessing me I was carefully removed from the field on a stretcher so the game could resume. My facemask had to be removed with a screwdriver to give me oxygen. The paramedics were worried about a head and neck injury, so they didn't want to remove my helmet.

    I was taken to the far end zone under the scoreboard, while they tended to me. I wasn't aware of what was going on because I remained unconscious. My mom didn't know it was me injured, so a coach had to go into the stands to tell her. My mom and Andre came down to where I was. She never wanted to come to my games because she feared for my safety. And there I was right in front of her, injured. Her worst fear had happened.

    A paramedic eventually asked me to move my right, then left foot, and I could. I was semi-conscious but I couldn't talk. I was loaded into the back of an ambulance headed to Sutter Davis Hospital. On the way I lost consciousness again, and they were unable to wake me.

When the ambulance arrived at Sutter Davis Hospital it sat in the emergency parking area for several minutes. The hospital couldn't take me because they were not equipped to handle my type of brain injury. The doctors made a decision. I had to be transported to UC Davis Medical Center in Sacramento. So the ambulance headed there. My mom rode with the paramedics.

Hours later, I awoke in the hospital. When my eyes opened I felt the worst crushing and exploding pain in my head I had ever experienced. My throat was dry and my eyes had trouble focusing.

Then I heard the bad news. I had a serious head injury, and they needed to run a battery of tests over the next few days. I would have to stay in the hospital. They needed to keep my brain swelling down and monitor it for bleeding.

Saturday and Sunday a battery of tests were run for a TBI, Traumatic Brain Injury. A CT scan and MRI were done. The crushing and exploding pain in my head persisted.

I don't think I understood the doctor when he told me I wouldn't be playing football again. It didn't register. I had to be out there with my friends.

Coaches Bev, Harden, and Newsom came to see me. They were a welcome sight. We didn't talk about the game. They just wanted to see how I was doing. I was comforted by their presence.

Monday morning I was finally released from the hospital. Look for signs of confusion, dizziness, and forgetfulness. Any problems, come right back. The doctor said no more football. I had a major concussion, and my brain needed time to heal. It couldn't withstand another impact from a hit without causing more serious damage.

The drive home from Sacramento with my mom was quiet. I didn't feel like talking, and the headache I was having was causing nausea. When we arrived home I went straight for the sports sections of the Saturday, Sunday, and Monday newspapers. I laid them on the dinner table and sat down to read the outcome of the game.

We lost, it read; and it wasn't close: 25-6. It was the worst loss in a game of my four years of football. I felt horrible for my friends and coaches. I felt like I let them down. I read every word closely, trying to soak it all in. My vision struggled to keep up. My head felt like it was in a vice and someone was tightening it.

Saturday and Sunday stories were read and set aside. I turned to the Monday analysis. I read the Vanden and Dixon game write-up. My eyes drifted down the page, and I saw my name listed in an article titled, "A True Competitor" by John Plain in his column, The Plain View. Who was this writer? I wondered. I did not know him personally. He seemed to know me, though.

His entire column, which was the width of the bottom of the paper, was about me. I read every word slowly. How did he know me, and how I was taught by Coach Kelly to play on the gridiron? I was stunned reading about what happened that Friday night in Dixon. It was all there. Near the end, eight words stopped me. "Unfortunately, he will be out for the season." There it was in print. It hit hard. I couldn't play with my friends and teammates again that season. I read the article probably a dozen times, trying to digest it. I felt nauseated.

A True Competitor

It happened suddenly. It wasn't premeditated. But when you play as hard as Jeff Rooney plays, chances are it will happen sooner or later.

Rooney, a standout player for Vanden High School, was leveled in the third quarter of a game against Dixon High School Friday night. A player as tough as Rooney can easily come back from most injuries and play with the same reckless abandon that led to the injury in the first place.

But Rooney didn't get up. A hush came over the crowd. Coaches, players and trainers surrounded the fallen player. "He's out cold," someone on the sideline said.

He was.

A coach never likes to see one of his players go down that way. The only way a player can go down that way is if he is playing as though every play will be his last. That's the way Rooney played Friday night. He's not afraid to run full-tilt into another player.

The final diagnosis, a major concussion. Rooney is okay. Unfortunately, he will be out for the season. But it could have been worse.

"You never like to see that happen to a player," Dixon Head Coach Bob Watkins said after the game. "I just hope he's alright," he added.

Football is a tough game. Jeff Rooney knows that now more than ever. But don't look for him to do too much complaining about his ill fortune. Fierce competitors like Rooney understand the risk they take when the pigskin flies through the air every weekend in the fall.

Above article courtesy of the Reporter.

I cut the article out, folded it, and put it in my top drawer so I could remind myself from time to time why I couldn't play football with my friends. I also wanted to motivate myself to do everything possible so I could join them again on the field. One of my worst fears had happened. I let my teammates down when I got injured. It ate at me. I knew I couldn't let that happen again.

That evening my friend and teammate of three years, David Reyes, came to my house to check on me. Even though he wasn't playing football that season in 1983, he was still my teammate in spirit. David asked if there was anything he could do, and told me if I needed help with anything to let him know. He was a true friend and the best teammate any football player could have.

When I went to school Tuesday morning, I was pulled out of my first-period class by Principal Juhl and Assistant Principal Sideris. They asked me to come to the office. Once there, they told me all my teachers had been briefed about my head injury and what to expect. I was told all my tests for the remainder of the year would be in class open-book, or I could take them home and do them there. They told me not to feel stressed over the school work, and if I was tired in class to put my head down on my desk and rest. They said they knew I had been a good student, and they didn't want my grades to suffer for something out of my control. The head injury I had was going to cause short-term memory loss and make school work difficult. I was then allowed to return to my class.

After school that day I headed to football practice. When I walked into the locker room my friends greeted me. Coach Bev waved me up to the coaches' office. I opened the door and he invited me inside. Coaches Newsom and Harden were there. All three said they were happy to see me. Coach Bev asked how I was doing, and I told him I was fine. He asked why I was there, because I couldn't play anymore that season. I needed rest and time off to recover, he said.

I told him I still wanted to be part of the team. I wanted to help any way I could and be there to support my teammates and friends. I could contribute. I could help set up equipment, warm someone up throwing a football, or maybe hold a bag on half-speed drills. I told him I understood I could have no contact. I could tell he was concerned for my safety, but he knew what the game meant to me. It was evident I wanted to be there. At that moment I needed the game more than ever, and he knew that.

After discussing it with Harden and Newsom, Coach Bev said I could help. I was still part of the team. That practice, I helped get equipment out and set up for the session. I watched my friends warm up, stretch, practice, and do their conditioning, preparing for our next opponent on Friday, River City of West Sacramento.

Mark, like myself, was out with an injury. His ligaments in his thumb would take a few more weeks to heal. That week, we watched our friends prepare for our next contest.

Friday came quick, and finally we were playing at Vanden on our gridiron, the George Gammon Field. I was excited. I wore my jersey and walked the sidelines while my teammates battled River City. We scored a touchdown in the first quarter from a four-yard run by Alvin, and took a 6-0 lead into halftime.

Mark and I would run water out to our teammates between plays, encouraging them. They were playing well. On the sidelines I cheered them on as loudly as I could. I began to have crushing pain in my head. I took my prescribed medication I kept in my pocket to help alleviate the headache. Dizziness followed as I became more animated throughout the game. "Slow down," I was told by Coach Newsom. "Take it easy," he said.

In the second half, Bryan took the kickoff at our 10-yard line and scrambled 90 yards for a touchdown. It was an impressive sight. River City battled back. On the first play from scrimmage, after receiving the next kickoff, Bryan threw off multiple River City Raider players and rushed 60 yards for another score. Alvin rambled in for the two-point conversion. Again River City began to battle back but Murdock intercepted a shuttle pass and returned it 68 yards to the River City's 30-yard line before being brought down in open field.

As I watched my teammates and friends from the sidelines, I realized I was their biggest fan. It was one thing to play with them on the gridiron, but it was another thing to watch them play. They were something to see that night. We went on to win, beating River City 22-14 in a hard-fought game. Thankfully, we had no injuries.

That weekend after our victory, our center, Jeff Martin, was involved in a serious auto accident. He wrapped his Monte Carlo around a tree and received a deep laceration to his chin. On Monday, Jeff showed up for practice sporting a bandage covering his injury. Even though the chin strap was going to agitate the laceration, Jeff wasn't going to let that stop him. We had another opponent that week, and Jeff would be there anchoring the offensive line. He wouldn't let us down.

I could tell something was wrong with me, and I didn't feel right. My balance and coordination seemed off. I went to the doctors at David Grant Hospital on TAFB begging to play football, though. I was told no. Not again this season, and maybe never. I was undeterred.

I went to every practice, and would go into school early to lift weights. I needed to stay in shape. I tried running, but headaches, dizziness and lack of coordination prevented me. That week I fell down the stairs in our home twice, rolling to the bottom and hitting the wall. Once was in front of my brother Tim. I begged him not to tell Mom. She would never let me play football again, I told him. Tim honored my request—he never told her.

I was scared. Everything I did was for the game, and I had spent a year preparing for the season. Then it was taken away so quickly. What would I do if I could never play again? I didn't know. I never planned for an injury and truthfully never thought it would happen to me. I was wrong. Now I was looking at losing the most important thing in my life forever. I wasn't ready to let go. The fear of the unknown was causing more pain than the concussion. I was wounded in more ways than one.

School work was hard. I struggled with trying to complete thoughts and convert them into words. I was thankful I could rest in class and take my tests home. I was feeling tired all the time. I struggled with sleep.

That Friday, we faced Justin at Vanden. They were a good team and outweighed our linemen twenty pounds per player. It was going to be a battle.

In the first quarter, Frank ripped a Justin player in the facemask, and broke his right hand. He kept playing until the hand swelled too much by halftime. He was pulled from the game and gone for the season. A huge loss for the team as Frank was a captain and a two-way starter. His leadership had been invaluable.

Darrick stepped up that game. He was a huge impact player like Alvin, Bryan, and Ronnie. He caught six passes for 70 yards. On defense Glenn and Darrick shut down the Justin run game. The contest was close, until the fourth quarter, when Justin blew it out. We lost 34-14. Bryan twisted his ankle severely in the last few minutes on a run up the sidelines.

We had a 2-3 record. The squad had lost Doug, Broyce, me, and Frank for the season. Mark was still out with his thumb injury but was expected back soon. Bryan, one of our two running backs, was now hobbled badly. The squad was limping but determined.

I was apologetic as I helped him off the ground. I could tell he was irritated. It wasn't what he'd asked me to do—but I had stumbled. Coach Bev had stepped in for Ronnie to direct a play at practice and he wanted me to blitz in (at half-speed). I did and lost my balance. I fell into his scarred knees knocking him down. "Take it easy!" he said. He wouldn't have to tell me twice. Thankfully, he wasn't injured, and he still let me assist at practices.

Darrick and Alvin took the reins for the squad. Both were two-way work horses. Darrick had great hands and had crushing hits. Alvin was fast and flashy but a back-breaker when he hit. Glenn wasn't going to let offenses roll over our Vanden defense. Murdock added another look to his personality: his game face.

The coaches didn't let any worries they had trickle down to the team. They remained positive too, like my teammates. Coach Harden could be heard encouraging the offensive and defensive lines. He had a way of drawing the best performance from them. Coach Newsom was directing the defense, and they were playing fearlessly. Coach Bev gave the guys the confidence to win.

That week the team had only 18 healthy players. At practice, the offense would run plays against half of a defensive squad, even with me holding a bag on half speed drills. Offensive plays would all be run to one side at a time because there weren't enough players to fill the defensive line and linebackers. The defense would then switch to the other side, and offensive plays were called in that direction.

Friday night, we faced Delta with our 18 helmets. Bryan, and Michael Brown, our fullback, were out. Our run game was missing some steam but we still had Alvin and Maurice. If needed, Glenn could run the ball well up the gut. Our safety, Paul Wilkerson, played the game with a broken nose. He injured it in the first few minutes of the contest. We beat Delta 20-8. The victory gave the team the self-confidence it needed because the mounting injuries were taking a toll.

I started jumping rope a little in my backyard, trying to regain my coordination affected by the injury. It was a struggle. I could only do a few revolutions before I would lose my balance. I knew I had a long way to go if I wanted to play football again. I was careful to hide the issues affecting me, because if my mom found out, she wouldn't let me play my senior season. Since I would be 17 years old, I still needed her approval.

I could tell that Mom never wanted me to play football again. She was worried. It made me think of the story I heard when my dad injured Tim when he was baby. Sean and Tim were only one year apart, and Dad used to swing Sean by his arms. Tim at the time was frail and Dad was worried about hurting him. One day Tim kept lifting his arms to be picked up and swung like Sean. When Dad relented and picked him up, he dislocated Tim's arm at the elbow. The news got worse when the emergency room doctor told my parents Tim would never use that arm again. It was paralyzed. That night my parents cried and prayed. When they returned to the hospital the next day they were informed Tim would be okay. He went on to make a full recovery. I could see that type of worry in Mom's eyes when I talked of returning to football. I understood her concerns but the call of the gridiron was too strong. I needed the game. It became part of me.

Our next opponent was John Swett, and we were to face them at Vanden. There would be no bottles thrown or crossing at the 50-yard line to avoid being hit by flying debris. It was our Homecoming Game, and Coach Bev stressed he wanted a score early. Alvin listened closely and he took the opening kickoff and rambled 91 yards for a touchdown. It was an incredible run. Coach Bev's request was fulfilled within the first few seconds.

Bryan played only a little because of his ankle injury, so Alvin had to carry the workload. Darrick stepped up to help him lead the team to a resounding victory. We won 43-0.

The team was over the .500 mark at 4-3, and we wanted to stay there. My friends and teammates of four years had never had a losing season, and we didn't want to have one now.

That coming Friday night we were to face our toughest opponent in Benicia. They were undefeated. We had to travel to their field to face them, and that gave them an advantage over us.

A good week of practice without any additional injuries, and Mark healthy and ready to play, gave the team confidence. Two weeks in a row with victories also helped raise spirits that Benicia could be the third win.

Darrick was leading the team defensively, averaging 12 tackles a game. He was all over the place, making things difficult for opponents. We knew if he continued to play like that, a victory against Benicia was within grasp.

The game at Benicia was a low-scoring battle. In the first quarter Darrick hauled down their top running back in the end zone for a safety. A few minutes later Darrick caught a pass from Ronnie for a touchdown. We won 8-0. Benicia was thrown for losses 14 times, and held to a total of 57 yards offensively. Our defense stepped up. During the last three games combined, our Viking team outscored opponents 71-8.

Our final game was against Rio Vista. We beat them 20-9. We ended our regular season with four straight wins and in a three-way tie for second place in SCAL. The team had pulled together and didn't let the multiple injuries deter them from winning games.

The league coaches had to vote which of the three teams that were tied for second place would go to the playoffs: Benicia, Justin, or us. The coaches chose us. We were scheduled to face the Oak Ridge Trojans the following week at their field.

The coaches and team prepared hard for the first-round playoff game for the Sac-Joaquin Section title against Oak Ridge. We watched game film on them and knew they were a big squad in weight and in number of players suited. We would be facing them with 19 players.

It was a wet rainy night when the team took the field to face the Trojans. It was going to be a tough battle. From the sidelines, Frank, Broyce, and I cheered on our teammates. It was a back-and-forth game with big hits and big plays. The guys all played well, but Oak Ridge overpowered our Viking teammates. We lost 27-12. It was a bitter end to a season of injury and loss.

When the team was decimated by injuries, the remaining players pulled together and played with heart, battling to a 6-4 record. My teammates were better conditioned than the opponents they faced but lacked in healthy numbers, which affected the outcome of some games.

It was sad to say goodbye to the seniors that would never play football again at Vanden: Broyce, Frank, Alvin, Darrick, Bob, Mike Farace, and others. I learned much from them that season. Mike Holovach moved away later that year. That season in 1983, my teammates made the Vanden football program proud. They showed character and played like champions. It was a setback for me and my friends. We lost games and I was injured. We had to come back. Our journey together had one last chapter and we wanted to make it memorable.

The above photo shows the 1983 6-4 Vanden Vikings varsity team which was riddled with injuries. The below photo shows the offense during the Dixon game. Shown (right to left) are Chris, me, Ronnie, Jeff, and Darrick. The photo was taken only minutes before I was injured. Both photos courtesy of Travis Unified School District and Vanden High School.

[1983 Vanden Varsity Coach]

(Coach Spotlight) - Ron Harden

As a freshman and sophomore on the JV squads, I watched Coach Harden direct the offensive and defensive lines on the varsity team. When I met and played for him in 1983 he was exactly what I had observed. He was an experienced and knowledgeable grizzled line coach. He knew what he wanted to do and how to do it successfully. Coach Harden worked with troubled students as a teacher, and as a football coach he developed name takers. I learned much from his direction, and he made my teammates and me better players. I never played for Coach Harden again. Thanks for the memories, Coach. You took names. Photo courtesy of Travis Unified School District and Vanden High School.

[Right Guard and Middle Linebacker]

(Player Spotlight) - Frank Reyes #54 - [Captain]
Right Guard, Middle Linebacker, and Specialty Teams

I played football for two seasons with Frank—on the 1981 JV Squad and on the 1983 varsity team. Frank wasn't a physically big player at 5'8", 170 lbs. but he would hit and tackle as if he were much larger. Frank was a devastating hitter and a teeth rattler. He was one of the best hitmen Vanden produced. Frank had an explosive blitz and played with reckless abandon, making his presence known every play. I admired Frank and tried to emulate him. I liked his style of play. It was old-school, hard-hitting, no-fear football. Thanks for the memories, Frank. You took names. Photo courtesy of Travis Unified School District and Vanden High School.

[Running Back and Cornerback]

(Player Spotlight) - Alvin Baldwin #28 - [Captain]
Running Back, Cornerback, and Specialty Teams

In 1983, Alvin was all over the field, making an impact. Alvin was also a member of the 220 and 440 Track Relay State Champions, so he was very fast. If you didn't tape your eyes open when playing with him you were likely to miss a big play. Alvin stepped up when injuries sidelined Broyce Batchan and Frank Reyes, and led the team with Darrick Peterkin. Those who were blessed to play with Alvin knew what a huge impact he made on the field. He was a fierce hitman and a vicious name taker. Alvin was the best at what he did on the gridiron. Thanks for the memories, Alvin. You took names. Photo courtesy of Travis Unified School District and Vanden High School.

[Tight End and Linebacker]

(Player Spotlight) - Darrick Peterkin #84 - [Captain]
Tight End, Linebacker, and Specialty Teams

Darrick was new to Vanden in the 1983 season. He came onto the campus, football team, and basketball teams, and instantly became a leader and a standout player. I have never played with another teammate who made a larger impact on the gridiron as a new player, in one season, as Darrick. A fierce hitter. He was a back-breaker when he stuck you. Darrick had sure hands and would catch, hold onto, and run with the ball as he powered over opposing players. He was voted the 1983 class 'Most Athletic.' I would say that was a good call. Thanks for the memories, Darrick. You took names. Photo courtesy of Travis Unified School District and Vanden High School.

[Running Back and Safety]

(Player Spotlight) - Broyce Batchan #21 - [Captain]
Running Back, Safety, and Specialty Teams

Broyce was a fierce name taker and someone to reckon with on the gridiron. He was a big playmaker. He ran a 40-yard dash in 4.2 seconds. In 1983, we had the chance to have Broyce and his brother Bryan in the backfield together. Sadly, Broyce broke his leg in pre-season play and was out for the year. If Broyce would've been healthy with Bryan and Alvin in the backfield with him, Vanden would have fielded the best backfield in its history. There is no doubt the 6-4 record that season would have been dramatically different with him healthy. Thanks for the memories, Broyce. You took names. Photo courtesy of Travis Unified School District and Vanden High School.

[Receiver]

(Player Spotlight) - Michael Farace #80
Receiver and Specialty Teams

Michael was a receiver on our team in 1983, and he had good hands and good speed. He was a friendly and could take it to opposing players for four quarters nonstop. Michael had an outgoing personality but when he stepped on the field he became something quite different. He was solid in all aspects of the game and he was the type of player who made our Vanden Viking squad notable. I only played football with him for one season, but I am honored I shared the gridiron with him that year. Thanks for the memories, Michael. You took names. Photo courtesy of Travis Unified School District and Vanden High School.

[Kicker and Lineman]

(Player Spotlight) - Mike Holovach #63 and #55 (81-82)
Kicker, Lineman, and Specialty Teams
Nickname 'Spartacus'

Mike played football with us for four seasons: on the undefeated 1980 11-0 Redskins; the 1981 7-0-2 JV squad; the 1982 9-0 undefeated and unscored-upon JV team; and the 1983 6-4 varsity squad. Mike was a fierce hitter, great tackler, and he gave his all from whistle to whistle, every play. Besides playing in the trenches, Mike was our field goal kicker up to 1983, and he could split the uprights down the middle. He kicked a 47-yard field goal in one game. Thanks for the memories, Mike. You took names. Photo courtesy of Travis Unified School District and Vanden High School.

That 1 Lace and 8 Stitches
Just one more time

Shoulder to shoulder with cleats dug in. Our eleven helmets versus their eleven. Reliance on each other to move the ball forward or stop its progress. Each having a specific task to do; a specific target to handle. Holding hands in the huddle—our circle wasn't broken. Mumbling with the mouthpiece in and trying to catch an extra breath. I missed them all. Just one more time, please.

The dizziness I had for several weeks slowed, and the bad headaches were becoming less and less. I struggled with sleep, though, and was always tired. I was able to rest but solid sleep evaded me. Retaining information was still difficult but seemed to be getting better.

I continued jumping rope in my backyard or garage daily. The more I jumped, the more revolutions I could do. My coordination was improving each week.

Mark, Joe, Jeff, and I began spending more time together. We were always hanging around each other at school, and every other day we would go to the gym on Travis AFB. David Smith and Paul Holes would join us.

We spent many hours at the base gym lifting weights. I liked that small gym, because there was no waiting for the equipment we wanted to use. I was strong; but I knew my physical size wouldn't standout on the field. That didn't matter to me. I wanted opponents to remember how I hit, tackled, and growled at them. I'd leave an impression they couldn't forget.

On our way to workout we began stopping at a new convenience store on TAFB to buy junk food. We would buy chips, candy, donuts, and soda to consume before lifting weights. We wanted to bulk up and put on weight for the upcoming football season.

It was during the trips to the gym that we talked about wanting to win the Sac-Joaquin Section championship and record another undefeated season. We had two previous ones and knew we could do it again. It wouldn't be easy, though. The odds really weren't in our favor. Less than one percent of football teams could claim that record, and most football players never reached that pinnacle. Just one last time I wanted to play with my friends, and just one more time we wanted to win together. There was only one season left to do both.

Track started once again. Jeff and I went out, and Joe joined us. We there to represent Vanden and fill open slots on the team. Glenn would come by and watch us sometimes. We practiced hard at the shot put and discus, but we were just average. We never won a track meet in our events. We didn't have the size and weight to throw either very far, and our techniques weren't as good as some of our opponents. Our hearts weren't in it—track wasn't football.

The above photo shows Jeff throwing the shot put, as (left to right) Joe, Glenn, me, and Tyra Williams, one of our football and track stat girls, watches on. Photo courtesy of Travis Unified School District and Vanden High School.

    I remembered every direction given. "Go like a Broke-Dick Dog!" That's how it was once described to me when pursuing a fumble. It might as well have been a hog covered in lard because that loose pigskin could be hard to grab as it bounced around. It was a balls to the wall compilation of madness and beauty that looked like wrestling and ballet combined. It was a free-for-all when bodies smashed into each other like a crash derby—and every bit as violent. That free ball was a trophy we all wanted. "Get it!" was the frenzied mindset.

    I was seeing Julie less and less. Not sure why, but it was because of me, and not her. I would go weeks without calling or visiting. She missed me and I knew that. I knew what she wanted to tell me the Saturday she called.

My heart talked to me as I drove to Pinole. I knew I had to be honest with myself. I just didn't have time for Julie to nurture our relationship. She deserved much better. The coming football season was just off in the horizon. I wasn't ready physically or mentally either. I needed to work on myself. When Julie told me she had met someone else from her church she cried. I held her and told her it was okay. Pursue the relationship and find true happiness, I said. Her teary eyes stayed with me as I drove home. Her angelic smile followed me when I closed my eyes. We never got back.

We were in our fourth year playing stuntmen on Vanden Road. Each ride was as exciting as the first one. The fastest time was something we all tried to capture, because it was bragging rights we wanted. The favorite car to use became a Ford Mustang my dad had purchased for us four brothers. It had the perfect size of a roof to hold onto, and it was easy to get on and off.

The above photo shows the Ford Mustang. Hundreds of trips were made speeding down Vanden Road at night on the roof tempting fate as stuntmen. Luckily, no one was ever injured during our escapades.

Joe wore his Alaskan roots well. At 6'4" he looked taller with his thick hair. He kept it fairly long so it almost looked like a lion's mane. He wore blue jeans and a sherpa-lined denim jacket and walked with a swagger. He had a loud deep laugh and was fun to be around. In his second year at Vanden, people gravitated towards him.

Joe came from a good family. His parents were still married and he had three siblings. They were all nice people. Whenever we were at their house on base we felt welcomed. Prior to going to the gym some days, Joe would fry up some 'Steak-umms' (sliced steaks), or he would make us sandwiches. His mom seemed to enjoy having us there.

Joe's confidence in himself started building as he put on weight from lifting. He hadn't played much during the 1983 season, but I knew he was going to be a great addition on the squad our senior year. We nicknamed him 'Big Joe' because he towered over us.

At the gym, Joe concentrated on 'bear curls' on a flat or incline bench, and curls for his biceps. He would do 15 sets alone for his arms. As Mark, Jeff, and I finished our workouts and left to play racquet ball and basketball, Joe would still be pumping iron. Jeff and I would play racquet ball together. It helped me with balance and coordination. Mark would be playing basketball with the airmen, and most of the time he was holding his own against them.

It was something like out of a movie. I didn't realize a finger could shoot blood like that when it happened. Joe was doing bear curls on an incline bench one session, and I was just a few feet away on a flat bench doing the same exercise. When Joe put down the dumbbells he was using, he smashed his right index finger hard between some weights. He let out a thundering yell and blood squirted out of the tip of his finger like a squashed ketchup packet. Some of the blood splattered the mirror in front of him. His finger was as flat as a penny. I think both Joe and I were in shock. We quickly wrapped it in a shirt and rushed him to David Grant Medical Hospital on the base.

Joe's finger was bandaged and splinted. The very next day he was back in the gym working out. He wasn't going to let his penny-flattened finger stop him. I respected his grit, and that only reinforced my belief that he would be a great addition on the gridiron.

Mark was different from Joe, Jeff, and me. We were all average in style, but Mark had his own look. He spiked his hair a little in the front and wore clothes like he was a punk rocker when he really wasn't. He would wear some old military jackets some days with patches. He didn't care what others thought. I respected that and thought his style was cool. He was just being 'Baro.'

Mark had a wild laugh, and when he started joking around you could see his mischievous side coming out. He was a good student in school, very intelligent, and he had a strong grasp on the subjects we shared in classes, but he was rebellious. He questioned everything.

Mark was the rebel in our group. He came from a military family, but his unhappiness at home caused him to act out. He wasn't close with his parents and they had a strained relationship. Mark had one sister several years younger than we were.

Jeff wasn't as outspoken as Joe and Mark. He was more reserved. He was your average kid from a middle-class family. His parents worked hard and instilled strong ethics in him. He had one older sister. Jeff's parents were very supportive of his involvement in football. Of us four friends, his parents were the only ones to attend games.

The four of us mixed well together, though, and the differences in us did not affect our interaction. We were the best of friends and spent most days together at school and away.

I still considered Glenn one of my closest friends, yet we spent little time together. I worked out a lot for football, and Glenn didn't like to lift weights. He didn't need to, because he was already built for the game. In the four seasons I played, I never met anyone who could scan the field better and know where the play was going. Glenn was the perfect linebacker. He took pain well and dealt out punishment abundantly. He took names, plenty of names, and stored them in a very large warehouse. I had never met a defensive player who was a bigger or more dangerous threat to running backs. Glenn's helmet was camouflaged in stickers. His hitting power and his big plays were displayed for our opponents to see. He was a General on the gridiron.

Glenn had an AMC Hornet. It was a light brown/gold color with wood trim. It looked like grandma's car, and Glenn drove it slowly, as if it were. I had to chuckle when I saw him behind the wheel. Here was this hard-hitting linebacker, but he had a retiree's car and drove like a little old lady. On asphalt—speed wasn't Glenn's friend.

Coach Newsom and I continued jogging together. I confided in him that I was struggling with sleep and was always tired. He told me it was important to get rest if I hoped to return to the gridiron. I also told him I felt it was wrong that I was chosen the most inspirational player for the 1983 season. The team going from 2-3 to 6-4 with an injury-riddled 19-man squad was inspiring. They deserved the recognition, not me. He just patted my back and said, "Keep jogging." As we jogged he said to me, "I wasn't always this big. I was once a football player. I played at Vacaville High and attended BYU on a football scholarship. That's where I hurt my back, and I gained weight due to the injury." His revelation stunned me—I admired him more—he'd been a name taker. It made me determined to help him once again feel like a football player.

One morning I was approached by Principal Juhl to be a 'Good Will Ambassador' between Vanden and Dixon Schools. They wanted me to meet the football player who ended my junior season. A school counselor took me to Dixon, and we met with the student leadership, and the football player involved. We spent four hours talking about how to improve relations between our schools and put aside any rivalry that was brewing.

Mark and I heard that Tom Kiefer was coming out of retirement to coach the offensive and defensive lines for the varsity football team our senior season. It had been eight years since he last coached. He had spent 1964 to 1976 coaching the lines for Vanden. The three of us became close. Mark and Coach Kiefer shared a connection that bonded them. They both had the same birthday. Coach Harden had retired from the football program after the 1983 season to join the administrative staff.

I saw the look on Mark's face. I knew what was coming and it was going to epic. David, though, was unaware of the dare he was about to be thrust into blindly. David Smith, our punter, joined us at the gym often. As he drove us there one day Mark taunted him to take the coming corner like "Speed Racer." When Mark began taunts they were endless and torturous. I knew David would fall prey to Mark and accelerate like he was in NASCAR. One day earlier Joe, Mark, and I had been on that very road, the first for any of us, and we noticed it had an extra-large speed bump. Mark knew what his taunting would cause, and so did we.

With Jeff, Joe, Mark, and me in the car, David fell for the dare and stepped on the gas pedal, flooring it. He took the corner fast, and we hit the speed bump and flew through the air like the 'Dukes of Hazzard.' We caught so much air the vehicle could've registered as a UFO on the base's radar system. The car slammed down in the center of a drainage ditch and slid to the curb. It stopped like it had been parked there, and the engine died. We all laughed hysterically while David tried to calm his nerves. His hands were still gripped to the steering wheel. When David tried to start the car it was dead. We had no choice but to leave it and walk to the gym. Mark's taunting of David still persisted as we walked. Eventually David found his flight time as funny as we did. At the gym we called a tow truck. When David's dad found out we had disabled the sole family vehicle he wasn't amused. David learned a valuable lesson—never let Mark taunt him again. Our Dukes of Hazzard flight only encouraged Mark more.

Coach Bev proved he was better than his first-year performance in 1982. He wasn't a 1-5-3 coach. Bev had a vision for Vanden's football program. A vision that would put us in the record books and cement us as champions. We just didn't know it yet.

I would go to bed early and even tried ear plugs. Nothing worked. My sleep was broken every night. I struggled to find comfort from the Sandman. It was as if the concussion had permanently altered my sleep patterns. In the mornings I was always exhausted. Mine wasn't your average concussion. It was the worst you could have without causing severe brain damage. It was affecting me daily. I had only one real concern though—would I play football again?

After track ended I started missing school days. Initially, Mom knew, because she would catch me resting on the floor of my closet, trying to hide. She would get upset and tell me to get dressed and go to school. I didn't understand why I was so tired and feeling lethargic. I couldn't hide in the closet anymore so I started climbing on the roof, by using the fence, and hiding behind the chimney (out of view) until Mom drove away. If it was raining I climbed up into the rafters in the garage and hid there until she was gone. I needed sleep. My body and brain felt like they were starving.

The school began questioning my absences, so I would write notes and sign my mom's name to them. It was inevitable: I got caught. My punishment was three weeks of Saturday work detail. Fortunately for me, Coach Newsom ran the program. During those three weekends he picked me up and dropped me off at my house. He drove a large car very similar to the one John Candy had in the movie 'Uncle Buck.' Coach Newsom's was dented and backfired black smoke also.

    I think he understood my absences because I was always tired, so he took it easy on me. On the way to Vanden where the students met to clean, we would stop at Winchell's Donuts. Newsom would buy a dozen donuts for us, a coffee for himself, and a milk for me.

    When we arrived at the school I became his trustee. He handed me a clipboard that contained all the names of the kids scheduled for work detail that day. I then met with them at the front of the school, checked their names off, and assigned duties. I would then return to Newsom's vehicle for donuts and my milk. Every 30 minutes I walked around campus and made sure they were all working. Then back to the car. I continued that pattern for the assigned hours, then released all the students to go home. During my tenure as a trustee for the program, none of the kids ever complained that I received special treatment, even though it was evident that I did.

    I may have slowed some but I was still the same guy that Jim knew. I had a wild streak in me, but it was changing. I was slowing down with my adventures, but I wasn't ready to quit and be normal. I still had my reputation to uphold.

    When he saw me he snapped his fingers and gave me that look. I knew I was in trouble, and like that 7th-grade kid, I didn't even get the opportunity to throw one water balloon. I climbed on top of the school with a bucket of water balloons and a mission. With a balloon in hand I spotted a target, as Vice Principal Mr. Sideris spotted me.

There I sat in his office awaiting my fate. Mr. Sideris chuckled a little and said, "If it was anyone else." He shook his head and looked at me. He went on to tell me that we were going to sit there for about ten minutes, so it appeared I was being disciplined. Afterwards I was free to go, but no more trouble. I agreed and thanked him. Ten minutes later I was released unpunished for my failed water-balloon attack.

My junior year was coming to a close. Coach Bev approached me to say Vanden, the athletic director, and the football program wanted to purchase me an 'Air Helmet' so I could play. It was going to be the first of its kind at Vanden. I told him I would try and get the medical clearance needed. I wanted to play one last time. There was a big hurdle, though: my mom.

Football was everything to me. It would always be my first love and I wasn't ready to end that relationship. I needed the game. So I had to make my mom understand how truly important it was to me. It wasn't just a sport. It was the first thing I thought of when I awoke and the last thing on my mind when I went to bed. I breathed football.

I knew she was scared. She told me more than once how worried she was that I would get hurt again, and maybe even worse. A brain injury wasn't fixable, she said. It could be permanent, she would say. I begged, I pleaded, and I talked about the difference between an air helmet and a regular one.

When I was a newborn I had contracted a strep infection, along with another baby, from a nurse at the hospital. We both became very ill. The other infant, a little girl who belonged to a neighbor and my mom's friend, died. That devastation stayed with my mom. She did not want to lose me at 17. Her maternal instincts said no to me playing. Her love for me to be happy said yes.

I had to pay a steep price, though. A price I was willing to meet. My mom made me promise I would never play football again after my senior year. I agreed and told her it would be my final season on the gridiron.

My dad was still stationed on Travis at David Grant Medical Hospital. I visited him often and had been making appointments to try and get the clearance I needed to play. I went multiple times, and was finally given the okay the last week of school. The air helmet was the deciding factor. It was set. I would be joining my friends again one last time.

I never divulged my concerns about my balance, coordination, and insomnia to the doctors or my parents.

That summer we continued to lift weights, and I jumped rope and played racquet ball. Each session we pushed each other to the brink because we only had the summer break left to prepare for the upcoming season.

Every morning during the week Coach Kiefer would meet us at Vanden and open the Shubin Sports Building for Jeff, Joe, Mark, Chris, and me. We pulled out blocking bags and laid them on a wrestling mat, and did various drills. For about an hour each day we worked hard, pushing ourselves. Then we would go outside to the varsity practice field and run wind sprints and gassers for another thirty minutes. At the end of our daily workout we were exhausted, sweaty, and more prepared.

We were on a mission. We wanted to be the best.

They were big odds we had to overcome—but the odds didn't know us. We weren't ordinary football players. We weren't extraordinary, either; but we were special when we played together. Life picked us to play the game with each other, and the gridiron saw something in us like Coach Kelly had. We respected it and gave it everything. The .0089 percent chance we had to win the twelve games without losing any by one point was fair money to bet on us. I knew my friends. With them and our coaches, greatness was within reach.

    At 16, I had lost everything that was important to me: football, the camaraderie in the huddles, and the feel of a hard hit. In one moment it was all taken away. I didn't have a warning or time to prepare for that loss. I don't think anyone really understood what I was going through with that loss either. I was injured more than physically. As a sixteen-year-old boy I didn't feel I could share those feelings with anyone. I wasn't that type of kid.

    At 17, I was getting a second chance to step on the gridiron. An opportunity I knew my mom, the doctors, Vanden, and Coach Bev were giving me. I was willing to do everything I could to help my friends and the team win. I was also willing to do everything I could to honor the game with my play. It had to feel my passion.

    I didn't count sheep when I closed my eyes. I counted that one lace and eight stitches on a football, over and over. We had been apart for too long. Soon we would meet again, and that reunion would be memorable and painful. I couldn't wait. I had missed my old friend. The game had been loyal to me, and it was time to return that loyalty.

576 Minutes in 1984
A coach's time, a team's chance and a player's return

This was my last chance and I knew it. It had been almost a year since that collision in Dixon. It was time to see if I was still a football player. Anyone could put on a helmet and shoulder pads. That was easy. Being a force on the field and a name taker wasn't. I was facing my greatest challenge as an athlete. Did I have the coordination to make an open field tackle, a crushing hit, or a devastating block? I wasn't sure. I remembered the hurt in my brother Sean's eyes when his dream came crashing down around him. He would wake up early to run, worked hard on the mat and pushed himself to be the best. Then he had his chance to show how good he was at the section wrestling tournament. He missed weight by 1/2 pound, and was unable to compete. Sean felt like he had let his team down. I knew that moment would follow him for the rest of his life. He couldn't escape it.

    I didn't want to feel his regret. I had this one opportunity left and I had to give it my all. I thought I heard

Maniac talking. I looked around. Jim wasn't there. I stood in front of the mirror alone. In the reflection I could see that old Psycho sweatshirt still hanging on the wall staring back at me. I could feel the pull of the gridiron and I could hear its call. It was time to return home.

Jeff's car horn didn't catch me by surprise. I had been ready. I grabbed my bag and headed to the door. Fresh air; the practice field impatiently waiting on us; coaches ready with their playbooks; our hearts and bodies prepared to give all; soon we would pump blood, hit bags, and crash helmets.

It was a comeback season for all of us. Coach Bev had something to prove to himself, the school, and our opponents: he was the coach to beat. The guys knew it was our time. We had to prove it though—with victories. I had something to face head-on. I needed the game, but I wasn't sure if it needed me anymore. I had to find out.

It was hot and sunny out, as we drove down Vanden road. The car windows were down, and the wind felt good on my face. It was finally that time again. Jeff, Mark, David Smith, and I were on our way to the Shubin Sports Building for physicals and weigh-ins for the 1984 varsity Vanden Viking football team.

We had driven on this road thousands of times over the years but this one meant the most. My trips on the Beast as a young Redskin were exciting and full of adventure. Our hundreds of trips on top of speeding cars were thrilling and adrenalin-filled, but this one seven-mile trip was important for me. I scanned the fields as we drove. Farmer's land and rock salt. (I smiled slightly.) The barbed wire fences knew Jim and me well. The cattle could've picked us out of a lineup. The smell of manure was welcoming. It was only fitting the road was called Vanden. Memories were made here, and good ones.

My head was outside the window when Jeff's windshield wiper fluid hit me in the face. It immediately reminded me of that water hose spray from the neighbor as Jim and I passed by his house. That summer afternoon four years earlier seemed so vivid as the car hugged the asphalt. Why would a 40-something-year-old man spray two teen boys for no reason? I still didn't know. It set off a back-and-forth month-long battle, though. He terrorized us and we retaliated. It was a classic Hatfield and McCoy feud, and Jim and I were determined to win at any cost.

Putting up a new mailbox was a mistake; since Jim possessed an M80 firecracker. His nickname was 'Maniac' after all, so it was inevitable what the response would be. The day it was installed, we turned it into a convertible. We could hear our tormentor's retaliation plans as we hid behind a car. It was important information that would end our quarrel in an epic fashion. He and his son were going to wait in their garage, with the big door open, and grab us when we went by. It was a simplistic plan that underestimated Jim and me. We were already in place to end this thing once and for all. When the garage lights went off and it got dark we became commandos. We were ready to make a statement: It's over, move on.

Getting to the side of the opened door was easy. I had the last of Jim's stash in my hand—a string of fifty firecrackers begging for their glory. I just knew the repeated thumb strikes to ignite the lighter (Shk! Shk! Shk!)

would be our undoing. Jim couldn't get a flame, and the quiet of the night couldn't hide each attempt. I knew the whole neighborhood could hear. I waited for a hand to come around the corner and grab mine as I held the little 'BOOM' sticks. Everything seemed in slow motion. I could see Cathy's dad chasing us and the base police in pursuit. I could see the cemetery and Glenn's poor aerobatic landing. I could also see our mug shots and juvenile hall in our future if we didn't put this battle to bed. Time to end it now, I thought, as Jim finally lit the firecrackers.

I tossed them and we ran across the street looking back. They exploded in succession. Fifty flashes illuminated the dark garage each time with an echoing boom. We made it to the open field and lay in the tall grass as the last flash ended. Our big bully wasn't so big as he ran from his hiding place with his hands on his head. His son looked even smaller. He was screaming wildly, "I thought they blew up my home!" He repeated it over and over. Vacaville police responded and they never went to my house. I think they saw it for what it was—a prank. We again escaped punishment and the feud became history. Our tormentor knew he had been beaten.

The curves and slopes of the road brought me back to reality. My friends had worked hard the past year and throughout the summer to prepare for this season. There would be no do-overs. If we screwed up or lost a game, our five-year-long journey would end with a last chapter none of us wanted to read.

As we passed under Black Bridge something caught our eyes on the left side of the road. What is that? I wondered. It looked like a small cow laying on its back with its feet straight in the air. Jeff hit the brakes stopping the car quickly. As we approached the animal it looked like a dog but it couldn't be—it was too big—it looked 200 pounds or more! We got closer. It was a dog alright, and it was dead. It was an unbelievable sight. Biggest dog I had ever seen.

After a few minutes of playing detectives we got back into Jeff's car and continued to the school. The dog's size and wondering what killed it stayed with me. There were no obvious injuries. It was a mystery.

There were about a dozen cars parked in front of the Shubin Sports Building when we arrived. Some players were outside, while others had gone in. I didn't see the coaches but their cars were there. We told the team about the dog. Mark persisted in telling the guys they had to see it. Physicals and weigh-ins hadn't started yet so we had time to go survey the scene and make it back. I think the curiosity got to them. Most of the guys loaded into vehicles, and we rushed back to the side of the road.

Oohs and aahs were heard, as the guys looked at the dog. It was big, they all agreed. Someone then yelled "Race you back to Vanden." It was if a whistle had been blown, because everyone rushed to their vehicles. Three cars took off before us loaded with players.

Big Joe was driving his dad's full-size blue pickup. It had a camper shell on the back and a large custom bumper on the front. It was a tank of a vehicle. We were yelling at the guys to hurry up and get in back so we could leave. We were going to be last back to Vanden. That didn't sit well with us.

Big Joe, Mark, and I jumped in the front seat, and

Joe slammed the pedal down to the floor. He wasn't going to be last without giving the other cars a run for their money. We took off with the tires spinning in the gravel on the side of the road. The truck roared as we flew down Vanden. We were in a 'Cannonball Run.' A quarter-mile off in the distance a stop sign stood watch over the coming intersection. It was warning us from afar.

Vanden connected with Peabody road, which was the main thoroughfare, leading to Vacaville from Fairfield and Travis AFB. Peabody was always busy with traffic. As you turned left past the stop sign there was a railroad crossing frequently used by trains. Anyone who went to Vanden, TAFB, or traveled back and forth from Fairfield, knew how frequently trains went through that spot. Traffic was regularly stopped by the flashing signals and downed gates as trains crossed. Many a time I had been on the bus going to school and we had to sit and wait for a train to pass.

The three cars filled with our teammates were stopped in front of us. I could clearly see cross traffic on Peabody. Joe still had the pedal pushed to the floor as the truck sped forward. I didn't need a crystal ball to see the outcome. I knew it was going to be bad. We had cut the distance in half to the stop sign.

I was sitting next to Joe in the middle with Mark to my right. I yelled at Joe to slow down because there was gravel on the road ahead. I anticipated the coming impact, so I put my feet up on the dash. I wasn't wearing a seatbelt. None of us were. I abruptly said to Mark, "Put your feet up on the dash!" He quickly did.

When we were about 40 yards from our stopped

teammates, Joe hit the brakes hard. It was too late. We slid hitting the car in front of us which caused all the cars to slam into each other, pushing the front two cars out into oncoming cross traffic. Like pinballs the cars collided in all different directions and spun around. Multiple cars impacted almost at once. A six-car accident.

The truck came to a stop. We were shaken but not injured. We jumped out. One helped the players out of the back of the truck, while others ran to the other vehicles involved. People were pulled from cars. Our teammates were all okay but rattled. Thankfully no one was seriously hurt in the multiple-car accident.

An ambulance was called and Sheriff deputies responded. Coaches Bev, Newsom, and Kiefer came to the scene. Players were sore and complaining of neck, back, and shoulder pain. The vehicles were damaged pretty badly, except for Joe's truck. The custom bumper didn't give, so there was very minor damage.

Coach Bev was upset. I couldn't blame him because Ronnie, his son and our quarterback, was in one of the cars we hit. Our backfield, linebackers, and linemen were all involved. Two-thirds of the team were in the four vehicles. All because of a dead dog and reckless driving, we almost lost our season before it started. We hadn't even weighed in or had our physicals yet.

Ninety minutes later with vehicles towed away, we returned to Vanden. Coach Bev was still upset but glad we were okay. He called the team together and sat us down for a talk. There was no hiding from his words. We needed to hear them. For that moment he wasn't only our head coach and counselor, but a concerned dad.

The physician who was scheduled to give us all physicals checked the players involved in the accident. None of us had any injuries or broken bones. We were then weighed and given clearance to play football.

The above photo shows the Shubin Sports Building. Photo taken and provided by Timothy O'Donnell #69 co-captain of the 1984 undefeated Vanden JV 9-0 team.

As we prepared for Hell Week I thought much about that accident. It could've been devastating. People and teammates could have died. I felt a lot of responsibility for the team going to look at that dog. We came close to destroying our season before it started. What was I thinking? I should've known better. We all should have been more careful. It was the last season of football I would ever play and my final at Vanden. I came close to feeling Sean's regret. I couldn't make that mistake again.

Sean and Tim had graduated and started their lives. That left Craig and me in school. Craig was just a sophomore so after I graduated he would be the sole

Rooney brother at Vanden. Was he feeling we were leaving him behind? I don't know but his actions were starting to show he felt even more lost than when dad left.

Craig had lots of friends and was well liked, but he was going through something none of us three brothers had. I guess it wasn't easy being the youngest and having to follow in the footsteps of Sean and Tim. I don't think Craig realized he didn't have to follow them. He had the talent and intelligence to plot his own journey. I still felt he was probably the best athlete of us four boys and he could've excelled in sports. All he had to do was try and he would've hit his mark dead center. Sadly, I don't think he saw it that way. Football had me so wrapped up I didn't see his struggles, so I was shocked when Craig transferred to Vacaville later in the year. I'm not sure why he made that decision, but he felt he needed to do it. After transferring Craig never returned to Vanden as a student.

I knew he was tough, but when I saw the gangrene on his leg, I realized he was even tougher than I thought. How a man with his large frame could stand on that leg and deal with the pain was incredible. I knew his leg hurt. It hurt me to see the infection. It was grotesque. I wondered how Coach Kiefer was able to teach all day and then coach us at practice. His limp showed the leg did bother him but it barely slowed him. His enthusiasm never wavered and he never sat during our summer practices. He was born to be a lineman coach.

I wanted to ask him how his leg became infected, but I never did. Maybe Mark asked him because they were close. The shared birthday really bonded them. Baro found a closeness with Kiefer he didn't have with his own father. Baro was able to bring Kiefer down to his level. They teased each other relentlessly. Both were quick-witted and they flung ribbing comments back and forth. It was like watching a tennis match between comedians.

    Buying my mouthpiece brought back the emotion I felt my first two years of football—an anxious excitement. I also bought new arm and hand pads. I was going to try and protect myself from injuries. I included some soccer shin pads I would wear under my socks during games. I remembered how a helmet to the shin felt the season before against Hogan, and I didn't want to feel that pain again.

    The first day of Hell Week was sunny, cloudless, and hot. It was early morning but I could feel the sun glaring down on me as I walked to the Shubin Sports Building. Many cars were in the parking lot so I knew when Mark, Jeff, David Smith, and I arrived we weren't the first, even though we got there early.

    David Reyes, John McClellan (our 'Murdock'), and a new student from Germany named Chuck Coates walked up to me. John was wearing his lucky game shirt he had worn for the previous three seasons, "I am not crazy, I just act it." I asked him why he was wearing it now and not saving it for the games. He stated he wanted to start the season off right and give us good luck. Murdock then slapped me on the shoulder and said he was going to do his part to win, and 'Psycho' had better do his.

    Walking into the locker room again as a player and not a spectator felt really good. I hit the metal partition with my clenched fist as I walked through the door. That was something all the football players had done when going out to games since my time as a Viking. It was only fitting to pound it as a welcome back.

The locker room was quiet as we walked in. Most of my teammates were already there and I saw a few new faces. There was a feeling of determination in the air. I knew it was our time to capture glory again. My friends and I had worked hard in the off-season preparing for these next four months. Four months in our lives that would have lasting consequences. We would either become champions again or live with the memories of why we hadn't. We lost four games last season and we had never been beaten before. It was a feeling we didn't want to repeat in our final year together.

The above photo shows the Vanden football locker room door and metal partition. Photo taken by and provided by Timothy O'Donnell #69 co-captain of the 1984 undefeated Vanden JV 9-0 team.

All the trenchers on the varsity squad, the offensive and defensive linemen, had lockers in the same area. The trench crew had always been a close-knit group, and I knew this season would be no different.

I walked around checking out all the players. There was a lot of talent trying out for the team. Eight guys had played on the 1980 undefeated Travis Redskins, the best Pop Warner midget team in the state, and twelve players had been on our 1982 undefeated and unscored-upon Viking JV team. All my former teammates were bigger, stronger, and faster. I knew if we could stay healthy we would be a force to reckon with on the gridiron. The guys were experienced.

The weight lifting for Joe, Mark, and Jeff had paid off, and they all put on weight with considerable muscle. Joe was 6'4", 195 lbs.; Mark 6'1", 190 lbs.; and Jeff was 5'9", 170 lbs. Chris came in at 6'0", 190 lbs.; John 6'0", 185 lbs.; and I was 5'10", 185 lbs. Glenn looked in good shape at 5'9", 170 lbs. Our backfield looked impressive. Ronnie, our quarterback, was 5'10", 175 lbs.; Maurice, our fullback, was 5'9", 204 lbs.; and Bryan, our tailback, was 5'9", 165 lbs. Bryan ran a 4.3-second 40-yard dash, so I knew he was going to torment defenses. Maurice was the only player over 200 lbs.

I took the time to meet the new players and find out a little about them. Chuck at 6'3", 185 lbs., wanted to play on the line. He looked like an athlete. Danny Miller, a new transfer student from the Philippines, looked like a linebacker. Cliff Roberts had transferred in from Okinawa, Japan, where he spent his entire life. He said he played running back and defensive back. He looked like a good running back. Felix Davis was from Fairfield, and he was hoping he would be a split end. J-p Smith came from Vallejo, and he looked like he was a hitter. He wanted to play defensive end or linebacker.

Two sophomores were trying out for the team, and they both looked like good additions. DeWayne Quinn was trying out for a slotback position. I knew him from my neighborhood, and he had been at my home several times over the years. I liked him, and I knew he was fast and an athlete. Sherman Pruitt was also going to try out for the slotback position, and he looked like he could play linebacker.

Eric Barnes, Ronnie's stepbrother, was going to be our tight end. He had great hands and good moves, and he was big at 6'3", 185 lbs. I liked Eric. He always had a story to tell, and with me he had an audience.

David Reyes was going to be a dependable cornerback like he always had been, Dave Haupt was a solid quarterback in his own right and a defensive end, and Darren Rysden was a shoo-in as a wide receiver. He had good hands and agility. I was glad Kye Purnell Jones was playing again. He was a great player and a true friend.

There were many more players who impressed me as I walked around. I had been blessed to play with great teammates during the past four seasons, and I knew this year would be no different. They looked like contenders that first day. I hoped I wasn't reading them wrong.

We all suited up. I put on my arm, hand, and shin pads. All the trenchers knew what happened last season with injuries—and how they decimated the team leading to those four losses—so they padded up like I did. They all wore hand, forearm, and elbow pads, too. Some even wore pads protecting their triceps. Some had neck rolls like I was wearing. We weren't going to take any chances this season.

    Wearing pads didn't mean we were afraid of pain. It meant we wanted to remain healthy for the full season. I knew how most of the guys played. They were taught to run through opponents and punish them. My friends were hitters; their helmets had been decorated with trophies of gridiron devastation. Those stickers proved they were hardened and battle-tested.

    I had my new air helmet, so I tracked down James Tucker, known as 'Tuck,' our equipment manager, to have him add air to it. I liked how the helmet fit, and it would shield my head. It came with a full face mask that would provide good protection. My helmet was like Thor's hammer. It would give me strength. The helmet was the deciding factor that my mom, and the doctors allowed me to return. I knew I was taking a risk with playing. My mom made sure to tell me that more times than I could count. I couldn't change my style of play or slow down, though. I wanted that championship.

    Coach Newsom came out of the office. He now looked 200-plus pounds lighter than when I met him in 1981. He was lean and his face was chiseled. He looked renewed. The football player and name taker in him was back. I could tell he was pumped and ready to direct us. My friend looked good.

    Coach Kiefer followed him. It had been 8 years since he coached last, but after following his direction doing drills all summer, I knew he would mold our offensive and defensive lines into great units. Vanden had captured one football Section Championship prior in 1975, the pinnacle of a winning season in our league, when Coach Kiefer oversaw the trenches. I hoped his past success would rub off on us.

Finally, Coach Bev came down from the office. At 37 years old he looked seasoned in his third year as head coach. He was only the second man in Vanden's twenty-one-year football program to lead the varsity squad. He also had played on the first football team for the Vikings in 1964, scoring the first touchdown in the school's history. As he walked he limped slightly because both his knees had surgeries to repair them. His gait was that of an athlete who had given his all in his younger days.

I had respect for Coach Bev because I felt he treated his son and our quarterback Ronnie no differently than the rest of us. I didn't see any favoritism. Bev let Ronnie direct the offense, and he did a great job doing it. In 1983, Ronnie was the first starting sophomore quarterback in Vanden's history, and he set two school records and tied a third one. He passed for 12 touchdowns and 1205 yards on 193 attempts and 81 completions.

The JV squad was called to "hit the field," and they hustled out of the locker room. Their 30-plus pairs of cleats thundering all at once made me smile. I had missed that sound. Their head coach this season was Gerald Hatcher, and I knew they would have a good year under his direction. He still looked like a little bull.

Coach Bev walked to the chalkboard in the front of the locker room. We all moved so we could see better.

Two decades earlier he had taken a knee on this same tile as a senior and listened to Coach Serpas. Coaches Newsom and Kiefer as young men too had gone through this same indoctrination. Coach Bev was about to lay out his vision for the program to us. We were to conform to his beliefs. The X's and O's he drew were like architect plans. Yet they weren't of some grand structure but the foundation to make champions. We listened intently.

We knew three-a-day practices were planned for the week. That was a first for Vanden. All former squads in the twenty years before us had faced the dreaded two-a-day sessions. We would be the first to see three. It was going to be grueling. No other schools in our area or section would face triple sessions. None of us players from different states and countries had ever heard of a squad doing what we were about to encounter.

There was a risk with doing three practices per day for a week. Injuries could easily occur. Practicing 7.5 to 9 hours daily meant players would be tired and may let their guard down during contact sessions. We had to be careful. In football, though, you couldn't tiptoe. You had to take chances, play with controlled chaos, and play recklessly. That's how champions were made. We knew it.

We had planned on staying at the school and resting and eating in between practices. It made no sense to go home, unless you lived on TAFB. Even then getting too comfortable could mean oversleeping and being late to practice. It was just easier to stay at Vanden.

Coach Bev began to speak and the room became quiet. He said we were no longer going to run the wishbone offense, instead we were going to employ an I-pro set to take advantage of Bryan's speed and Ronnie's passing. The new setup was also a first for Vanden. We were abandoning a twenty-year format for a new untested one. He said the guards would be pulled and trapped often. Ronnie would be running a read option. Coach Bev explained that's why we needed to do three practices a day because we had a lot to learn in a short amount of time. We had only one week to digest all the new changes. We had to adapt quickly. Time wasn't on our side.

On defense we would employ a 5-2 and 5-3 setup, five down linemen and 2-3 linebackers would be utilized. Our goal line defense would be a 6-5. Lots of blitzing and stunting to confuse our opponents. Keep them on their toes, he said.

I looked around. This season would be no different from the rest we had played together. We were a racially mixed squad. Equal parts of black and white, Asians, and one Hispanic, David Reyes. We were vegetable soup, and we were going to be the best darn soup our school and our opponents had ever seen. We all bled green and gold, and we knew we needed each other to win. Our trust would be forged in pain and sweat.

"Hit the field" was called, and we jumped to our feet and scrambled out of the locker room. Some players pounded the partition as we exited. I didn't. I wanted to save those future pounds against the metal for our opponents to hear. It was a battle cry that became our calling.

We spaced ourselves out on the practice field. The JV's were already warming up next to us. The grass was green under our feet. As we began to stretch I could smell its freshly cut scent. I missed that aroma. It was one of those things that stayed with a football player. The smell of the gridiron, the feel of a hard hit, and that visual through a facemask. I felt at home with that inescapable scent. It smelled better than perfume.

Stretches came next, and as we rolled around on our helmets facing up at the sky, it looked so blue. It was so clear and lasting. I had stared at that sky hundreds of times over the years while stretching my neck. It was like an old friend. It was comforting. I was already sweating and the perspiration on my back was causing the grass to itch my skin. Our practice jerseys were a mesh material so you could feel almost every single blade of grass finding its way through the holes.

Leg lifts and mountain climbers weren't as easy as they looked after ten minutes of stretches and exercises. I started grunting a little. To my left, right, front, and back grunts were heard. We were all feeling the pain.

Finally, break into offensive groups was called. Coach Bev and Coach Newsom took the quarterbacks, receivers, and backfield. Coach Kiefer took the trenchers. Players who wanted to try out for certain positions went with the group they wanted.

We went to the far end of the practice gridiron. The George Gammon game field was to our backs, separated by bushes, trees, and a chain link fence. We had some shade where we set up. Tuck and his equipment assistant Eddie had laid out some blocking bags there for us. Like our summer sessions, Coach Kiefer had drills planned for us to perform.

There were ten of us trenchers there. Jeff, Mark (AKA 'Baro'), Big Joe, Chris, David Smith, John (AKA

'Murdock'), Chuck, Derrick Davis, and Eugene (Burton) van Eikenhorst and myself. Derrick and Eugene were the only juniors. We were a small crew.

    We did drill after drill, blocking and hitting. Dozens of hard collisions. We were all going full bore. Impress Coach Kiefer rang through my head. Make a statement; I wanted to play and start. I knew Jeff would be our center for sure. A decade in the trenches and each season he got better at that position.

    Thirty minutes later, break off into defensive groups was called. All ten of us stayed where we were. I was told earlier by Coach Newsom I wouldn't be playing linebacker this season. They wanted me as a nose guard. When he told me that, I had to digest his words. I loved being a linebacker but I couldn't have another head injury. I think I understood the change. The coaches wanted to protect me. I wouldn't get as much velocity charging in from nose guard as I would as a linebacker. I wore an air helmet for a reason.

    Once again we went through drills and defensive schemes. Hard hits and blocking ensued. All the guys seemed quick off the ball. Everyone wanted to play and start. Unfortunately, that couldn't happen. Stick marks were already showing on our helmets from the collisions. Murdock loved his stick marks. They made him grin.

    "To the sleds" was called by Coach Newsom. The dreaded sleds. I had never been a fan of them but knew the importance of pushing them. Coach Noos, the nickname we started calling him, jumped on the eight-man sled. He wanted to be at the helm as we pushed it with him barking at us.

Big Joe, Baro, Jeff, Chris, Murdock, Chuck, Glenn, and I were called up first. We knew the drill. Get into our stances and at the whistle hit the sled fast and hard while driving our legs. Keep driving forward until the whistle was blown. The sleds were my least favorite thing in football, so I was already dreading the push.

Coach Noos blew his whistle, and we slammed into the sled propelling it forward. It seemed so heavy as we pushed. We drove our legs as hard as we could and our shoulders leaned into it. I waited to hear the whistle and it didn't come. I looked at Noos, and he was snarling. "Drive!" he barked—so I growled as I drove harder. Finally he blew it. Just in time. We were all exhausted after pushing it about 30 yards. Oh, I really didn't like those sleds, I thought, as the next group was called up to hit it. Three times in all we pushed the sled with Noos barking at us. I glanced up at him, as I grunted, and I thought I saw a smile through his snarls. He loved tormenting us, but I knew it would make us better football players. There was a reason for pushing those sleds—they taught us to drive hard into a player and push him backwards.

We broke off from the sleds and lined up for some tackling drills. Coach Bev wanted to see who the hitters on the team were. I could've told him Glenn would be at the top of the list. Four bags were laying on the grass, about two yards between each one, near the goal line. The four bags symbolized three holes a runner could choose from.

Half the team was chosen as runners and half as tacklers. Later we would switch sides. When the whistle was blown the ball carrier would run towards a hole and try to cross into the end zone. The defender would try to stop the runner from scoring a touchdown. I always liked the drill because the impact awakened my senses. It was like sniffing smelling salts.

I was picked to be on the tackler side. I was ready to try my air helmet. I told Bryan I wanted to go against him. If there was anyone to test myself against it was Bryan. He had the fastest feet and the quickest moves on the team and was extremely hard to tackle one on one. When Bryan hit you, it felt like a sledgehammer. Many opposing players found that out the hard way the previous four seasons. It usually took a minimum of two, if not three players to take him down. Bryan had power like a freight train. Right before contact he would stiff arm or lower his facemask, causing the tackler to end up on his back as he literally ran him over. I witnessed that happen many times as Bryan gained yardage leaving cleat marks on the chests of our opponents. He had to be my test.

The ball carrier and the defender each started at the first bag about five yards back. Coach Bev blew his whistle and one after another my teammates collided into each other. There was some hard-hitting, good running, and great tackling going on.

There is a distinct sound made by shoulder pads colliding and helmets crashing together. It is a sound that every football player never forgets. As I watched my teammates slam into each other I knew how much I had missed making those sounds from the sidelines last season.

It was Bryan's and my turn. I was pretty nervous, I did not want to embarrass myself. I was not sure if my balance and coordination were up to par and ready for the likes of Bryan. He was becoming legendary at Vanden as a running back. I felt I had lost a step because of the injury. I knew I still had the heart, and that fire burned inside. Football had raised me and I couldn't quit on it. If I wasn't careful Bryan would leave cleat marks across my 55 number.

I told myself to follow what all my coaches had taught me about tackling: watch the waist, lower my body, put my facemask in the numbers, wrap my arms, and drive backwards. I knew Bryan would lower his facemask to meet mine. It would be teeth-rattling and jarring. (I couldn't wait.) Bryan knew me well—I would be there at that hole waiting for him.

One of three things would happen from our collision: it would awaken my senses; make my legs wobbly; or knock me unconscious like last season. I certainly did not want that, but with Bryan charging towards me any of the three were possible. I was wearing an air helmet and it would give me the best protection I could have, so it was time to test it. It was also time to see if I was still a football player.

Coach Bev blew his whistle and Bryan began moving forward and along the bags. I slid my feet, keeping pace with him. Bryan turned upward at the center bag. I exploded forward into him. Our bodies, helmets, and facemasks crashed hard into each in the center of the hole. I wrapped my arms as Bryan drove forward. Neither of us gave an inch. I stopped him from scoring but didn't drive him backwards.

The whistle blew and we broke off from each

other. I was seeing stars, and my vision was blurred from the impact. Bryan had hammered me—I was wobbly. I went to the back of the tackling line. I was worried as I slowly collected my thoughts. Could I handle hundreds of collisions during the season without getting hurt? I wasn't sure if I could. This was my final season with my teammates though, and I wasn't going to watch it from the sidelines again. Football was the game my friends and I chose to play, and I wanted to share the gridiron with them. I could still contribute and would, no matter what. I told myself to suck it up and be quiet.

I did not tell anyone of my concern and the result of the impact between Bryan and me. I decided I would keep that to myself. Nothing was going to stop me from helping my friends win. Nothing.

Coaches Bev, Noos, and Kiefer had sized us up. They knew who could block, run, catch, hit, and tackle. They saw a lot of heart that first practice from my teammates. They had a team that wanted to win.

The whistle was blown and the most feared words at a Vanden football practice were heard, "Line up at the 40." What we all wanted to avoid but knew was necessary to make us the best-conditioned team: wind sprints. As we lined up at the 40-yard line, I was sweating from the heat, as was everyone. It was very hot out. There was no shade and no one to protect us from the awaiting dashes.

Everyone needed to hustle or we would do more. That's how Coach Bev ran the conditioning program. If anyone on the team slacked, we all suffered. Coach Bev ran a strict disciplined program. He was like a drill instructor. He wanted the best-conditioned team in our league and section. He was determined to make us champions.

He blew the whistle and we ran. Time and time again. Twenty-five 40-yard dashes. I was sucking wind, and my side hurt. I bent over a little, then took a knee. I looked around. All my teammates were in the same condition. We were hurting and the pain was just beginning.

"Line up at the goal line" was called. We hadn't recovered from the dashes. 'Gassers' were next. The feared 200-yard timed runs. Like the 40's, if anyone slacked we ran more. Coach Bev was at one end zone and Coach Noos was at the other, to make sure no one would cut the run short. We had to touch the goal line before turning to run back. We had 45 seconds to make the run but it better not take that long. Run hard. We knew the drill with Coach Bev and what he expected.

Once again the whistle blew and we took off running as hard as we could. Make sure to touch the goal line, I told myself. We all made it back with plenty of time to spare. We had nine more to go unless someone screwed up. At number eight it happened. One of the players didn't step on the goal line before turning. We had an additional gasser to do. Players were pissed and yelling at others to run hard. I was frustrated. I looked around and couldn't tell which player failed us.

Sweat was dripping into my eyes. They burned. Both of my sides were cramping, and I was not far from vomiting. We ran the next two gassers. We made it. I waited for the call to bring it in. It didn't come.

Coach Bev barked a word that was new to us, "Progressives." He explained at the whistle we were to run to the 5-yard line and back, then to the 10-yard line and back, and so on, until we touched the end zone and returned to the goal line. He blew the whistle and we ran as hard as we could. It was torturous. At the end of the progressive a few players took their helmets off and vomited. I wanted to join them but kept my helmet on.

"Bring it in" was finally called and we all ran to the coaches and took a knee. Coach Bev commended us on a good practice. All the coaches spoke, then they dismissed us to rest before the afternoon session. We made it to the end of our first practice of the three scheduled that day. We had 14 more to go before Hell Week would be over. Though the session pushed us all to the brink physically, I was loving every minute of it. We wanted to be champions and it wasn't going to be handed to us on a platter. We had to earn it the hard way.

Players struggled to eat during the break due to nausea. We all needed to get used to the conditioning program. It was going to take time to get accustomed to the dashes, gassers, and progressives.

Bruises were already showing. Even though we wore extra pads we were still blessed with the benefits that came from good hard hitting. I missed those bruises, pain, and soreness. That was football, and that's why my friends and I enjoyed the game. We liked the contact and brutality of the sport.

After that first practice I knew we would have an unstoppable backfield. Maurice was a powerful runner, and with him as our fullback running up the gut or blocking for Bryan, he would devastate linebackers. As our heaviest player and one of the fastest, he would make his mark that season. Bryan was just an animal on the field and our collision together during the pick-a-hole drill reminded me of why he was one of the best running backs in our area and in the state. Ronnie was very seasoned as a junior. His ability to scramble during a quarterback option made him a major threat to defenses. He had a rifle for an arm, and the 200 to 300 passes he threw weekly during the summer break had improved his accuracy and strength. Day one he was ready to go.

I knew with Glenn leading the linebackers and defense we would be a nightmare for the opposing offenses we would meet. The offensive line with the trenchers we had would be quick off the ball. Jeff's decade in the trenches, Chris's natural ability as a tackle, Mark's unchained aggressiveness, Joe's strength and grit, John's unpredictability, Chuck's desire to make a difference as a new Viking, and David Smith, Eugene, and Derrick's desire to be the best, would make our trench crew notable. I wanted to remain healthy and contribute with them.

The end to our break came too soon. Time for the afternoon session. Coach Bev called us out to the practice field. We all took a knee. He explained with our new offense and defense we needed to speed things up. We had much to learn in five days. He named the team captains. Ronnie was to be our offensive captain and direct our attack. Glenn was chosen as the defensive captain by Newsom to spearhead our Viking defense. Both good calls, I thought. Coach Kiefer picked me to lead the trenchers. I felt honored to be chosen to head our trench crew. They were a great group of guys and fierce competitors.

We stretched, warmed up, and broke off into our

groups. Coach Kiefer explained that since our line wasn't very big we needed to be quick, aggressive, and outthink our opponents. Weight and size weren't on our side. He went on to explain he had devised an idea he thought would give us an advantage over the larger defensive linemen we would battle.

Kiefer stated we were going to use "movie-character names" to confuse defenses. We would use these names to remember when the ball would be hiked and distract the players on defense by pointing at them and yelling one of the names before the snap. He went on to explain in that short moment before the ball would be hiked, the defensive players would be thinking about the name or names we had just yelled, giving us an edge when the play started. Coach Kiefer stated we would start employing that idea in practice so by game time it would be second nature.

The starting offensive line was picked. Jeff was to be our center, Chris the right tackle, Baro the right guard, me the left guard, and Big Joe the left tackle. Kiefer explained that the offensive plays would involve much use of the guards being mobile. Baro and I were going to be pulled and trapped often, almost every other play. We needed to be quick and unforgiving.

We were lined up in our positions, and Kiefer walked Mark and me through how he wanted us to pull and trap. On pulls, we had to move quickly to get around the corner the play was going. Ronnie, Maurice, and Bryan were very fast, so we had to be quick to get out in front of them to take on the defensive ends, linebackers, and cornerbacks. On traps, he wanted us to stay low, bent at the waist, and move fast. An unexpected defensive tackle would be left free to penetrate into the backfield, and we were going to light him up. Hit him square in the numbers hard and intimidate him, making him wary to cross into the backfield, Kiefer said. Control the line of scrimmage through aggressiveness, he stated. "Be mean, just downright fearless!" he growled.

Next he explained how he wanted us to maneuver in pass protection. He instructed us to step back first with our outside foot, then the inside, and go back a few paces and square up. Bend at the waist with arms bent and palms flat, facing the approaching defender. Protect Ronnie at all costs, Kiefer stressed. We were his bodyguards and needed to keep him protected and healthy. "Do not fail!" Kiefer snapped as he glared at us.

Coach Kiefer had a barbaric attitude when it came to the trenches. He had battled there himself and he knew we needed to be relentless. He was molding us to be disciplined and unyielding. We were to be his Vikings and his muscle—unwavering for 48 minutes of play. We were to rule the gridiron and give no ground.

We switched to the defensive side. Dave Haupt was brought over, along with J-p, Eric Barnes, and Maurice. Jeff, David, J-p, and Eric would share the defensive end positions. Jeff and David would start but that may change sometimes. J-p and Eric would see plenty of action. Chris, Baro, and Chuck would share defensive tackle duties, with Chris and Baro starting. I would start as nose guard but Maurice and Murdock would share duties. We would mix it up. If Maurice was in as nose guard, Murdock and I would be rotated in as defensive tackles also.

David Smith, Eugene, and Derrick would back us up. They needed to be ready to go at any time. As I listened, I told myself, they would step up. I knew those three were going to be as good as any opposing players we faced. As juniors Eugene and Derrick were tough. They were formidable opponents for us in practice, and David Smith had guts to take on anyone in the trenches.

The entire team was then brought together, and we started working on offensive plays. We needed to get our timing down for the coming Watermelon Scrimmage, which was five days away on Saturday, against Armijo.

Play after play we went over to understand them and get the timing right. Coach Bev was a stickler for perfection. Perfect practices would make champions, he would tell us. This was a whole new offensive scheme we had to learn. It was a first for Vanden so it took concentration to understand Coach Bev's vision. Some plays we would go over as many as ten times (or more) until we got them right. At points Coach Bev would jump in as the quarterback and walk us through the play. He was hands on, and becoming a master of developing a football team.

We had the best coaches the previous four seasons, but this season Coach Bev seemed on his 'A' game. Not only was the team out to prove itself so was Coach Bev. It was obvious to me. I was a visual, soak-it-all-in type of football player. I believed I could learn from every player and every coach. As I watched Coach Bev closely that practice, a label kept coming back to me. He was 'Mr. Football.'

The squad was coming together, and during this second practice there was something different about the team. I could feel it. It was something I felt on the 1980 Travis Redskins and on the 1982 JV team two years earlier. There was an allure about this group of players and these coaches, along with our new offensive scheme and movie-character name-calls that made me believe the stars were aligning for us. A feeling inside kept tugging at me. It said something special would happen this season.

We switched to defense, and Coach Newsom took the reins. He laid out what he wanted to see from us. He wanted to see five or more players in on every tackle. He wanted us to be relentless. "Take names!" he would yell over and over.

Coach Noos had already picked his linebacker crew. Glenn would lead them. Danny Miller, one of the new transfer players, would plug the center as the middle linebacker. Glenn would anchor the left side and Sherman Pruitt would be the right side. A good accomplishment for a sophomore. Ronnie, David, Cliff, Felix, and Louis would be cornerbacks. Our safety would be a player named Steve Crittenden, another transfer student.

During the practice, Coach Noos offhandedly called the linebacker crew "The Orient Express" because they would blitz often and all three were part Oriental. The nickname stuck. The three relished that given name and it became their moniker. They wore it with pride.

Some passes were thrown for the defense to try and shut down. Darren had matured as a receiver. He had good speed, ran a good route, and had good hands. He also had a natural skill to run well after a catch. He was going to be a huge plus for the offense. Eric was big as a tight end and when he jumped for a ball, even harder to stop. He showed he too had great hands, and would be a strong offensive threat.

I was seeing very little that our opponents could exploit. The team was solid in all areas and each player was eager to prove he wanted to play. There was no lollygagging. I saw only hard work, determination, and hustling each play until the whistle was blown.

Next we went to specialty teams. David Smith proved to have the strongest leg for punting. He could send them high and long. Dave Haupt earned kickoff, field goals, and extra points. He too had a strong leg and accuracy. Glenn was picked to hold the PAT's (points after touchdown) for Dave.

The starting five linemen, Jeff, Baro, Big Joe, Chris, and I, would spearhead kickoff returns, with the linebackers, Glenn, Danny, Sherman, and John, with Bryan and Cliff back deep to receive.

On kickoffs, Jeff, Chris, Baro, me, Sherman, DeWayne, Darren, Chuck, Murdock, J-p, and Dave Haupt were chosen.

It was that time again: conditioning. We lined up and ran our dashes, gassers, and progressives. It was as painful as the morning session. The first 40-yard dash was easy; but by the end of the progressive, my legs were spent and screaming "UNCLE!" It was even hotter out, and my head was cooking inside my helmet. It felt like it was in an oven. At the end of the running I joined some of the players and vomited.

After taking a knee to listen to Coach Bev, I took my helmet off. My hair was soaking wet like I just got out of a shower. After we were released from the mid-day practice all the players and I made sure to drink plenty of fluids to stay hydrated. Cramps were starting and we couldn't afford any pulled muscles.

During the break some of the players slept. I couldn't blame them. I wanted to stay awake though, because I didn't trust Mark or John not to pull a prank.

Maybe I was being paranoid or overly cautious but I had Tuck add some more air to my helmet. He was 'Johnny on the Spot' for anything we needed. I wanted to make sure I had the proper fit and protection after colliding with Bryan that morning. Tuck and Eddie would do whatever we wanted and get what we needed. They both were willing to assist the best way they could. They knew a football team was only as good as all aspects of it, and that included the equipment and management. We were lucky we had two great guys to assist our squad.

During the break I made the mistake to go to the bathroom and leave my helmet unattended. I should've known better. When it was time to return to practice I had a surprise waiting. My mouthpiece had been switched with another player's. I wasn't sure which one did it, Murdock or Baro, but by their snickering it could've been a collective effort.

By the evening session we were all tired. It had been a long day. After running offensive and defensive plays we did pursuit drills. Half the team was lined up against the other. One line was to run straight down the field, while the other would pursue at a 45-degree angle from the other side and try to catch the runner.

Of course Ronnie, Bryan, Maurice, and a few others were fast. I knew they would be. Derrick and Eugene both surprised me how fast they were, along with David. For a smaller player he could hustle, and when his shorter legs scrambled down the field and caught the runner he was chasing, I was impressed.

Surviving to the end of the first day with no injuries and no players quitting was an accomplishment. We learned much during those first three sessions. As we changed and headed to our vehicles to go home a grin joined the sweat on my face.

That night I still struggled with sleep. My insomnia was difficult to overcome. I did get some rest though, and felt pretty good by morning. When I rolled out of bed and felt all the aches, I smiled. It felt good to hurt because I was playing football again, not just watching it. I really was enjoying these times with my friends.

It was another hot day when we arrived at practice. All 33 players showed, which was a positive note. Spirits were high and no one was complaining. We were on a roll. As we jogged out to the practice field the sun was still rising. I could see the sunshine glisten off the dew on the still wet grass. As we got into position to do our stretches and warm-ups the glare from my teammates helmets could be blinding. The sun captured every movement—like a photographer looking for the right shot.

When we stretched our necks and I looked up at that blue sky with no clouds, I felt relaxed. Certain things stayed with me. That sky, the feel and smell of the grass, the sound of pads and helmets crashing together, the thundering of the cleats in and out of the locker room, and the view through the face mask.

Looking through the vertical and horizontal bars

was one of the best views in my 17 years of life. I loved that visual when wearing a helmet. That to me was one of the great things about football.

After hitting the sled we ran full-speed offensive and defensive drills. It was time to learn Coach Bev's full book of plays. Yes, many included traps and pulling like Coach Kiefer said they would. Mark and I were going to be running a lot and hammering defensive tackles and linebackers on the run. We liked that idea.

As we ran the plays Coach Kiefer kept barking at us to go downfield after dealing with our initial defender. That meant moving on from the defensive line, to the linebackers, then cornerbacks. Keep moving and blocking until the whistle was blown. Bryan, Maurice, and Ronnie were explosive as runners, so they could use us in the secondary mowing the field. We were expected to keep the defensive players scrambling. (We would.)

From my four previous years playing football I knew it was important to be quick off the ball and quick sideline to sideline. Quickness for most players was more important than speed, unless you were a ball carrier. As a lineman or defensive player, though, you needed to be quick. Being aggressive, quick, and playing with heart could beat a larger, stronger, faster player who was a better athlete. Your physical size really didn't matter. It was the desire of your conviction to win and intensity until the play ended that made the difference. The best eleven athletes on either side of the ball did not win football games. It was the players who trusted each other and played as one—and not eleven—that would prevail.

Our team was small in size and numbers. Maurice

was our anvil at 204 pounds. I knew though, from playing with these guys for four practices, they were going to be as good as the 1980 and 1982 teams—or even better. You could see it in their eyes, the way they hustled, and the echoing of the pads and helmets as they collided. My teammates were name takers.

On the offensive line we were enjoying using the movie-character names at the line of scrimmage. It was really unique. In my short football career I had never seen anyone else employ that idea or heard of it being used. It was going to make our team standout. We had a surprise for our opponents, and they had no idea what was coming.

Not sure why he started doing it but I liked it. In huddles Eric (or 'Big E' as I called him), would nod at me right before we broke to head to the line of scrimmage. In a way it became our bond. Like clockwork I could always count on Big E's nod. It was constant, and always made me want to play harder.

Ronnie was cool and calm running the offense. You could tell he felt at home there. In his second year at the helm on varsity he was very seasoned. He ran a great option, and if he decided to run with the ball he would be extremely difficult for our opponents to stop.

Bryan and Maurice worked well in tandem. Maurice was a devastating blocker and excellent at pass protection. If Bryan hit an open hole he was gone in a flash. If he turned the corner to take the ball upfield, he was at home there. He owned the outside. It was his slaughterhouse.

In my three years of battling in the trenches I had

not played with a more cohesive unit than Big Joe, Jeff, Baro, and Chris. We were learning what to expect from each other. There were no chinks in the armor. Baro was going to level anyone who got in his way, Big Joe and Chris were rock solid as tackles, and Jeff was proficient in his techniques. From the outside we probably looked like quite an assortment of mongrels—well-trained and disciplined—but we bit; hard and often.

J-p, Dave Haupt, Jeff, and Eric were all formidable at containing the outside on defense. All four were as solid as defensive ends as there were in our league. They could contain the run and shut down the pass.

The Orient Express was a close-knit group. They took pride in their name and play, and they were very good. They were hard-chargers and hard-hitters. The more physical the play, the better they got. It was like they enjoyed the challenge. I respected that in them.

The defensive backs were led by Ronnie. Cliff, Louis, DeWayne, Felix, and David were all hitters who hustled to the ball. Quarterbacks were not going to have an easy time completing deep passes.

After struggling through conditioning that session, I was thankful when practice was over. I was learning and remembering the offensive plays, so I knew my memory retention was fine. I did feel my balance was slightly off and it was most noticeable during pass protection drills. Sometimes I felt wobbly.

During the lunch break some of the players lifted weights in the Shubin Sports Building where we rested. I was using the bench press when one of our junior players named Stephen Harrison came over and was egging me on to lift harder. I wasn't working hard enough, he kept saying. I told him to quit multiple times. He persisted.

When I got up from the bench I grabbed him in a bear hug and carried him over to the wrestling mat. I asked some of my teammates to assist me. We rolled Stephen up in the 38-feet-by-38-feet 1-inch wrestling mat, leaving just his head exposed. He looked like a cannoli. We weren't only football players but Italian bakers.

Break was over and we headed back to the practice field. I left Stephen in his wrapped confinement. As we stretched, Coach Noos would do a head count every practice. He counted bodies and kept coming up with 32, one short. He asked us who was missing. No one said a word. (We chuckled, though.) Noos went down the player list calling names, and we were instructed to respond when ours was called.

When he got to Stephen there was no response. Noos asked if he had quit. All the players chuckled again. Noos was getting irritated, and he asked where Stephen was. I could tell he wasn't in a joking mood, so I spoke up and said he was in the Shubin Sports Building.

Noos told me to go get him. I jogged inside and unrolled him from the mat. We returned to practice together. I think Stephen learned his lesson because he never bugged me again when I was lifting weights. We became friends, and he would joke periodically about his time spent as a cannoli.

The rest of the week the team worked hard, trying to understand and memorize the new offensive plays and defensive schemes we would use. We wanted perfection. We heard Coach Bev each time he stated, "Perfect

205

practices will make you champions!"

I didn't care how we did it. Inch by inch; foot by foot; yard by yard, as long as we crossed the end zone. I didn't care what the final score read. Just be a victory. I wanted payback for 1980. I wanted something for the unconscious faceplant in Dixon. I'd be willing to take good memories with my friends and the title in return.

As we took a knee the last of the three-a-day practices of Hell Week, the coaches looked content. In that short time frame of five days and fifteen practices, we had learned most of the new system designed by Coach Bev. We were ready to face Armijo within 24 hours for our annual Watermelon Scrimmage.

The locker room was quiet as we dressed the next morning. It was time to take everything learned during Hell Week and utilize it against the Armijo Indians. The trenchers helped each other taping pads in place. We were as prepared as we could be.

From the first whistle starting the scrimmage to the final play, we battled back and forth on the varsity practice field. When it was over we were ahead on points. There were no injuries for either team and no fights. It was a good end to Hell Week. It was the last one that my friends (who were seniors) and I would enjoy.

Once again Jeff's, Bryan's, and Chris's dads were there cutting the watermelon, along with a few other parents. It was nice to see the support the football teams had from the school, the athletic program, and the families.

As I left the locker room that day I was happy the team had played well and was coming together. I knew there was something special about the squad and how we trusted each other. Walking to the car to leave I felt a sadness too. I would never attend another Hell Week at Vanden. As much as the five days of three-a-day practices had tested us physically and mentally, I was going to miss that annual first week of football as a Viking.

That evening was a time for celebration. I played my first week of football with my friends again, and we were all injury-free. We were feeling invincible—so we spent the evening on top of speeding vehicles on Vanden road. Though Coach Bev had made some changes to the program, we weren't ready to change our weekly routine. We were still stuntmen and needed to feel that rush.

A sophomore a year ago, Vanden's Ronnie Beverly was under a lot of pressure as the team's starting quarterback. Now, a year older, he's hoping to lead the Vikes to the SCAL crown.

Vikes Will Sport New Look

The above pre-season image shows Ronnie at one of our three-a-day practices during Hell Week. Photo courtesy of the Reporter.

I knew during their time at Vanden my brothers had been rock stars. Sean looked like a teen idol with his letterman jacket, feathered hair, and his girlfriend, the head cheerleader, Dana Wilson, on his arm. Tim was no different. Both of them proudly wore their letterman jackets showing their varsity letters in wrestling.

Jeff, Chris, Murdock, Glenn, and Big Joe all wore letterman jackets, too. Baro didn't have one and I don't think it was his style. It would've clashed with his original look. Maybe if he put military medals or chevron ranks on one it would've worked for him. I still couldn't see him wearing one, though. He was too rebellious.

When my mom offered to buy me a letterman jacket, I thought about it. I was an athlete and similar to the jock in the movie 'The Breakfast Club.' However, I didn't feel the need to wear my football record for all to see. I felt more comfortable showing it on the field. I also knew finances were tight in our home and I wasn't working. I had put all my free time in preparing for this final season and I was always exhausted after practices. Between football and school I didn't have time to work. I didn't feel right having my mom buy a letterman jacket or even a school ring for me, so I passed on both.

We four boys kept my mom on her toes. From the time we were little we were a handful. I had to laugh when I heard the story of my mom flying back from Japan when Craig was an infant with us three boys in tow. We were only 4.5 years apart and rambunctious. From airport to airplanes back to airports. How did my mom keep a safe eye on three little boys who were so high-spirited? With harnesses and leashes that looked like octopus arms moving in all directions. I don't think the woman who complained had a clue about the difficulty and struggle it had been for my mom with four little boys. Her sarcastic comment, "Those aren't puppies" deserved the dirty look my mom gave her.

It was not far from where we had our six-car accident at the intersection of Vanden and Peabody Roads. It was just on the other side of the railroad tracks where Big Joe jumped into action. It was before school started one morning, and the two-car accident was only 1/4-mile from Vanden. Big Joe was the first one on the scene and became an instant hero by safely pulling the injured from the vehicles involved. It wasn't going to be his last 15 minutes of fame, either. We still had a football season ahead where records would be broken and unforgettable memories made.

I was hearing the different stories of their exploits. They were like Jim and me, just older. I wasn't surprised when I heard Coach Noos caught Big Joe and Baro behind the Shubin Sports Building with a beer bong. He thought they were doing drugs. When he realized it was just beer, and they offered him a try, he wasn't amused and declined. I also wasn't surprised when I heard Big Joe and Baro took a vacuum and sucked some goldfish from a fish tank while drunk at a party on Travis AFB. They were making names for themselves, and a perfect fit for a squad. We may have been Air Force brats—but we weren't lily white. We were just teenagers trying to find our way through football, girls, adventure, and fun. Along the way we would make some wrong choices, but they became memorable ones.

School started, and Baro and I had Coach Kiefer for U.S. History. He would joke with us daily before class. Kiefer was a diabetic so he drank lots of fluids. He kept two big plastic containers on his desk. At the beginning of class each day he would have Baro fill both with water. I think Coach Kiefer singled Mark out because they shared the connection of the same birthday, and Baro played the same trencher positions—right guard and defensive tackle—that Kiefer had at the University of San Francisco.

Our lunch breaks were spent in the senior quad area. A lot of the teammates would spend time together during that period. We were the best of friends on and off the field.

My preferred lunch was a burrito, french fries, and a frozen chocolate malt. (I wasn't that health-conscious.)

Above photo shows Cliff (left), our new transfer teammate from Okinawa, and Glenn (right) during a break at school. Photo courtesy of Travis Unified School District and Vanden High School.

The cheerleaders at Vanden made the football program better. Their dance routines were fun to watch and their spirit uplifting. Hearing their cheers always made us battle harder. Our victories were theirs, too.

Top photo (L to R): Michelle Paisley, Phyllis Betsill, and Sherri Takahara. Bottom photo (L to R): Kim Tatman and Michelle Paisley. Top photo courtesy of Travis Unified School District and Vanden High School. Bottom photo courtesy of Kim Tatman.

Off the field and away from school I couldn't get enough of anything related to football. I was constantly reading the newspapers about our Viking team, those opponents we were slated to face, and the other local squads.

I never missed an article in any of the newspapers. I could be found glued to the sports sections. That time alone was something I liked. It gave me time to study our opponents. I also knew the clock was ticking until my football career would be over. There was about three months until the sand ran out of that hourglass. We had 9 regular season games and if we did well there would be an additional 3 more games for the playoffs. I had 12 games left, and that would be it for me. I wanted to get my fill during those few remaining months; so the Vacaville Reporter and the Fairfield Daily Republic newspapers became my daily companions.

I never liked the limelight much as a player. It made me feel uncomfortable. Our success as a team and as friends is what I cared about. I was a chest thumper during a game if I became upset or the contest was trying. That was personal motivation for me. I was never one to pat myself on the back or run around after a big play, though. It wasn't my style. I just wanted wins in our column, not personal glory.

One morning prior to the start of our regular season I saw my name in an article about our team and the changes being made to our program. As I read that article I was surprised at what Coach Bev thought about me as a player. It made me feel proud. It was my last season and I had to give it my all. I needed to (for me).

Beverly put his team through triple sessions this summer because the Vikings have a new offensive and defensive system. Vanden will run and pass out of an I-formation as well as a split backfield. "It will be a pro look," noted Beverly, who scrapped Vanden's traditional wishbone in favir of the I.

Defensively, the Vikings will employ a 5-2 and a 5-3 setup. As usual, opposing offensive units will have to be on their toes. Vanden likes to blitz and stunt a great deal.

Watch out for Jeff Rooney. He's a two-way starter, at offensive guard and defensive noseguard. "Rooney's an animal," Beverly said out of respect.

Last season Rooney suffered a concussion during the Dixon game and missed the rest of the season. He was badly needed considering the lack of depth on the squad. The Vikings finished last season with 19 players.

The above paragraphs are from a pre-season article. Courtesy of the Reporter.

Our annual Quadraplay was scheduled that Saturday at Vanden. We were to face Dixon and Benicia on the George Gammon Field. Hogan was to participate but cancelled attending the event at the last minute.

The two teams arrived that morning to face us. We dressed in our practice uniforms and took the field. It was the first time I would face the Dixon squad since my concussion. I was anxious as I awaited that first contact.

The rules were set. Each of our offenses would get two series of 20 plays starting at the 50-yard line, and only three plays to score a first down. A touchdown or a turnover would move the ball back to the 50-yard line.

In the first series we faced Dixon with them on offense and us on defense. I was playing nose guard. We stopped their first play, which was a pass attempt. On the second play they ran off the right tackle, and we again stopped them for a one-yard gain. Glenn, Jeff, Chris, and I hit their running back, burying him. A large mass of bodies slammed hard into each other.

As I got up from the bottom of the pile a Dixon player shoved me back down stating they would knock me out again like last season. I lost my composure, and I slugged him with an uppercut. A brief fight ensued between both teams with my teammates coming to my defense.

The meeting I had attended the previous spring at Dixon as a 'Good Will Ambassador' between the Vanden and Dixon schools, to subvert any brewing rivalry, had failed (on the second play) against them. Coach Bev was upset and pulled me from the scrimmage for three plays. He let me return, and we outplayed both their squads.

"Things are getting a little physical out there. It was supposed to be a friendly scrimmage and people are getting into fights and everything."

The above quote was from Coach Bev during the Quadraplay scrimmage at Vanden. Article and image courtesy of the Reporter.

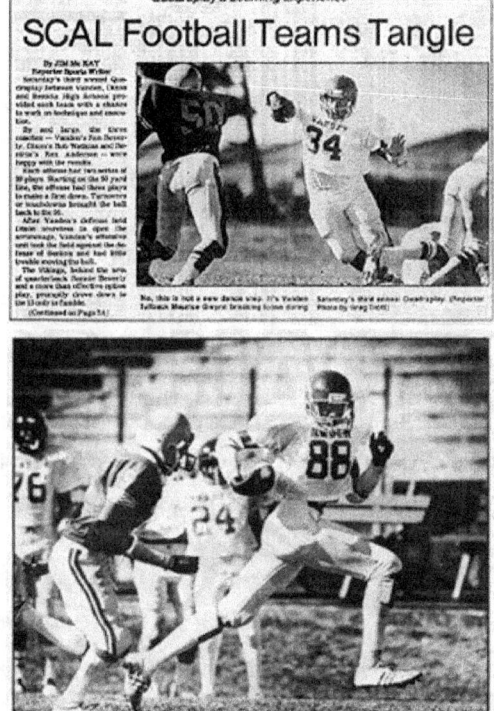

Our squad did well against both teams. Maurice is shown at top and Eric ('Big E') below during the Quadraplay scrimmage at Vanden. Both photos courtesy of the Reporter.

That week at practice we worked hard preparing for our first opponent that coming Friday. We were to face Galt at Vanden in a non-league contest. We knew the game would be a hard-fought battle because most of their 9-1 winning JV squad from the year before were on their varsity team. They were almost a mirror image of us. We had most of the players from the 9-0 undefeated and unscored-upon JV team from two years prior. The Galt Warriors were going to have to play their best to beat us.

I asked my mom to come to the game and she said she couldn't do it. She said she couldn't handle sitting there. I knew she was having regrets about letting me play. She was still terrified I would be hurt again or worse. I told her it would be okay and hugged her. I was wearing a special helmet to protect my brain, and the air would cushion my head during contact, I said. I don't think my words comforted her or eased her worries. I was a football player though, and dangers came with the game I loved. I was willing to take that risk. She wasn't.

That Friday morning before school the entire football team and coaches met on Travis AFB to attend church. The service was performed by Maurice's dad. It was during that mass I realized Maurice got his outgoing personality from his father. I drew strength as I listened to his words. I knew it wasn't right to pray for a victory—as the Galt Warriors would be doing the same—but I told myself it couldn't hurt.

We wore our football game jerseys to Vanden that day. I could see the looks and feel the vibes. Classmates looked at us a little differently knowing we were football players. When teachers asked me if I thought we would win, I responded yes without hesitation. I knew how my friends played.

We had practiced how we would head to the field as a squad. We were there to play, entertain, and win. Our entrance needed to have an impact, and we wanted it to be an impressive one. How we looked and acted would be a preview to how we played. Our cheerleaders would be working hard to keep spirits high during the game. Our school band would also be entertaining at halftime, so the football team needed to do its part to put on a good show for those who came to watch us.

The JV game was to start at 5:45 p.m., so we got there early to wish them good luck. We warmed up, ran some mock plays on the practice field and watched the first half of the JV game. After their halftime we started getting suited and ready for our contest.

As I sat in front of my locker I put on my equipment slowly making sure everything was perfect. I put on my shin pads under my socks that I had taped up, hip pads, football pants, and cleats. I put on my shoulder pads with neck roll and jersey over it. I then put on my elbow and forearm pads, along with a pair of baseball gloves with hand pads over them. The gloves made it easier to grip an opponent. I was the only player on our team to wear them. Once fully dressed, I felt like a Titan.

I reminded myself eyes and fingers were the key. The eyes told the heart of a player. They gave insight to him. Was he a fighter or easy to roll? The fingers told the intensity. If they were moving and antsy, he was ready to explode at the snap of the ball. If they were still, I had him in my trap. I knew to watch them both.

The other trenchers dressed in a similar fashion, putting on arm and hand pads as I had. We couldn't take any risks with injuries this season. We wanted to win, and to do that we had to stay injury-free.

  I tracked down Tuck our equipment manager, and had him add air to my helmet. I told him to check it at halftime also. I hadn't forgotten that concussion. I wasn't going to slow my speed or shy from contact. If anything, I planned on ramping it up.

  After dressing the trench crew helped each other tape our arm and hand pads securely in place. The mood was serious. I looked around at all the faces I could see. I didn't see any smiles. We were about to battle our first foe together. We smacked our fists against each other's shoulder pads, prepping ourselves mentally.

  Coaches Newsom, Kiefer, and Bev all wore yellow shirts with light gray pants. We were wearing our forest-green jerseys with gold numbering. The coaches went up to their office, which overlooked our lockers, for one last strategy session. I glanced up at them.

  I walked around checking on my teammates, as did other players. I saw many feet tapping in anticipation. I made sure Murdock was wearing his lucky tee shirt under his pads. He was. Murdock walked around head butting other players as soon as they put on their helmets.

  Nights in bed or the long bus ride to school put thoughts in my head. How would I feel if I was able to return to football? I was willing to give my left arm to get back to the game—and here I was. Those thoughts that had come to me easily during those quiet moments were silent now. All I could hear was my heartbeat.

The Orient Express—Glenn, Danny, and Sherman were ready to cause destruction. The TTB—Triple Threat Backfield (Bryan, Maurice, and Ronnie)—were ready to take apart their defense. All the guys were ready for the contact awaiting us. I knew many helmet stickers were going to be earned. I also knew that the Galt Warriors would remember our Vanden Vikings.

The coaches came down from their office, and Coach Bev walked to the chalkboard and went over the game plan they had devised. His hand was fluent with the X's and O's. He tapped the chalk board as he spoke. You could've heard sweat drop, we were so still. He was calm in his speech, yet firm with his words. We were better prepared mentally and better conditioned physically. We had heart and desire to win. He told us we had the plays, skills, and knowledge, and all we had to do was combine those with hustling and we would win. He was right. It was our time as 'No Names' to start being recognized.

It wasn't just our quest back to glory; it was Bev's too. The decades hadn't erased his memory of his time on the gridiron. He remembered wearing shoulder pads and a helmet. So did Kiefer and Noos. They became coaches for a reason. They loved the game and needed it, like us. They were still football players in their hearts. Our victory would be their victory.

We knelt for prayer, then rose to our feet for a team cheer. We were ready to go. As we exited the locker room the cleats on the tile echoed. Each player pounded the metal partition outside the door, adding to the thundering sound of 33 Vikings preparing for battle. I hoped the Warriors could hear us coming.

It was still light out but starting to turn dusk as we lined up in a straight row with the captains in front, Ronnie, Glenn, and myself. We readied ourselves for what awaited us on the gridiron. The fourth person in line was picked for big plays the previous contest; so since Bryan had a great scrimmage during the Quadraplay, he was the fourth Viking. We walked towards our field slapping our thigh pads in unison. It must have sounded imposing as we slowly worked our way along the 125-yard path towards the George Gammon stadium.

Once we arrived at the rubber track surrounding the football field we crossed over some padded runners that protected it from our cleats. As we hit the grass we (the captains and Bryan) turned left and jogged towards the goal line, and spun backwards in, separating ourselves by five yards. Our next four teammates jogged to the five-yard line, spun backwards in, and separated themselves by five yards, lining up straight with the captains. The rest of the team continued doing that five yards further down the field. When finished we had four rows, eight deep, with one extra player at the end.

Bryan and we three captains then yelled, "What time is it?" The squad thundered back, "Showtime!" Ronnie started us off with stretching; then Glenn, Bryan, and I directed our teammates. The movements were choreographed well and the team looked disciplined. I knew we looked sharp.

After stretches and warm-ups we broke off into groups. I went with the trenchers. Coach Kiefer directed us to the Vanden side of the visitor end zone. There he had us do bear crawls, loose football scrambling, and other controlled drills. As we completed our preparation and I stood up, I could feel the butterflies in my stomach. Adrenalin had taken over and the combination of the two caused me to throw up in my mouthpiece. I spit the vomit on the ground and shook the guard out and put it back in. I knew that was football, so I wasn't going to rinse it out. I wanted that sour taste to remind me it was a violent game, and to be the aggressor at all times. My body was cautioning me that anything could happen on the field—I had better be prepared.

There was no doubt I was nervous. It wasn't from worry or fear for what awaited us on the field. It was because it was my first time under the lights in almost a year. Spectators and fans came to watch us, and I didn't want to disappoint them, my team, coaches, or myself.

Our squad was waiting in anticipation. Minutes seemed like hours. It was torturous. Some of the players were bouncing slightly, but for the most part the team looked professional. Under those well-trained quiet exteriors something else was brewing. I heard the sound of them crashing together at practices. I knew what they could inflict. They should've been on chains—leashed. The calm demeanor everyone was seeing was dynamite waiting to explode. We wanted a victory and we would accept nothing less. I knew the guys suited around me were ready.

Bryan, Glenn, Ronnie, and I went out for the coin toss. We met the Galt Warriors. Our real introduction would be made shortly in a very physical fashion. I made a point to make eye contact. Set the tone for what is coming, I told myself. I knew it would be fun.

After the kickoff it was a back-and-forth game. Galt came out with a single-wing offense. We had never faced a team using that offensive configuration, so we had to adapt throughout the contest. The center was offset on the line and from the quarterback. The fullback and tailback were offset from the quarterback and each other. It was a confusing for us, but we adhered to the basic rule: follow the football.

End, Guard, Center, Guard, Tackle, Tackle, End

Wingback

Quarterback

Fullback

Tailback

(Single-Wing Formation Offense)

Galt got on the scoreboard first, and we were losing 7-0 at the end of the first quarter. On our first possession in the second quarter, we went 62 yards on 9 plays for a touchdown, when Ronnie threw a 10-yard score to our tight end and his step-brother Eric. We missed our extra point. We held Galt on their next four plays.

Our very next possession Bryan broke free on a draw play and went 80 yards for our second touchdown. Ronnie kept the ball and scored on a two-point conversion. We took the lead at 14-7. The third quarter was scoreless.

Galt scored first in the fourth period with a touchdown. With their own two-point conversion they regained a 15-14 lead. That seemed to stiffen our resolve. On the ensuing kickoff, Cliff, our new transfer student, caught the ball on the run. He started left, then went right, crossing the field and dodging tackles. He scampered 82 yards for a touchdown. It was an incredible run. We scored another two-point conversion, recapturing the lead. From there we held Galt and went on to win 22-15.

On 42 rushing carries we held Galt to 119 yards. Bryan rushed for 134 yards on 11 carries, with another 46-yard run called back on an illegal motion penalty. On offense we fumbled four times, losing 3 of the 4, from mishandling of the ball.

I was impressed with the whole team. The trenchers played with grit. Big Joe looked massive in his uniform, and on the line he opened big holes. Mark was a battering ram when he pulled. Chris kept the Warriors at bay, making it easy for Bryan to turn the corner on the right side, and Jeff kept Ronnie safe from the blitzing linebackers. On defense my Viking teammates showed Galt they were hitters, holding them to 2.8 yards per carry.

DAILY REPUBLIC   SUNDAY, SEPTEMBER 4, 1984

Roberts keys 22-15 win
Vanden beats Galt on 82-yard return

Above headline showing our win and Cliff's run is from an article in the Daily Republic. Courtesy of the Daily Republic. Used with permission.

On the ensuing kickoff, Vanden's Roberts took the ball at his 18, started up the middle, cut to his left near the 30, then broke back to the right and scampered down the sideline for the winning score.

Above paragraph detailing Cliff's kickoff return, from an article in the Daily Republic. Courtesy of the Daily Republic. Used with permission.

Vanden ground game eats up Galt, 22-15

Above headline is from an article in the Vacaville Reporter. Below photo shows Ronnie, our quarterback, as he kept the ball on a run. Both images courtesy of the Reporter.

Vanden's Ronnie Beverly dives forward to help the Vikings beat Galt. (Reporter Photo by Dan Trevan)

As was customary with every football game I had ever played, we shook hands with the Galt Warriors and thanked them for a hard-fought contest. They were our first notch. We needed eleven more to get the crown.

In the locker room the players and coaches were ecstatic. We played well and prevailed against a tough squad, which used an offensive scheme we had never seen. I was happy as I changed and headed to the car. I was too tired to celebrate riding on top of a vehicle speeding down Vanden Road, so I went straight home to shower and rest. It had been a great day of football with my friends and my first game back as a Viking. I could see his smile—Psycho was happy.

Under Coach Hatcher's direction Vanden's JV squad won their game too, beating the Galt Warriors 30-14. It was a good day for our Viking football program.

That Monday at school Coach Kiefer wore a grin from ear to ear. He was happy with how the trenchers performed on both sides of the line. When he saw us he slapped us on the back and told us we played well. Before class started he joked with Mark and me about how Galt thought they would confuse our defense with the Single-Wing formation. Yet it was we who confused them with the movie-character names. It worked perfectly. Kiefer's unique plan made the Warriors stop and think right before we hiked the ball. It gave us an edge.

After school the entire team met in a classroom in the freshman quad area to watch game film of our performance against Galt. Watching the video gave the coaches the opportunity to look for issues that needed to be corrected, or praise players for their play. We always watched game film the following Monday after facing an opponent. That was standard in football and we were no different. We needed that time to make us a better squad.

The above photo shows (left to right) me, Jeff, Chris, Baro in front, Murdock behind him, Big Joe, Ronnie and a few other players, while Coach Bev is preparing the VCR and TV to watch game film. Photo courtesy of Travis Unified School District and Vanden High School.

At the start of practice that afternoon coaches Bev, Noos, and Kiefer told us we needed to prep hard all week for our coming game that Friday night at Vanden. We would be facing one of the toughest teams we would meet on the gridiron, Hogan. Hogan was in the MEL league and they had four to five times as many students as Vanden. They would be physically bigger than us and have more bodies suited on their squad. They had a deeper bench and a better crop of athletes.

Even though Hogan was part of our annual Quadraplay, Vanden had never prevailed against a MEL school in an actual game. Ronnie, J-p, Eric, and Coach Bev were all from Vallejo, where Hogan was located. They lived in the same neighborhood as many of the Hogan players. Coach Bev wanted to win badly because it was bragging rights. After the loss to Hogan the year before, Ronnie had been given a hard time in the neighborhood, so he wanted a victory over the Spartans.

Coach Kiefer repeatedly stressed we had to be explosive off the ball and continue to utilize the movie-character names on offense. On defense we had to penetrate into their backfield quickly because their tailback and quarterback had great speed. We needed to shut them down to give our offense under Ronnie a chance to put points on the scoreboard.

Jeff was instructed after the first series on offense to let Coach Bev know if he could handle their nose guard alone. Whether he was able to control him or not would affect the offensive play selection.

That week at practice Baro wore his cleats without socks. It looked uncomfortable to me; but he liked it. It became part of his persona when we practiced. The coaches made a point to tell him he definitely needed to wear socks for games—it wasn't debatable—so don't ask.

I became a prank victim again midweek when Murdock put Icy Hot in my jock strap. I didn't know it until I started warming up during leg lifts. I squirmed and rubbed as Coach Kiefer asked, "You have ants in your pants Rooney?" Somewhere from behind me David Reyes yelled out, "Yeah, fire ants!" The whole team laughed as I jumped up and ran to the ice water jug for relief. As I was shoving ice down the front of my pants the cheerleaders rounded the corner of the building. Their giggles said they saw me. I spent a few minutes tap dancing with my cleats. My middle finger told Murdock what I thought. My laughter joined theirs as parts of my body warned me to watch Murdock and Baro MUCH closer.

Friday evening when Hogan arrived at Vanden and exited their bus they looked so much bigger than us. I counted almost 60 players versus our 33. They looked like they had over a dozen players over 200 pounds, to our one, Maurice. We were in for a game, and I knew that as I looked at the Spartans.

Sometimes as I left the huddle heading to the line of scrimmage I could hear the coaches talking to me. Coach Kiefer would say, "Push off fast! Drive hard into him! Push him backwards!" Coach Noos followed with, "Our jogs together taught me you won't let me down." And Coach Bev gave me direction, "Jeff, we need this first down. Turn the corner quickly and take out their linebacker so Bryan can make the turn!" Did I really hear their voices? No. But, I thought I could—and it gave me the fuel to do what needed to be done. Against Hogan I knew I would need that encouragement.

> **The Vikings have failed in five attempts to beat an MEL team since the inception of the league in 1976. Vanden is a member of the Superior California Athletic League.**

The above image is from an article written in the Vacaville Reporter. Courtesy of the Reporter.

After the JV halftime my teammates and I followed the same quiet preparation in the locker room as we dressed to face our much larger foe in Hogan.

There were no mischievous laughs or pranks but slow movements putting on our equipment. As I put on my shin guards I remembered how a helmet against them felt the last time we played the Spartans. I didn't care if I was upended on another hit from their squad but my shins wouldn't suffer the same fate.

After we finished dressing, Coach Kiefer instructed us trenchers to follow him. The entire trench crew followed him into the main gym area of the Shubin Sports Building. He told us he knew we were about to face a very tough test, and we should reflect quietly about the challenge ahead. He said he wanted us to take time alone from the rest of the team. Just our crew and twenty minutes of darkness. Listen to your hearts and prep yourselves mentally, he told us. No coaches, no players, no cheerleaders, or refs would bother us. In twenty minutes he would return. "Take your Zen time," Kiefer stated. "You need this time alone to find your inner strength," he said, and left us. He later returned. I think he was right because I felt a calm I hadn't in the four previous seasons before a game. The look in the other trenchers' eyes said the same thing.

Our Zen time became a pre-game prep for the rest of the season. Twenty quiet minutes alone to find ourselves. It made us better players. Coach Kiefer knew the game of football well and how to mold linemen. His 'movie-character name-calls' and 'Zen time' brought us closer together as a crew, and victories were to follow.

His hand was steady as he wrote the X's and O's on the chalk board. I think Coach Bev purposely wrote ours smaller than Hogan's because he wanted us to understand the challenge. They were big. We were about to meet a huge hurdle in our comeback. All three of their faces—Bev's, Noos's and Kiefer's—couldn't find a smile. They set the mood: be prepared to dig down deep and find that inner strength.

I think the clenched fists pounding on the metal partition sounder louder, meaner, more menacing. I was sure the Hogan Spartans heard our battle cry. They knew we were coming. Maurice joined Glenn, Ronnie, and me taking the team out to our field. We moved together in tandem, as we slapped our thigh pads and our cleats thundered together on the cement and asphalt.

When we arrived, the Spartans were already there. As we lined up to do warm-ups I couldn't help but notice how big they looked and how many Hogan uniforms there were. They had more than our team, coaches, equipment assistants, stat girls, and cheerleaders combined. It was just a number, I told myself. I had vegetable soup on my side. Air Force brats who were stuntmen. Some wore no socks and others were named after TV characters. Our backfield was black, our line white, and our linebackers Asian. We all liked each other and we were friends. We bled green and gold, and we played as one. The Hogan Spartans were about to see why our 1984 Vanden Vikings squad was unstoppable.

Football was just a game to them. To us it was much more. It was everything. It bonded us—and we weren't prepared to lose it all to them in game two of the season. I remembered being that 13-year-old kid peddling fast down Vanden Road in uniform. I loved football and rode the 'Beast' back and forth, braving speeding cars and exhaustion to play with my buddies.

Those same guys were still here, except for Jim, ole Maniac. Damn I missed him, I thought to myself. Glenn, Jeff, Baro, Murdock, and Bryan had a true respect for the game. They knew every aspect of it and how to win. Twice before we had been champions together. I knew we could do it again.

The lights were shining down on us, and the stands were full. We were like actors in a play but our outcome wasn't predetermined by a script and a writer. It was going to be determined by hard hits, crushing tackles and those sleds I hated.

I looked at Bryan. He had this piercing look in his eyes. I had seen it many times before, and each time it was intimidating. I knew decades later I would still see it.

The above photo shows our route to the George Gammon Field from the locker room. Provided by Timothy O'Donnell #69 co-captain of the 1984 undefeated Vanden JV 9-0 team.

After warming up with the trenchers doing scrambling drills, the combination of butterflies and adrenalin once again filled my mouthpiece. In the four previous seasons I had played football that had never happened. I wasn't sure what was causing it but I shook it out and put it back in. I had bigger worries facing me across the field than the sour taste in my mouth.

Meeting the Spartans at the 50-yard line told me we weren't going to be sharing pizza after the game or inviting them to join us as stuntmen on Vanden Road. They didn't like us much and it showed. We won the coin toss and opted to receive the ball. During our first offensive play, the huge defensive tackle lined up against Chris and Baro fought them off on a high/low block, and ran down Bryan from behind as he turned the corner on the opposite side of the field. When we went to huddle for the next play, all we could talk about was how big, strong, and fast that Hogan player was. We could not believe he was able to catch Bryan. We knew we were in for a fight—it was going to get bloody.

In the first quarter Hogan's running back scored a touchdown on a 64-yard run, and their extra point was good. After we failed to move the ball during our series Hogan scored another touchdown after driving 67 yards. We were able to block the PAT (point after kick) but were losing 13-0 with little over two minutes left in the first period. We had to turn the game around and gain our footing. "Remember your Zen time," Kiefer told us.

Jeff told Coach Bev he could handle Hogan's nose guard one on one, so Baro and I were free to pull and trap. We were ready to swing that hammer. Being

13 points down didn't rattle the team. We weren't the surrendering type. We were ready to dig in.

From my three-point stance I would stare directly into the eyes of the defensive tackle lined up against Joe and me. I refused to break eye contact. I wanted him to know we would not cower or turn tail. My look said it wasn't us that needed to worry about the outcome of the game. We were just getting started. For the rest of the season he would remember how we buried him in the turf, and how he needed dental floss to remove grass from his teeth. Payback was coming.

Big Joe and I repeatedly hit him hard, high and low, the same as Chris and Baro were doing on the other side of the line. We pounded him fast and deliberate. Explode off the line, I kept telling myself. On pulls Mark unleashed his fury at the Hogan players. When I followed him he cleared the path like a bulldozer. All I had to do was clean up the remnants. Joe, Jeff, and Chris controlled their larger opponents when Mark and I were on the move. We started firing on all cylinders.

Our offense drove 67 yards and scored on a two-yard run up the gut, as Maurice buried the Hogan defenders trying to stop him. We were on the scoreboard the first play of the second quarter. We tried a two-point conversion but it failed. We were down 13-6.

On defense I made sure to get as close to the center without crossing the threshold of the line. I growled at him. That old 1981 Psycho character wanted to make his presence known. He was back.

When I was pulled off defense for a breather, I was impressed at how fast Murdock and Maurice were able to penetrate into the backfield as nose guards. Dave Haupt, J-p Smith, Eric Barnes, and Jeff started containing the outside from their defensive end positions. Our Orient Express linebackers, Glenn, Danny, and Sherman were making big sticks. Ronnie, Cliff, Louis, David, and Felix were shutting down Hogan's passing game. We were turning the tide.

After stopping Hogan's control of the ball we drove downfield and Bryan scored on a 28-yard run. Our two-point conversion failed. On our next possession, Dave Haupt kicked a 32-yard field goal to give us a 15-13 lead going into the halftime break.

In the locker room Coach Bev and Coach Kiefer came to me and said it was time to set the tone. We were going to run three traps in a row towards the large defensive tackle lined up against Chris and Mark. They wanted me to hit him hard in the numbers and make him wary to penetrate into the backfield. Punish him, I was told. Lead by example were the unsaid words.

After the kickoff, and when we were on offense, I knew the coming play selection. Our movie-character names were having an impact, confusing the Hogan defense. I knew it would give me an edge as I went to trap the monstrous Hogan tackle. From my three-point stance I told myself, turn fast, stay low, and explode hard. Be a battering ram. The coaches were watching and counting on me. I knew the Hogan tackle was much bigger, faster, stronger, and a better athlete. He wouldn't prevail, though. Goliath was about to meet David. I didn't have a slingshot. I had a 185-pound frame ready to strike.

Jeff hiked the ball and I flew down the line as

Chris and Mark let the defensive tackle through. I hit him hard in the numbers with my facemask and clenched fists. I launched my body at him and my feet left the ground. He went backwards onto his back, with me on top of him. The metal braces he put on during the halftime break (because of the high/low pounding from Chris and Mark) weren't going to help him from an impact to the chest. The next two plays ended with the same result. Each time the defensive tackle cursed at me to get off him. He was pissed, embarrassed, and wary.

Coaches Kiefer and Bev were right. The three hits slowed the defensive tackle down. He didn't want to be trapped again, so Bryan was let loose on the right side of the field. Bev's playbook was opened up, and our Triple Threat Backfield ran wild. It was an ugly sight if you were a Hogan fan. The Spartans were against the ropes being pummeled.

The second half was all us. We held Hogan scoreless while we put 15 more points on the scoreboard from two touchdown passes from Ronnie to Eric. For three quarters we shut out a MEL team with players much larger and stronger than us and a deeper bench to pull from. The Spartans had had a painful introduction to our squad. We scored 30 unanswered points.

With two minutes left in the game Hogan's quarterback ran the ball on a keeper and tried to turn the right side of the field. Glenn and I pursued and buried him hard along the sidelines. It was a punishing hit. As we stood up I noticed I had blood on my uniform. I wasn't injured. I looked at Glenn and asked if he were okay. He said it wasn't his blood, either. I looked down and was stunned.

The quarterback's leg was broken with a bone protruding through his sock. He must've been in shock because he was quiet. Medical staff rushed onto the field and he was taken off on a stretcher. He left by ambulance. Our sideline collision ended his season.

We won 30-13. Ronnie threw for 113 yards with three touchdowns and Bryan rushed for 101 yards on 18 carries. Maurice added another 30 yards on 4 runs. Coach Bev, Ronnie, Eric, and J-p were happy. They had bragging rights in their hometown. We were now 2-0.

Vanden's JV squad won too, beating Hogan 7-0.

Vanden quarterback Ronnie Beverly (11) eludes the rush of a Hogan defender during the Vikings' 30-13 win over the Spartans Friday night. (Reporter Photo by Dan Trevan)

The above images are from an article in the Vacaville Reporter. Courtesy of the Reporter.

Beverly leads Vikes to comeback victory

The above image is from an article title courtesy of the Daily Republic. Used with permission.

"This team's got a lot of heart," said Viking head coach Ron Beverly, the quarterback's father.
"They've got a lot of togetherness and they won't quit.
"We had a lot of incentive tonight," the head coach continued.
"A lot of people were picking us to lose big.
"Plus, I live in Vallejo, and I told the team I wanted this one real bad," he added.

The above image is from an article courtesy of the Daily Republic. Used with permission.

The game was marred when Hogan quarterback Chris Day broke his leg after being tackled on a quarterback run with only two minutes left in the game.

The above image is from an article in the Vacaville Reporter. Courtesy of the Reporter.

That game against the Spartans, Big Joe came into his own. He, Jeff, and Chris solidified they could handle any opponent one on one. The Orient Express showed our opponents they were the linebacker squad to beat in our league. The rest of the team showed what hustling from whistle to whistle and a strong conditioning program would do in the second half and fourth quarter.

Our win against Hogan was like climbing Mount Everest. It was overcoming insurmountable odds and it felt great. I was feeling the pain of our hard-fought battle and it made me smile. Each ache brought a grin because I was playing football again—and we were winning. I planned on having a quiet weekend at home to reflect on our victory.

It was a revolving door in our house among our friends. Friday and Saturday nights it was a given I would see current and former Vanden alumni. Lee Stanton, Wes Cleveland, Al 'Barney Rubble' Baker, Rich 'Breeze' Quinn, and Bill Green should've been charged rent they were over so often. So that weekend was no different.

My reflection time was spent upstairs in my room. I tried to rest but I was still struggling with sleep every night. I wasn't dreaming anymore and that worried me. I knew that wasn't normal.

Everything about the Hogan game was replayed in my mind. The coin toss to the kickoffs. The huddles to the sidelines. Using oxygen, to drinking Gatorade. The sound of the cheerleaders and the fans in the stands. The movement of the chains with each yard gained. The stat girls keeping track and the coaches directing the play. The atmosphere of the replayed scenes was addictive.

The game was becoming a drug to me and I was an addict. I just couldn't get enough of the visuals flipping through my mind. I want more, give me more, tapped on my shoulder.

I loved those coin tosses. They were like parlays of warriors before a siege or an onslaught. Those kickoffs always brought butterflies while waiting for Dave Haupt to launch the pigskin, then we took off running as fast as we could to tackle the runner. Hit people hard on the way to the ball. The kickoff returns always brought apprehension. Waiting for the football to be kicked and then dropping back to cross block our designated targets. Level someone and protect the ball at all costs.

The huddles were intense yet quiet all the same. A board meeting, a military operation, and a break with my friends combined. The sidelines were chaotic and filled with desire to be on the field. Each teammate there breathed unspoken words that said, "I want to play."

A dry throat screamed for Gatorade as thirst became too much, and the oxygen tank replenished my depleted wind. Both gave that battery charge to go more.

The cheerleaders were like an adrenalin shot and a comforting hug. They gave us the ammunition to continue our forward offensive or build a strong defensive stand. They were our mortar.

The fans and their craving for those four quarters. For the girls, was it a subconscious reminder of a fairytale they were read when young, of knights in shining armor? Or how we looked in our uniforms? For the parents, did it take them back to a simpler time before they had to grow up and face the world? For the moms were they reminded of pep rallies and cheers of their own? For the dads did they still miss the game and the feel of those shoulder pads? Their gasps and claps echoed through our helmets like speakers. Play harder, they are watching, was whispered.

The sound of the yardage chains movement was like Christmas paper being ripped from a present— Exciting and what did we get this time? The stats girls looked like reporters preparing a great story. The truth will be told on those sheets, of who did what and when. All will know what happened here.

The coaches sideline movements were slow at times and rapid at others. Each animation copied the mood on the field. Things are going well or not so good. Just watch the coaches, and they will tell you how the game is going. They reflect each play.

My three-point stance prepared to pull, trap, block down, or drop back for pass protection. Only I knew what I was going to do, and the defensive players would pay big money for that knowledge. Protecting the goal line in my four-point stance was predictable. It was obvious what I was going to do. Stuff that hole so it can't be breached and stuff the ball carrier so he can't score.

My eyes were getting heavy but once again the sandman was sleeping on the job. He failed me, so I counted that one lace and eight stitches over and over until the Hogan game was no more. Let it go, we won, I repeated till I drifted off.

I perched on the couch that Saturday morning to watch TV. I found a Clint Eastwood movie about him besting a bully. Clint always won. I chuckled; so did Jim and I. Hard to believe it had almost been four years since we watched that senior in the quad tormenting some freshmen. It didn't sit well with us. We hated bullies. Our motto was, they needed to be taught a hard lesson.

Teaching him one was easy. We knew his name and the phone book gave us his number. Call after call of "I heard what you said about me, and I am coming to get you" were made. I told him I was from Fairfield High and that my name was Mike Stoner. I will meet you at Vanden. Be there tomorrow. Then a no-show was easy to explain. A teacher was there or the principal walked by. You were lucky; tomorrow punk! I told him what he wore that day because Jim and I had the bully in PE.

Weeks of torment took its toll on him. Looking around corners, checking strange cars. He was scared. He was being bullied back, and by an unknown assailant. Our torment was finally effective, because his pushy behavior towards other students ended. Was it cruel? Yeah, but it worked, and it protected freshmen. The bully learned a valuable lesson. He didn't like being bullied. Our prank was therapeutic—and a definite cure.

I enjoyed our second win for the rest of the weekend. R&R, good ole rest and relaxation. I had earned it. I knew a new opponent was lining up to take his shot. I wanted to be ready; and after climbing Mount Everest I needed time to heal.

Monday morning at school, Big Joe was limping. He had injured his leg during the game against Hogan, and had a bruise the size of a large squash on his calf. It looked really painful, and by his slow-limped walk, I could tell that it was. Baro made sure to imitate Joe's gait. You want a pacifier with that gimp? Baro taunted. It was unforgiving and funny, but Big Joe didn't like the teasing. I had to laugh.

When we watched game film later that day Coach Kiefer was more excited than I had ever seen him. He told the entire squad there was something he wanted to show us on the tape. He then played the film. It showed us on offense. The starting line: Jeff, Baro, Chris, Big Joe, and I were shown moving downfield in tandem several yards apart, almost in a straight line. After taking care of our initial defenders, we moved on to chase Hogan's linebackers and cornerbacks. The film showed us running over the linebackers, with the cornerbacks scrambling to get out of our way. Their safety wanted no part of the field being mowed.

Coach Kiefer kept replaying the sequence, claiming it was the best blocking he had ever witnessed in a football game. He was grinning ear to ear as he played it over and over, and he acted like a proud newborn's father. Someone should have handed him a cigar. He needed one.

At practice that day everyone seemed to have an extra bounce in their step, except Joe. He was still limping and walking slowly. Baro and Murdock were relentless in their teasing of him. Suck it up cupcake, it is only a bruise, they would say. The taunts continued throughout the practice, and all the trenchers joined in. That is how the crew dealt cards. Bite the bullet and keep quiet about the pain or hear about it from our close-knit group.

As the leader of the Orient Express, Glenn reminded me of the character 'Ponch' from the television series 'CHiPs.' He was Vanden's Hollywood CHP in the making. They had the same giant personality, same grin, and the black-feathered hair. If you looked closer you would swear they were from the same litter. The twin closeness the two shared made Glenn not only a standout on the field but also in the halls of our little school. His future career was probably predestined to be in law enforcement because he mirrored that character so closely.

I enjoyed my lunch breaks because all the guys on the squad were fun to be around. With the personalities of Kye, Darren, Reggie, Cliff, and Chuck and the others, you couldn't help but have a great time. They were good kids and great Vikings. We were having the time of our lives. And it really showed with Cliff. His style stood out with me. He was giving the squad something we needed: pizzazz.

The above image of Coach 'Bev' Beverly is courtesy of the Reporter.

Just because I didn't hang out with teammates like Louis, Stephen, Eugene, or Derrick didn't mean I did not like the guys. I liked them a lot. They were my friends and teammates. I trusted and respected all 32 Vikings on our small squad. We couldn't win games without them, and our time at Vanden wouldn't have been as memorable. I was no better than them—but they made me better.

That Friday we were to face John Swett at their field in Crockett, so I knew we would have to cross at the 50-yard line again to avoid thrown bottles and other debris. It had been two years since Coach Moore launched the helmet with a swift kick. I smiled remembering that moment. That was football. It wasn't a princess sport. It was punishing and bloody, and I savored its violence.

We knew John Swett was probably the weakest team in our league but we also didn't want to overlook them. They were always hitters. The coaches stressed any team could be beaten at any time, so don't let our guard down. John Swett could beat us, they kept saying.

We practiced hard all week with the conditioning ramped up. Any points scored against us by our opponents were added on top of the twenty-five 40-yard dashes, plus 10 gassers and progressives we had to run. Since Hogan scored 13 points against us we ran 38 40-yard dashes, along with our gassers and progressives at the end of Monday's practice. Big Joe escaped the conditioning program that week due to his bruised leg.

Friday came fast, and we followed our weekly routine. I went to church with the team and coaches to hear Maurice's dad speak. Afterwards we went to school wearing our game jerseys.

After school we met at the Shubin Sports Building. Since the JV game began at 5:45 pm, and John Swett was about a 45-minute drive, we were in a hurry to leave. We placed our shoulder pads, helmets, and bags in the storage compartments underneath the bus. Even though it was John Swett and our last trip there involved the school bus windows being shot out by a pellet gun, Coach Bev was assured by their school administrators that they had taken the necessary security steps to insure our safety when we arrived and left.

It was fun traveling on the bus with the team, coaches, cheerleaders, and stat girls for our first road trip. The mood was animated, and laughter could be heard throughout. Coach Kiefer sat in back with the trenchers. He wanted to go over blocking strategies and the game plan we would utilize, plus he felt immense loyalty to us. He was a lineman still in spirit. The trenches never left him. Riding with us in the back of the bus was something Coach Kiefer would do for the rest of the season. He was part of our group and led it.

Our arrival at John Swett was uneventful even though we still crossed at the 50-yard line to avoid any thrown bottles.

Vanden had faced John Swett in 11 previous outings, with us winning 9, losing 1, and tying another. Prior to the start of our game that evening, Ronnie had thrown 16 touchdowns in his last 12 games as our quarterback. It was a new Vanden record, beating the 15-TD mark that had been set during the 1964–1966 seasons by Larry Gaddis. The first touchdown Coach Bev had caught for the football program in 1964 was thrown by Gaddis.

Vanden High School quarterback Ronnie Beverly, (11), directs the Viking offense tonight in their Superior California Athletic League opener against John Swett.

"I have been blessed with a good team this season and barring any injuries, we could be tough."

And Beverly indicated that being a Vanden offensive lineman is no easy task.

"We ask a lot of our linemen," Beverly said. "Because of the I, we ask linemen to sustain their blocks longer on running plays. And because we like to throw, they have to protect the quarterback."

The photo above is from an article before the John Swett game. The photo shows Ronnie and me blocking. Courtesy of the Daily Republic. Used with permission. The quotes are from an article in the Vacaville Reporter. Courtesy of the Reporter.

The Vanden JV team defeated John Swett 14-0. Their win put them at 3-0. After their contest Coach Hatcher headed to the announcer box to spot for our squad. He would call down to coaches Bev and Noos what he was seeing on the field, and any adjustments he recommended. Hatcher began doing that at the start of the season and would continue it for the rest of the games we played.

Our battle against John Swett was one-sided. We beat them 29-0. The score didn't reflect the hitting power of the Indians. It was a bare-knuckle fight at times. When we were in a pile-up or had a John Swett player buried in the turf, we knuckled him. We weren't dirty players (the trenchers) but we weren't by-the-book players either. When we felt we needed to retaliate we threw one or two quick punches when the refs weren't looking. It was a brutal sport and we were brutal players. Winning wasn't always easy. Did we cheat? No. We would've never cheated the game we loved. We respected it. We knew it was violent, so we had to engage in violence to prevail. It's just the way it was. The Indians weren't the first we had to knuckle and wouldn't be the last.

From the start of the third quarter on, Coach Bev made sure all the players on the team saw plenty of action. There was no need in running up the score with his starting squad. It wasn't Coach Bev's style. During the John Swett game Bryan rushed for 134 yards on 11 carries. Ronnie threw for 127 yards and two touchdowns, going 11 for 16. He broke another Vanden record, becoming the all-time passer. Ronnie surpassed the career total of 1452 yards set during the 1968–69 seasons.

Bryan, Maurice, Big E, and DeWayne Quinn all scored touchdowns. Cliff and Sherman Pruitt accounted for a safety for two more points.

On defense we held the John Swett Indians to minus 8 yards total. Yes that's correct, a minus 8. They had passed for 39 yards through the air but we held them to minus 47 yards on 25 carries on the ground. On 21 different plays we held their running backs and receivers to minus or no yards gained during our contest. Danny had a big game stopping the run.

Early in the third quarter, Ronnie was injured on an option play when he was tackled hard. He left the game with possible bruised ribs heading to the hospital for X-rays. Dave Haupt stepped up to take the helm for the rest of the game and performed well. Watching him direct the offense gave me confidence he could lead us to victories like Ronnie. Dave was a better quarterback than most of the ones we faced. The final 29-0 score could have been even higher too, but a dropped catch in the end zone and a missed 49-yard field goal kept it down.

Against John Swett, Murdock played the entire fourth quarter as nose guard, and was in the backfield so often he could've been mistaken for living there.

Coach Kiefer was proud as he rode home with us in back of the bus. We were now 3-0. Not a bad start to a long season ahead.

What was Coach Bev thinking? I wondered. He was off to his best season start in his third year as skipper. I knew one thing for sure, he wouldn't let it go to his head or let up on us. He was going to work us even harder. He wanted champions. I always watched him closely, because I knew he would make us better players. In his eyes I could see the forecast ahead—conditioning, pain, and victories.

One of the many things that drew me to the game was the play on the gridiron. Having a front-row seat to the action on the field was something I would've paid to watch. To see Bryan make a long run look easy; Ronnie throw a perfect pass or easily juke a linebacker in open-field; or one of my teammates make a crushing block or a devastating hit close-up was indescribable.

I was only feet away as my teammates would do things most people couldn't do. It was awe-inspiring at times. It was also humbling to share the same grass with them. I knew I had been blessed to have a second chance to play. I also knew I was playing with guys that honored football with their efforts. I was sharing the field with legends, and I knew it.

Vanden 3-0 after 29-0 victory over John Swett

The above article headline is from the Vacaville Reporter. Courtesy of the Reporter.

> Vanden defenders Pruitt and Cliff Roberts then burst through the John Swett line and tackled Shawn Norris for a safety with 6:22 left in the third period.

The above paragraph is from an article in the Daily Republic. Courtesy of the Daily Republic. Used with permission.

> The drive was highlighted a 24-yard pass from punter David Smith to Steve Crittenden on fourth and 14 at the Vanden 37.
>
> "Smith did quite a job avoiding the rush on that play," commented head coach Beverly. "He saw their two lineman were close enough to block his kick, so he just sidestepped the rush and let Steve know he was going to throw it."

The above paragraph is from an article in the Daily Republic. Courtesy of the Daily Republic. Used with permission.

That Monday at practice the three members of the Orient Express—Glenn, Danny, and Sherman—were all given 'HITMAN' and 'ORIENT EXPRESS' tee shirts from Coach Noos. He said they had earned them for their hard hits and outstanding play in the first three games.

Since we shut out John Swett, we avoided additional 40-yard dashes during conditioning that afternoon.

Our upcoming game that Friday was going to be against Dixon at their field, where I was injured one year earlier. That injury and the memories of it still stuck with me. I don't know if I wanted retribution, reckoning, or just another win. I wanted the Rams to recognize me, though, because I hadn't forgotten about them and that game.

Ronnie was back but questionable to play. The

rest of the team was healthy and ready for the challenge against the Rams.

Mark and I met at the same bus stop every morning for the long ride to Vanden. It was just around the corner from my house. One cold morning the wind was blowing wildly as we waited. Thankfully we weren't wearing roller skates or we would've ended up on the east coast and in the Atlantic Ocean, because the wind was so strong. Mark's girlfriend at the time was much shorter than he was, and Baro had long legs. As the winds pushed us around she wrapped her hands around one of his thighs, holding on tightly. I noticed her long fingernails clutching his jeans. I made the comment that her fingers looked like rat claws clinging onto his leg, so as not to be torn away by the gusts.

Mark laughed loudly and so did I. She didn't find it funny, and slapped Mark hard across the face. He looked at me and laughed again, causing me to laugh once more. That morning riding the bus to school, Mark and I were both in the doghouse; but by the grinning on his face I don't think it bothered him much.

Were football players dumb jocks? Not the guys I played alongside. Were we superficial? I wasn't. I noticed all the small things that gave the game color: The refs studying closely before each play; how the chalk lines on the gridiron looked like a well-defined map that could lead to treasure; the upward tilt of Coach Bev's cap while he contemplated his next chess move; the way rain or mist were highlighted by the stadium lights; the changing facial expressions of those watching us; how the varying noises sounded like an orchestra; the stare from a young kid who wanted to be like us; yes—I saw them all.

Friday morning we learned Ronnie would be playing. Though I had great confidence in Dave Haupt to lead us, I felt better knowing we had two quarterbacks in our stable versus one.

On the bus to face Dixon it was quiet. We remembered the last time we were there. We lost 25-6 and I was seriously injured. Our last visit to their field wasn't a good memory. We knew they weren't happy after our Quadraplay. I had punched one of their players and they had lost. We knew the game would be tough. We had survived three-a-day practices during Hell Week. We also had Bryan. The Rams couldn't stop us.

The JV game wasn't close, as they beat their Ram opponents 36-0. They were looking strong at 4-0.

Coach Hatcher took his place to spot for our team. We took the gridiron. Late in the second quarter, we received a Dixon punt, placing the ball at our 5-yard line. On a designated play where he followed me on a trap, Ronnie ran 90 yards before being tackled. He was within 5 yards of Dixon's goal line. On the next play he kept the ball and scored a touchdown. We were first on the scoreboard. Ronnie's pass for a two-point conversion failed. We were up 6-0.

Dixon retaliated and drove 63 yards, scoring their own TD with little over a minute left in the first half. Their extra point was good. They took the lead 7-6.

In a matter of seconds we battled back after receiving the kickoff, when Ronnie threw a 45-yard pass to Eric. Bryan then ran the ball in from an option pitch to put us back in the lead at 12-7. We again went for a two-point conversion but it failed. Ronnie was hit hard on the pass attempt and went down. He was injured.

Coach Bev and medical staff rushed onto the field. Ronnie was taken off on a gurney and away by ambulance with a concussion. With the hit, Ronnie and I now had something in common. We were both injured with a concussion by Dixon players at their field—taken away on a gurney by ambulance—one year apart. Fortunately, Ronnie never lost consciousness.

With Ronnie out, Dave Haupt stepped in and took the reins for the offense for a second week in a row. Vanden's JV quarterback Alan Casner was pulled from the stands and told to dress in case Dave was injured. We knew we had to protect Dave at all costs.

After the halftime break, we kicked off to the Rams and held them on their series, forcing them to punt. From the 20-yard line we drove 80 yards in just six plays to score a touchdown and further our lead to 19-7.

The Rams took little time to strike back. From their first play from scrimmage they called a halfback option pass and it worked. They caught our defensive backfield, which Ronnie normally anchored, off guard for a quick score. That narrowed the game to less than one TD.

We fought off Dixon for the rest of the game with neither of us scoring again. We went on to win 19-14 in a close battle. Dave stepped up when we needed him and directed us to a victory. He proved his strength as a Vanden quarterback. We were lucky to have him.

During the Dixon game Bryan rushed 23 times for 160 yards to lead the ground offensive. Ronnie rushed for 105 yards on 5 carries.

Vanden hangs on, tops Dixon 19-14

The younger Beverly scored the game's first touchdown with 4:34 left in the first half on a five-yard quarterback keeper. On the play preceding the touchdown, Beverly had raced 90 yards from the Vanden 5 to the Dixon 5 on another quarterback keeper.

"That's a designed play," explained the head coach. "We trap the tackle and Ronnie cuts right off the guard's block. After that, it's a foot race to the end zone."

The above headline and excerpt are from an article courtesy of the Daily Republic. Used with permission.

After scoring on a 5-yard run late in the second quarter, giving Vanden, now 4-0, a 12-7 lead, Beverly suffered a concussion when he was hit on an attempted pass play for the 2-point conversion. Beverly's pass fell incomplete and Vanden led at the intermission 12-7.

The Vikings, led by reserve quarterback David Haupt, came out fired up in the second half, and after holding Dixon on four straight downs, the Vikings marched 80 yards on six plays for the score and a 19-7 lead.

The above paragraphs are from an article courtesy of the Reporter.

> "The kids really got up at halftime," said head coach Ron Beverly, the quarterback's father. "They pulled together and decided they wanted to win it for Ronnie. There was a lot of character shown out there tonight."

Above image is of a paragraph from an article courtesy of the Daily Republic. Used with permission.

    Coach Bev handled Ronnie's injury during the game like a true football skipper. He stayed with the team while Ronnie was rushed off to the hospital. He didn't abandon us even though the dad in him was worried for his son. He didn't know what Ronnie was facing or whether his football career was over as the ambulance drove away. He had a responsibility to his son, but also—a job to do. He did the job like a champion coach. We had eight more victories to go to hand him that title.

    It was obvious the Dixon fans were not happy with our win. It was getting rowdy as we hurried to the bus to get out of town before our vegetable soup tangled with cowboys. The coaches wasted no time in getting our bus driver George to leave a dust trail as we sped away.

    There was only one problem. We left Tuck our manager behind, and no one knew. He was retrieving footballs and equipment as we drove away. With arms full he saw the bus leave. He was alone and on his own with an angry crowd. They knew he was a Viking and he was their target. The refs and line crew came to his rescue, hiding him in the custodial closet.

Our arrival at Vanden was typical. We off-loaded, put gear away and went home. Tuck's mom stood outside the bus asking Bev where her son was and Bev kept calling Tuck to hurry, his mother was waiting. When Bev finally realized Tuck wasn't there, full panic ensued. No one knew why Tuck was missing. Prayers said, a hurried call to Dixon, and a rush there retrieved him safely. Tuck learned his lesson. Our remaining trips that season, he was the first person on the bus. He wasn't going to be left behind again.

Saturday morning, I awoke with soreness all over from the Dixon game. I appreciated that feeling. From my ankles to my neck I was reminded of the night before. I replayed the collisions and tackling in my mind and how my teammates pulled together when Ronnie went down. I was proud to be a Viking and thankful I made it through another game without an injury.

After going to the hospital for medical evaluation, Ronnie was listed as doubtful to play that coming week. He had suffered a concussion but thankfully not as severe as mine.

Monday came quickly. I saw Ronnie at school, and he looked good. He was sore and wasn't sure if the doctors or his dad would clear him to play for our upcoming game.

Coach Kiefer told Baro, Big Joe, Jeff, Chris, and me that he was happy with our blocking against Dixon. As trenchers we were becoming closer as a group. We all liked each other, and disagreements were few on the field and off.

At practice we had to prepare ourselves to face

Justin of Napa. They were the defending Sac-Joaquin Section Champions, and had won 14 of their last 16 games. They were a very good squad, and we had to play them at their field. Not on Friday evening—on Saturday afternoon. It was going to be our only Saturday day game during the season.

If Ronnie could not play I knew we would be okay, because we still had a very potent offensive attack with Maurice and Bryan. Both were devastating runners who could easily outrun or overpower defenders. Plus, we had Dave. He hadn't failed us and wouldn't. I knew that. Dave Haupt had proven his worth as our quarterback. He could run our offensive plan, and he had a stable of good receivers in Big E, Darren, Reggie, Sherman, Felix, Kye, and DeWayne. They all had good hands and good speed.

Like the trenchers coming together and working as one group, the Orient Express was the best combined linebacker unit I had played with in my five seasons of football. Maybe it was their Noos-appointed moniker that solidified them—along with their shared Asian heritage—that made them dangerous. They fed off each other on the field and played better together as a group.

In the trenches, that was becoming the case with us. On either side of the ball we played better together as a combined unit. Each lineman made the others better. The controlled chaos, intensity, and our perseverance was all ramped up because of each other. None of us in the trenches wanted to let our teammates down, so when the ball was hiked it became a feeding frenzy—with our opponents as the food.

Joe's swagger became a little more evident at

school. He was enjoying the spotlight of being on an undefeated football team. His stature, his hair, and his personality were all big. On the campus he stood out. So did Kye, Maurice, and John, too. They all had huge personalities. I knew anytime I was with Kye I would have fun.

From the teachers to the administration and students, we were being elevated almost like movie stars. When you walked from class to class, sat in a classroom, or ate lunch, eyes followed you.

Jeff, Glenn, Chris, Baro, Bryan, David, Reggie, and me didn't relish the limelight. It wasn't our style. Let your play speak for you, I told myself many times. Don't pat yourself on the back. Make big plays; then go back to the huddle without celebrating.

Three of my teammates were recognized by the student body for their personalities and interaction at school. Cliff was picked friendliest, Bryan as most athletic, and John as biggest flirt. None surprised me.

Baro, Jeff, Dave Haupt, and I shared Physics and Calculus together. I had to rely on all three for assistance because they had a better grasp of the topics than me. We were often given assignments in Physics that would test our imaginations and engineering skills.

Our Physics teacher, Mr. Stasi, asked us to build a bridge solely out of straws and glue that could withstand weight and force. Everyone completed the assignment, but Mark's stood out. You could stand on his bridge and it didn't give an inch. The whole class gave it a go, along with Mr. Stasi. It was impressive.

For another assignment, we had to build a compartment that would hold an egg we could drop off the top of the football bleachers to the ground without breaking it. Jeff, Dave, and Mark did well with their construction for protecting the egg. Mine broke when it hit the ground. With the heat on the pavement cooking it, I toyed with eating it for lunch.

When Mr. Stasi was punched by a student and knocked unconscious Baro and I took it personally. We respected Mr. Stasi so we went looking for the kid. We never found him, and he never returned to Vanden. He must've been expelled and probably arrested. Lucky for the kid—if we would've found him we would've sought our retribution for his cowardly attack.

Chris as the only junior on our starting line was proving he was a great addition. He was the best natural tackle I had played with or against in my five seasons of football. He was one of the few two-way starters on the team that included Baro, Jeff, Ronnie, and me.

I liked our new teammate Chuck. He became close with David and Murdock. Most weekends David and Chuck were always together, so Chuck had become part of our secretive stuntmen group that tested speed and daring on Vanden Road. Chuck could fill in well at either tackle spot during a game and not miss a beat. I had to snicker when I saw David and Chuck together, because one was short and one was very tall.

'Mr. Cool' was cool. No doubt about it. The name fit his personality. He was a collie mix the size of a German Shepherd. When I got him as a puppy I could tell he was different so picking his name was easy. Sean taught him to climb our six foot wooden fence, and he did with feline grace. His balance and agility were cat-like.

After Cyclone's passing he became Shadow's partner and a member of our family. I would come home to see him perched on top of our fence. We never had any problems with him escaping the backyard and running off. He was a good dog and made our lives better.

Friday we were told Ronnie had been given medical clearance to play with us on Saturday against Justin. That extra day before the game would also give him more recovery time. We didn't know if he would start.

Justin was in Napa, so about a thirty-minute trip on the bus to battle our league opponent. That morning Coach Kiefer took his spot with us in back while Coach Bev and Noos sat up front. Last-minute strategy was forged. Confuse them with the movie-character names, because they are a good squad. Only two losses in their last 16 games, so play hard-nosed football. Coach Kiefer was our biggest cheerleader and pep squad, and he also reminded us that Justin had prevailed over us the last time we faced them on the gridiron, 34-14.

> Justin, the defending league and Sac-Joaquin Section Class A champion, has won three in a row since a season-opening 20-12 loss to Fairfield. The Braves have won 14 of their last 16 games coming into today's action, including a 34-14 decision over Vanden last season.

Above image of a paragraph is from an article courtesy of the Daily Republic. Used with permission.

It was already hot out when we arrived in Napa. As we dressed in the locker room most of the players were covered in sweat. Thankfully, Coach Bev cleared us to play in our practice jerseys, which were mesh, but most of the numbers didn't match our game jerseys. I was wearing 75 instead of my game number 55.

After dressing, the trench crew and I sat in the shade in an alcove outside the locker room door. We needed our Zen time alone to find ourselves. As we sat there fully padded, and sweating, I looked around at my friends. They were good football players. Though not big, averaging 186 pounds per player, they were the best offensive line around as a combined unit, and it made me proud to lead them.

Coach Bev called us inside for last-minute game preparation and prayer. "If we don't play our game, they will bury us," Bev warned. "They are one of the best teams you will see all year," he reminded us. "Fight hard to the last whistle and play like champions!" he barked. We then lined up and smacked our pads as we walked to the gridiron to battle the Justin Braves. Chris joined us in leading the team.

Taking the field for warm-ups during the day time was similar to practice. I had to keep reminding myself it was a league game. Justin had a nice field, and Bryan commented he thought he could cut well on it. I hoped he was right, because when he had the ball and room to run he couldn't be stopped.

As we rolled on our necks stretching, the sky looked so blue. It was the same visual I became familiar with many times at Vanden. It was comforting to see.

The above photo shows the team stretching at Justin prior to the start of the game. Photo from a yearbook courtesy of Travis Unified School District and Vanden High School. The below photo shows Dave Haupt practicing PAT's and field goals before the game as Glenn held the ball for him. Photo courtesy of Dave Haupt.

After the coin toss we lined up for the kickoff. Those butterflies again tried to escape my throat. We knew the drill. As Dave Haupt ran forward to kick, we would take off running as fast as we could and run over anyone who got in our way. Pursue the ball.

We didn't have to pursue far, as the ball was fumbled by Justin. Sherman Pruitt jumped on the loose pigskin and recovered it at the 15-yard line. Two plays later, Bryan ran in for a quick touchdown. Our PAT attempt missed, so we led on the scoreboard 6-0, 77 seconds into the game.

I was knocked down—which was embarrassing. It was humbling and maddening, and there would be a swift response. The first play on offense I lined up in my three-point stance, and thought I was ready. The Justin player across from me was larger but I wasn't intimidated. When the ball was snapped he immediately caught me under the chin with a forearm rip and knocked me on my back. That had never happened in my years of football. Like 'Murphy's Law' it had to occur during the first play, during daytime, while we faced our sidelines. There was no hiding the fact that I just had my ass handed to me, and everyone saw it. I had grass stains on my back for the first time. "Damn!" I cursed. I was disappointed in myself.

In the huddle I heard and felt the wrath of the trench crew. It was merciless. I became Big Joe with that large bruise on his leg. Instead it was my pride that had been bruised, and I knew it hurt worse than Joe's leg. Snickering, laughing, and taunting came from Baro, Big Joe, Jeff, and Chris. There was no way I could handle a second round from them, so I was ready to get even.

On the next play, as I pointed at the Justin player yelling a movie-character name, I added that it wouldn't happen again. He knew I was pissed. I lined up in my stance and stared him directly in the eyes. I knew the outcome before it happened. When Jeff hiked the ball I returned the favor, hitting him hard with a forearm. He went backwards landing on his back, and I came down on top of him. Facemask to facemask, I snapped, "You'd better get used to the view!" I made sure to keep that promise, too. Two thirds of the remaining game I fulfilled it.

In the second quarter from their 13-yard line, Justin did a reverse handoff and took it the full length of the field, going 87 yards for a score. With their successful kick they were ahead 7-6. After moving the ball back and forth by both our teams, the Braves got on the scoreboard again from a 32-yard field goal. They extended their lead over us 10-6.

A few minutes later Ronnie found Bryan open across the center of the field behind their linebackers, and threw a 15-yard pass to him. Bryan added 45 more yards, taking it in for a touchdown. Ronnie's two-point conversion gave us a 14-10 lead going into halftime.

Adjustments were made during our break. Noos, Kiefer, and Bev instructed us what they wanted us to do in the remaining two quarters. We knew we were a second-half team. It was just our style; and I'm not sure why we were either. Maybe we liked to play with our backs against the wall because it made us reach deeper inside, or we liked keeping the coaches and our fans in suspense. For whatever reason, we knew the remaining two quarters of a game we owned. We were better conditioned and better prepared to play those 24 minutes.

We put Justin away in the second half, scoring 18 more points on touchdown runs by Maurice (17 yards) and Ronnie (2 yards), and a 25-yard field goal by Dave Haupt. Louis Adams pulled in an interception.

When the final buzzer sounded we won 32-10 against the defending Sac-Joaquin Section champions, handing them only their third loss in 17 games. We scored 26 unanswered points against the Braves.

Our win against Justin put us at 5-0. Bryan rushed for 202 yards and two touchdowns, with Ronnie throwing for 6 of 10 completions and 152 yards. Maurice proved he could block for Bryan and run himself, by adding 40 yards on the ground.

Vanden atop SCAL standings

Batchan shines; Vikes rip Braves

The above image is from an article title Courtesy of the Reporter.

The above photo taken during the Justin game shows Bryan running the ball. Image courtesy of the Reporter.

The above photo shows Maurice on the move against the Justin Braves. Image courtesy of the Reporter.

The above photo shows Bryan preparing to turn the corner against Justin. He is seen right with Maurice, our fullback, about to level the Justin player. Mark 'Baro' Baranowski is shown burying another Justin player in the turf. Photo courtesy of Travis Unified School District and Vanden High School.

"If you give him daylight, watch out," Beverly warned about Batchan. "He's very explosive.

"Switching to the I-formation helps our attack. That's why we disbanded the wishbone," Beverly added. "In the wishbone, we couldn't get the ball to Bryan as much."

"We came together as a team today," Batchan said. "We were pumped up. We made the big plays when they counted."

The above photo and article images are from an article courtesy of the Daily Republic. Used with permission.

The above photo shows 'Baro' stepping over his downed opponent and Dave Haupt going for a sack against the Justin Braves. From an article courtesy of the Daily Republic. Used with permission.

That evening we wanted to celebrate, so Jeff, Chris, Baro, Big Joe, and I made our first trip to the Bay Area together to try Blondie's Pizza in Berkeley, and then to San Francisco. It was the first of a few adventures to the Bay Area we would make that season as friends.

After enjoying pizza and gawking at the strange characters we encountered, we went to the Berkley campus. We heard loud music coming from a quad, and thinking it was a party we walked closer. A large crowd of intoxicated male students (about 25) saw us coming and started cursing us. Without provocation they charged in our direction. We took off running, jumping over fences to avoid a confrontation—because we were sorely outnumbered. We didn't know why they chased us, and we felt it was best not to stop and ask them. It brought back vivid flashbacks of Cathy's dad and the base police pursuing me as a 13-year-old.

Vanden was welcoming. It offered a clean homey friendly environment, and it was an extension of the family for many students. It embraced us, and the teachers really cared about our lives. We didn't have gangs or lots of fights, and if there were drugs they were few. The school was intimate, and basically a pleasant place to be. We were very fortunate to be part of the Travis Unified School District. In Northern California it was one of the premier schools. That was evident to anyone who saw the daily interaction on our campus or sat in a classroom.

That week was Homecoming, and we would be facing Benicia at Vanden. The school had planned a full calendar of fun events for the students. Coach Bev allowed us to wear our football jerseys to school every day during the festivities.

We enjoyed tug of war between the seniors and juniors, watermelon-eating contests, races drinking chocolate milk through baby bottles, and 'Buy a Senior' day. That day consisted of renting a senior and having that person at your service all during school hours. Many of my teammates were dressed up as girls by the female students who rented them. I got lucky. The girl who rented me asked me to dress as the Tom Cruise character from the movie 'Risky Business.' I was happy to oblige—I didn't have to wear a dress, makeup, and pantyhose—like Murdock, Jeff, David, and David Smith.

I played the Tom Cruise character to the hilt, and in our little school, stole his thunder for one day. I enjoyed portraying him too. I kind of felt during the 1983 movie

'All the Right Moves' that his character paralleled me as a football player with his gridiron attitude and love of the game. It was only befitting to return the favor. I also found it ironic that the movie came out the year I was injured.

Above photo shows me as the Tom Cruise character from the movie 'Risky Business.' Photo courtesy of Travis Unified School District and Vanden High School.

The school was to vote on the Homecoming King and Queen for the halftime event during the varsity game against Benicia. We were all called into the auditorium and read the results of the votes cast by the students. I was chosen King, and Lesly Barnard—my good friend I stood up escorting as the Homecoming freshman attendant three years earlier—was picked as Queen.

It was an embarrassing moment for me. What should've been an exciting time made me feel awkward. I never liked the limelight and now I was thrust into it. As I walked down the stands to the center of the auditorium to be congratulated I became even more uncomfortable. I was wearing shorts and my football jersey hid them. I thought to myself I looked naked under my 55 number. I felt like that streaker in Village East, yet unlike that moment of only one car seeing me run naked, I was walking in front of the entire school—and it appeared I wasn't wearing pants. I wasn't the nervous type but as I stood there in front of my classmates I was sweating—and not from the heat. I also didn't feel I was the right choice to be Homecoming King. There were other guys I thought would be chosen. I guess the students felt differently. Thankfully, Baro and Murdock didn't shout something to make me feel worse. I dodged a bullet from them.

There was a chance it could happen again. I knew I might stand her up once more and she may not forgive me this time. Twice I had the opportunity to escort Lesly during Homecoming, and there was a possibility I would go 0 for 2 in my duties. Coach Bev told me if the Benicia game was close at halftime he would need me in the locker room to listen to any changes and strategize. I was a captain, so my first responsibility was to the team. Losing wasn't an option, so I understood what he was telling me. Football was still my first love, so Lesly would have to understand if I couldn't be there. At least I hoped she would. What really were the odds I would stand her up again? A 50-50 chance.

Wearing our jerseys to school that Friday was exciting. The school had its annual Homecoming Parade planned for the day. It was the fourth year we would drive around the streets of TAFB so that the personnel and their families could watch and enjoy the festivities. Besides graduation, Homecoming day was the biggest celebration for Vanden students throughout the year.

The band led the procession and thousands came out to cheer and wave. It was amazing, surreal, and a success. It put us in the right perspective to battle the Panthers that evening.

Benicia always put up a good fight, so our contests were never boring. I had a gut feeling our game that night would be no different. I just hoped we would be comfortably ahead at halftime so I didn't have to face Lesly again for being absent. Lesly and I were close friends since 4th grade, and she was important to me. I really needed to escort her. She was relying on me to not let her down.

The above football parade photo courtesy of Vanden High School and Travis Unified School District is from a yearbook. It shows (left to right) Danny Miller, David Smith, Purnell Jones, DeWayne Quinn, Reginald Stover, Eric 'Big E' Barnes, Glenn (Kelly) Barretto, and Louis Adams, on one of the flatbed trucks during the annual Homecoming event.

The Vanden JV team continued winning under the direction of Coaches Hatcher and Ordez. They easily beat their Benicia opponents 24-0.

When we took the field to face the Panthers, there was excitement in the crowd, with it being Homecoming. Our games were typically packed with our fans, but on this evening the stands were overflowing. It was standing room only.

We needed to play well because Benicia had a tough program. Their mascot name was a good fit for their style of play. The Panthers were hitters and didn't quit. They wouldn't be easy to beat. We needed another win—and to stay injury-free.

The above photo shows Mark 'Baro' Baranowski before the Benicia game Homecoming Night. Mark played right guard and defensive tackle. He was a two-way starter. He patented his 'Tilt and Glare' look. It was unique and something to see. Photo provided by Baro.

We kicked off to the Panthers, and during his pursuit of the ball Baro collided helmets with a Benicia player, resulting in Mark's eyebrow splitting wide open. Blood poured down the side of his face.

I followed him to the sideline and he approached Coach Kiefer. Kiefer told him to get back on the field because we needed him. That didn't sit well with Baro. He could be known to question authority, and he only listened to our three coaches and me. Ronnie was lucky if he could get Baro to follow his direction. Mark was one of our two wild cards, with Murdock being the other.

Baro took off his helmet revealing his injury. Knowing both Coach Kiefer and him, and their close relationship, I knew the interaction was going to be epic. Instead of heading to the defensive huddle I had to watch from the field just a few yards away. I didn't want to miss this. There are few times a player gets to see a funny moment during a game—this would be one.

Kiefer barked at Mark to get back on the field, and Baro argued back, "What the hell, do I look like Superman?" I burst out laughing. They sounded like an old married couple. Kiefer looked at me with a scowl. Before I could face Kiefer's ire for thinking it was funny, I rushed to the huddle. I was glad I stopped to watch their quarrel. It was epic alright. Coach Kiefer was not amused by Mark's response, and benched him for four plays while medical staff looked at him. Murdock was called to replace me as nose guard, so I could fill Baro's defensive tackle spot.

Benicia came to play. We battled back and forth the first quarter, neither of us scoring. Late in the second quarter with a little over two minutes left before halftime, we finally got on the scoreboard by extraordinary circumstances. We had driven 47 yards to within one yard of Benicia's goal line. Ronnie attempted a quarterback sneak up the center and fumbled. Maurice picked it up, and with a Panther around his ankles trying to bring him down, he tossed the ball back to Bryan who ran around the left side of the field, into the end zone. Our 'Triple Threat Backfield' used a three-pronged effort and scored. Our two-point conversion came up short.

We were ahead 6-0 when halftime was called. I remembered what Coach Bev had said to me. Even though I was Homecoming King and supposed to escort Lesly as the Queen I jogged straight to the locker room. I knew she had a backup plan but I wasn't sure what it was. I figured she would be disappointed. I also knew she would never give me a third chance. Too bad the game was close, I thought. I really wanted to escort Lesly and ride around the track and football field in that convertible.

Adjustments were made for our offense and defense during our break. The team physician and Tuck attended to Mark using butterfly bandages to keep his laceration closed. We needed him on the field and the "Suck it up, cupcake" taunts made him want to play.

Halfway through the third quarter Benicia scored a TD of their own, when on 4th down and five yards to go at our 25, they completed a pass on blown coverage. Their extra point missed its mark and the score was 6-6.

In the fourth quarter we took the lead for good when we drove 86 yards and Bryan ran in for a touchdown from 30 yards out. Our two-point conversion was successful, and we went on to win 14-6. Bryan rushed for

151 yards and Maurice added 68 yards of his own against the Panthers.

After the game we showered in the locker room and went to the school dance. Later that night we celebrated our victory and 6-0 record playing stuntmen on Vanden Road. We felt like superheroes.

Batchan sparks 14-6 Vanden win

The 1-yard TD, which came with 2:37 left in the first half, came at the end of a 47-yard drive on a somewhat bizarre play. On third-and-goal inside the Benicia 1, quarterback Ronnie Beverly tried to sneak the ball through the middle of the Benicia line into the end zone. He fumbled the ball, fullback Maurice Gwinn picked it up, and with a tackler hanging on his ankles, pitched the ball back to Batchan, who sprinted around left end into the end zone.

"That was smart thinking on Maurice's part," said head coach Beverly. "He made a real heads-up play there."

The above two images are from an article courtesy of the Daily Republic. Used with permission.

The above photo shows Jeff and Ronnie during the Benicia Homecoming game. They worked well together. We couldn't have had a better combo. Courtesy of the Daily Republic. Used with permission.

> Brian Batchan, recognized as one of the state's leading rushers, scored both the Vikings' touchdowns on runs of 1 and 30 yards.
>
> Batchan upped his season rushing stats to 882 yards after piling up 151 against the Panthers.

The above image is from an article courtesy of the Reporter.

The above photo shows Bryan running the ball during the Benicia game. The below photo shows me blocking for Maurice at practice, during Homecoming week. Both images courtesy of the Reporter.

We were three games away from breaking a Vanden record set in 1975 by the first and only Sac-Joaquin Section Championship football team. They finished their regular season at 8-1. No football team from our high school had ever finished the regular season undefeated. We wanted to be the first. We had three opponents left to grab that record.

Coach Noos could not be prouder of the defense and the Orient Express. The team doing well and the weight loss gave him a renewed look. The way he carried himself he gave off the impression his glory days on the gridiron weren't behind him. He looked and acted as though he himself were ready to join his famed linebacker unit on the field and take names. During games he walked back and forth on the sidelines, and during practices he was like a general directing his troops. Our 1984 season looked good on him.

Coach Kiefer was happy. He was happy he came out of retirement, and he was happy with the conviction and determination of his linemen. He knew what it meant to battle in the trenches and the brutality there. His loyalty to us at school, at practices, in games and on the bus trips to face foes was paramount. Even though he was a big man, he seemed to stand a little taller around our close-knit group. It was evident he took pride in coaching, and he favored his trenchers. We knew he cared for us, and we felt the same for him.

Coach Bev, in his third year of directing the varsity squad at Vanden, had seen the worst season of a head coach in 1982, and now was looking at the best season just off in the horizon. His Fu Manchu mustache could not hide his grin because the team was performing so well. Yes, he knew we had setbacks, but he also knew we wouldn't quit on him. He was our skipper, and we wanted to play the best we could because he was watching. On the sidelines in games he was calm, and anyone who saw him there directing us knew he was Mr. Football. We were fortunate he was our head coach.

Big Joe's 18th birthday that year was something to see. His mom invited the starting offensive trenchers to celebrate with him. When Jeff, Chris, Baro, and I arrived at Joe's house, we laughed when we saw what she put out for us to eat.

They had cleared out their front room, and she had two tables covered thick with food. There were two very large thick-crust party-size meat pizzas—each looked three feet in diameter—one half-dozen bowls full of chips, numerous dips, salads, cases of sodas; and Joe's birthday cake was three-tier and the size for a wedding celebration. It was an unbelievable sight.

I looked at the cake in awe. It was made entirely out of Hostess products—Twinkies, Ding Dongs, Cup Cakes, Ho Ho's, Sno Balls, and Fruit Pies—layered in three tiers. There must've been 100 or more Hostess goodies for us to enjoy.

Joe's mom knew how to throw a party but overestimated what we could consume. We did our best, but only put a dent in the food. I was thankful Joe had three siblings and his parents to handle the leftovers.

That Friday we were going to travel to take on our next opponent: St. Patrick's of Vallejo. They were new to our SCAL league.

Monday's practice was like the others throughout the season. We worked hard to make it perfect. We heard many times from Coach Bev that perfect practices would make champions. We would soon find out if that were true. Conditioning included the extra dashes for the 6 points Benicia scored against us.

Though we would get out of practice about 5:30 at night, Big Joe, Jeff, Baro, and I still went to the gym a few times a week on TAFB. We didn't want to lose the strength we had gained from the many hours lifting there.

Teachers no longer waited to approach me on Fridays to talk about the game. Most of the times I passed one I was asked my thoughts about the upcoming opponent. What did I think about the team and could we beat them?—were the favorite questions. My response always stayed the same. They're beatable and yes, we would win. Six games into the season asking me those questions, I think they knew what my response would be, but they enjoyed hearing it. The teachers at our small school were mostly 20-year employees from when Vanden opened, and they wore their pride as Vikings also. Their desire for us to win was as great as ours.

One day it occurred to me Coach Kiefer had been Coach Bev's line coach for the first football team at Vanden. I'd never put that correlation together before that moment. I wondered what they both remembered about that season. Player and coach to head coach and coach had to mean something. I hoped it meant good things were coming for our squad. We could use the good luck.

Friday morning came, and I was ready to put on my game jersey. I took pride in my number 55 and wanted our opponents to remember that number (and me) after taking a beating from our squad.

It was humid when we arrived to meet our seventh opponent, St. Patrick's. We were playing them at Corbus field in Vallejo where we had faced Hogan the previous season. Though our coaches had scouted the St. Patrick's Bruins we still knew very little about them, since they were new to the SCAL league. We found out pretty quickly they had a good team. They had some guys who would give us a great fight.

Ten minutes into the first quarter we got on the scoreboard first, when the Bruins' quarterback fumbled the ball on their 8-yard line. John McClellan (our 'Murdock') recovered the loose pigskin. Two plays later Bryan spun off two St. Patrick's defenders to score a touchdown. Our PAT missed the mark and we were ahead 6-0.

Big Joe and I, along with Jeff, Baro, and Chris, were having a tough time with the defensive tackles lined up against us. They were big, tall, athletic, and strong. They were also very quick off the ball. We struggled containing them on outside run plays and on pass protection. Those two defensive tackles were the best we had faced all season, and they worked well in tandem. Both were equally good. The trenches became a hard-fought battle.

After our score the Bruins struck back on their next possession. They completed a 61-yard pass to tie the game. Their PAT was blocked, and we stayed tied at 6-6. Five minutes before the half, Ronnie threw a 31-yard pass to Sherman Pruitt, and he went in for a score, dragging a Bruin defender with him across the goal line. It was an impressive sight. Our PAT was good and we once again took the lead at 13-6.

When halftime was called and we jogged into the locker room, I approached coaches Bev and Kiefer. I wanted to tell them we were having a tough time containing the two defensive tackles on outside runs by Bryan. They were too quick sideline to sideline and our high/low blocking was having little affect against them.

I told them we could push the defensive tackles outside, freeing the run up the gut. I recommended letting Maurice loose, with two back-to-back dives off the left and right side of Jeff's hips. As a captain on the team the coaches did listen to Glenn, Ronnie, and me when we gave input, so I hoped this time would be no different.

When we returned to the field after halftime we received the kickoff and returned it to the 30-yard line. The very first play from scrimmage, Maurice was given the call for a dive up the gut to the left side of Jeff. At the snap Jeff and I fired hard into the defensive tackle. We pushed him outside, and Maurice bulled up the middle between the linebackers for a 25-yard gain. The very next play was the same call but to Jeff's right side. Mark and Jeff pushed the other defensive tackle out, leaving Maurice a large hole to scramble through. He barreled up the field for a 45-yard touchdown. In those two plays Maurice moved the ball 70 yards and furthered our lead to 19-6. We attempted a two-point conversion but it failed.

Bryan had struggled gaining yards on the outside because of the two defensive tackles and defensive ends clamping down. When Maurice took control of the center of the field, the Bruins were pushed back in their game plan. Their defensive strategy crumbled.

Seven minutes later after a 60-yard drive, Maurice again scored a touchdown up the gut on a 7-yard run, as he bulled over their linebackers. We increased our lead to 25-6. St. Patrick's scored a TD of their own in the 4th quarter, narrowing the game to 25-12, after their two-point conversion failed. When the final seconds ticked off the clock, we won 25-12. It was not the hardest-fought game for our team, but in the trenches it had been for us linemen. That day we battled better trenchers than we were at Corbus field. We still prevailed—because we outsmarted them.

Maurice ended with 130 yards on 10 carries and two touchdowns. He put our future opponents on notice, that the inside, like the outside, were major threats to them. Our backfield had wheels and power. That Friday against St. Patrick's, Maurice reinforced the fact that Vanden had a TTB, Triple Threat Backfield. Bryan ended the day with his lowest yards gained during the season. He had only 83 on the ground, but he accounted for one of our touchdowns. Ronnie had been hampered by a thigh injury, slowing his mobility against the Bruins, but he was still able to direct us to another victory.

My teammate and friend Paul Holes was injured that game. He would watch the rest of the season from the sidelines. Football was a violent sport that could cause injuries, but it was because of that contact that my friends and I played the game.

At 7-0 we were getting closer to that championship title. We had five opponents left before we could capture it. Except for Paul we were still injury-free.

Gwinn sparks Vikings past Bruins, 25-12

"Toward the end of the season, the other teams have been keying on Bryan so I'm getting the opportunity to run the ball more," Gwinn explained. "I didn't expect to carry the ball this much."

Batchan, who ran for a moddest 83 yards, got the Vikings rolling in the first quarter after Vanden's John McClellan recovered a Rod Gover fumble at the St. Patrick's eight-yard-line.

The above two images are from an article courtesy of the Daily Republic. Used with permission.

The above photo shows Murdock #65 after recovering a fumble. Glenn and Danny are shown congratulating him. Courtesy of the Reporter.

> The start of the second half featured two fine runs by Gwinn. The 5-foot-10, 205 pound fullback rambled for 25 yards on Vanden's first play from scrimmage in the second half. With the ball resting at the Bruin 45, Gwinn again got the call and this time covered the distance for the score. Vanden had increased its lead to 19-6.

The above image is from an article that is courtesy of the Reporter.

    The JV squad continued its dominance of the teams they faced by beating their Bruins opponent 7-0. Like us they were also sporting a 7-0 record.
    I coveted those open field tackles. It was one on one. No one to help but training and experience. They were symbolic of one's strength. Missing could mean a score. Each movement was strategic, and we became the only two on the field. Everyone was watching and would see the victor. "Don't miss"—echoed in my head. I wouldn't miss. I would destroy him. Hit him hard, wrap my arms, pick him up, drive him backwards, and bury him in the turf. Send him to Valhalla to meet Odin and leave a Tiwaz (Norse symbol for conquest) where I took his name.
    Our next opponent was Delta, and they were coming to Vanden to face us. We knew they, like John Swett, weren't a very strong team, but the coaches again stressed they could beat us. Coach Bev, Noos, and Kiefer

warned us of becoming complacent.

That week Bryan was suffering back spasms and wasn't listed to start. Cliff was going to take the reins as our tailback. If his 82-yard kickoff return against Galt in game one was a preview of how he could maneuver with the ball, we would do well.

A sophomore wide receiver was promoted from the JV team to join our stable of targets for Ronnie. Coaches Bev and Noos wanted Chris DeForge to see some action in regular season on the varsity level. We had already secured a spot in the playoffs for the Sac-Joaquin Section title, and they were wanting to utilize three receivers at once during those games. DeForge would join the other sophomores playing on our small squad, Sherman Pruitt and DeWayne Quinn.

As we prepped for the game in the locker room that Friday night the mood was light. The team was feeling good about our prospects. We dressed, had our Zen time alone, and waited for the coaches to give us our pregame talk.

How did one thing become my everything? I didn't know; but it did. Football had this hold over me. I felt real when suited—comfortable and complete. The first time I met it, it embraced me. I had a clean slate with it and there was no prejudging who I was. It allowed me to define myself; because of that we had an instant connection. A connection that was new but seemed old. Delta would soon see the connection I had with the game.

I glanced over at Baro. He and I had forged a bond as the pulling and trapping guards. We were constantly on the move on offense and defense. On offense we both relied upon each other more than any two-player combo I had been part of or seen in my five seasons of football. Yes, Glenn and Danny, 2/3 of our Orient Express, relied heavily on each other in a 5-2 defensive setup, when they were the sole plugs in the middle. I knew their bond was very strong, but with Mark and me it was different.

The success of many of our offensive plays relied upon us. That was a heavy burden to carry. We had to quickly get around corners, blocking for Bryan or trapping a defensive tackle, so Ronnie, Bryan, or Maurice could take advantage of the open hole where we just buried our target.

We faced many players larger than we were, and we had to be fast because our Triple Threat Backfield would run us over if we didn't open a hole quickly. That constant reliance forged a bond between Baro, me, and Coach Kiefer. We took pride in that bond.

Joe and I as the left anchors on the line also forged our own close bond. I relied upon his grit and strength when the play of the gridiron got rough, which was often, to hold strong and not let the line collapse. When Mark and I were gone and on the move, Joe, Jeff, and Chris were left to their own accord and skills to handle the defense, which included blitzing linebackers. Big Joe towered over all of us, on the line and in the huddle. I had to look up at him to make eye contact. There was a large difference between his 6'4" frame and my 5'10" one.

The coaches finally came down from their office. Play hard, hustle to the last whistle, and do not let your guard down, they said. We could be beaten, they told us.

That kept us grounded, because there is a belief in sports and especially in football, when a good team faces a basement squad, the good team underperforms, while the basement squad plays better. We had to be careful, because Delta could slay our undefeated season and championship quest.

Then the good news came. Bryan's back had loosened some, so we were notified he would play but see limited action. An injured Bryan was still better than most healthy running backs on other teams. I would take his limited capabilities over any player an opponent could throw our way.

Our Vanden JV squad had little trouble dispensing with their Delta foes, as they won 54-14, putting their record at 8-0. Their unblemished record was a reflection on the capabilities of coaches Hatcher and Ordez.

We were stuck in that theory of underperforming. Our first quarter of play was marred with turnovers, and it took over five minutes into the second period for us to score first on a four-yard run up the gut by Maurice. With Dave Haupt's extra point kick we led 7-0.

Within five more minutes we drove 80 yards in four plays to score our second touchdown. Fifty-seven of those yards came on one play when Maurice scampered over Delta players. Bryan scored the second TD from eight yards out. We were leading 14-0.

Dave Haupt tried a 57-yard field goal on the last play of the half but missed—barely. It was still worth giving him a shot because in practice he had kicked successfully over 50 yards through the uprights.

After our break and halftime talk we returned to a

scoreless third quarter. We were playing flat like Coach Bev warned us. I think we knew the outcome was inevitable so subconsciously we didn't have to dig down deep.

On the first play of the fourth quarter Bryan took an option pitch from Ronnie, racing 32 yards for our third score. Dave's PAT was good and we extended our lead to 21-0.

Less than eight minutes later on our 6th play of a 63-yard drive, Ronnie scored our fourth touchdown when he faked dropping back to pass, then followed my block over the left guard position of the line, racing 38 yards to the end zone. Dave again kicked the PAT, putting the score 28-0. All my teammates were then given a chance to play. With only (three) seconds left in the game Delta avoided a shutout with a 24-yard touchdown pass.

For the second week in a row Maurice led our ground game by rushing for 108 yards on 10 carries. Bryan added 75 with limited play, and Ronnie rushed for 94 yards and passed for another 83. Our offense rolled for 277 yards on the ground.

The win against Delta was significant for several reasons. Bryan crossed the 1000-yard mark for the season at 1027 yards. We tied the school record with most consecutive wins in a regular season, 8, and with the win secured home-field advantage for the first round of the Sac-Joaquin Section playoffs. Our win also gave us a share of our SCAL league title—a first since 1980—and a first since Coach Bev took over the head coach position. The last time Vanden Vikings had clinched the SCAL title, we were Travis Redskins playing for the California State Championship.

Coach Bev, Ronnie, and Eric became the first father-and-son combination to win a varsity title in any sport in Vanden's history.

We were forced to play the game against Delta without a functioning game clock when it quit working before the start of the kickoff. The referees on the field, along with the coaches, kept the time.

As Coach Bev talked to the reporters after our win, we picked him up and carried him to the showers, throwing him in. When he returned to the interview he was soaking wet but smiling. He was having fun.

Vikes rip Delta 28-7, clinch SCAL crown

Vikes improve record to 8-0...

The above two images are from article titles courtesy of the Reporter.

The above photo shows the offense, as Ronnie drops back to pass. Left to right: Maurice #40, Ronnie, me #55, and 'Baro' #64 are shown from an article courtesy of the Daily Republic. Used with permission.

It had been a long journey since my first play on the Travis Redskins. My respect for the game had grown, and the memories my friends and I had shared over the past five years were fresh. We were getting closer to another undefeated season. What Jeff, Big Joe, Baro, and I had talked about in the gym on Travis AFB was materializing. Forty-eight minutes against our next opponent, the Rio Vista Rams, would determine our fate.

If we prevailed a new chapter in our journey would begin: the playoffs. We would meet some of the best football teams in our state and get our chance to see how good we really were. That championship title was getting closer, but it wasn't going to be easy to capture.

My birthday like Big Joe's was memorable that year. I, too, had invited the starting offensive trenchers for a small close gathering. Jeff and Chris couldn't make it. For dinner my mom made Baro, Big Joe, my brothers, and me taco salad and strawberry-covered angel-food cake. We ate our fill.

Afterwards, I wanted to catch a movie with the guys and then find something exciting to do. My mom let me borrow her little four-door Toyota Tercel. She was off for the night and would be getting some much-needed rest from her busy work schedule.

When we left for the movies the plan changed. We decided to head to San Francisco. Once there, we walked around the Wharf, China Town, Ghirardelli Square, and just wandered like 18-year-olds—with freedom and car keys. At midnight one of the guys tossed out the idea that we should go to Tahoe. It sounded like an adventure worthy of us. Off we headed without thinking too much about the winter weather and how the little four-cylinder Toyota, with no tire chains, would do driving three hours north.

We made it to within ten miles of Tahoe and were turned back by too much snow. Baro and Big Joe wanted to get out and play in it. They were acting like children and I felt like their father. Okay kids, for ten minutes, then we have to head home, I told them. It was about 3:00 a.m. I stopped the car and we got out and played in the knee-high snow. It was cold and we weren't smart enough to take winter clothing. It reminded me of those wet practices in the rain where my entire uniform down to my socks became soaked. After some snowball fights and tackling it was time to head back to Vacaville.

As we drove down the mountain with no cars behind us it was snowing fairly heavily. There was about ten inches on the highway. I was driving slowly in the tracks other vehicles had left. Mark was in the front seat and Joe in back. Stay in the tracks, Big Joe kept repeating. He sounded like a parrot. He knew how to drive in the snow, being from Alaska, he bragged. It became too much. I turned around and told him, "Of course I will stay in the tracks! What am I, stupid?" As I turned back my tires slipped from the tracks to the snow. Just like that, "I told you so" flew from Alaska Boy's parrot mouth. I wished I had a cracker to shut his beak. He continued to squawk.

I lost control of the car and it began to slide without me driving. We slowly turned sideways with the passenger side taking the lead going down the mountain. Thankfully, there were no other vehicles in sight.

We saw it coming. My mom's car hit the center cement guard separating the lanes. It stopped like David

Smith's 'Dukes of Hazzard' flight. "No, no, no, no, no, no, no!" flew out of my mouth. I knew my mom was going to be really upset. I couldn't easily explain how a movie trip turned into San Francisco, Tahoe, an accident, and damage to her only car.

We scrambled out and the front rubber bumper was laying on the road. There was no time, stuck in the middle of the highway, in the snow, in the middle of the night to play mechanic trying to put it back on. I placed the bumper in the back of the vehicle. I wondered how the three of us could be involved in two auto accidents in three months. Both accidents were our fault under careless conditions and driving our parents' vehicles.

Those dreaded sleds with Coach Noos were going to come in handy. The three of us put our shoulders into the car and pushed, driving our legs in the snow. Our feet slipped, but we kept pushing. We were able to maneuver it back into the tracks made by other vehicles.

Thankfully the vehicle started. My luck had been better than David Smith's—we weren't going to need a tow truck. We carefully drove down the mountain to Placerville. I stopped in an empty parking lot to try and get the bumper on. We didn't have tools, so it had to wait.

We made it to Baro's house and arrived at dawn. My mom would be up soon. As Joe and I put the bumper back on Mark washed and dried the car. We hurriedly jumped in the vehicle and drove down my street, stopping before the court to push the car up into the driveway. We snuck in the house and up the stairs minutes before my mom awoke. We slept only a few hours, with Mom thinking we'd slept in.

She never noticed any damage to the car. There wasn't any, except for the bumper, and I never told her what happened. It wasn't the first time I had had an accident in her car and didn't tell her.

"Back up. Glenn's in the driveway," Mark said as we drove by. I hadn't seen him as we passed in the dark, driving to Big Joe's. I put it in reverse and hit the pedal. Coach Hatcher, who had been my driving instructor at Vanden, and Coach Kelly, my Redskins skipper, wouldn't have been happy with me. I didn't use the side or rear mirror as I accelerated the fifty feet backwards. A blind man on Mars could've seen what would happen next.

I backed into the rear bumper of Coach Kelly's truck as it sat in front of their house. Glenn ran towards us as Baro and I jumped out. The heavy bumper protected Coach Kelly's vehicle. My mom's wasn't so lucky. To the right of her license plate a one-inch-by-one-inch 'nub' that protruded out had been pushed flat. I wasn't sure what the nub was for, as there was one on each side of the plate. They didn't house lights to illuminate it. One thing is sure, if Coach Kelly had seen the accident, I would've been running laps as punishment.

I was trying to find the right time to tell Mom when she came home from work a week later and said, "Let me show you what happened to me at work today." We went outside to the rear of her car and she pointed at the smashed nub. She stated, "A lady at work hit my car. When I went to leave for lunch I saw her vehicle pushed up against my parked car. I went back inside the hospital and located whose vehicle it was. The lady didn't argue and paid me for the repair costs."

I didn't know what to say, and I knew I couldn't tell her the truth at that point. I had waited too long, and some poor lady paid for my mistake. My mom never knew I was the cause for the damage. (She does now.)

Those three were some of our best, and I knew without them we wouldn't be the team we were becoming. Ronnie, Big E, and J-p were the nicest of guys and the best of football players. Everyone liked them, and they could be seen walking the halls of Vanden wearing wide smiles. Students gravitated to them and I was no different. We were lucky to have them on our 33-man squad.

Outside of Bryan, Ronnie was the best athlete I knew. He was equally good as a quarterback and a cornerback. He was the leader of our Triple Threat Backfield and held a winning hand full of threats. Ronnie could throw accurately; move like a running back in open field; hit like a linebacker; catch like a receiver; run like a sprinter; and think like a coach. He was as tough as they came and never got rattled. His presence was reassuring and play unforgettable. He was a natural leader. He was the best all-around football player I had ever seen. He was a standout and could turn the tide of a game by himself. He would also be picked the small school player of the year for the state of California. Ronnie was that good.

Eric was Ronnie's stepbrother but in reality just his brother. You could tell they were close. He would always make me smile or laugh with one of his stories. Eric was a good kid with a big heart, and he made Vanden a better school. As our tight end and defensive end he was an impact player. He had made many big plays for our squad. When we needed that important catch, Big E would pull it in. His hands were sure and his jump remarkable. I needed that nod he gave me in our huddles. It was something between us that said 'Let's get this done.' It always made me play harder.

J-p was an all-around good kid that strengthened our team. In his short time as a Viking he made us all better. I never saw him down or angry, just uplifting and ready. Who couldn't appreciate a guy like that? He was a tough football player who liked to hit. My type of teammate. I liked his never-surrender attitude. The Alamo could've used him. He would've made Texas proud.

I was enjoying my life and our football success but I spent a lot of time looking back. My wild escapades had slowed, so I would spend more time alone. I was becoming a little withdrawn. Maybe because of my head injury, or I just liked to reflect on days past. Much had changed in my life in a few short years. My family broke apart, girlfriends were gone, and Maniac had become a memory. I had a good childhood, though. My brothers and I grew up in an era of innocence. We played outside until the street lights came on. A dinner bell was rung to call us to supper. As military dependents we stood when the National Anthem was played before a movie at the base theater. We played 'Hide and seek,' 'Red rover, red rover, send someone over,' 'Dodge ball,' and 'Crack the whip.' We had traveled all over the U.S. and Japan with my dad's military career. I had been blessed.

I think it was his subconscious reaction to dad leaving. He never started them, but Sean began getting into fights. He hadn't fought when dad lived at home, but almost overnight Sean started using his fists to settle grievances. He was very good with his hands. They were quick and accurate and put down all who challenged him. He never lost. In our town of Vacaville his reputation grew and his name was recognized. I don't think he realized it but those bare-knuckled battles were like therapy sessions. Each punch thrown was a "You'll be alright" reassurance from a counselor.

Outside our Vanden friends some guys from Vacaville High could be found at our home often. Rich Chandler, Todd Harris, Sean Feeny, and Jerry Gray became regulars. Some of those guys we played baseball with growing up. Todd and I were on the same little league team that his dad coached. While playing baseball at Keating Park together we could see inmates from CMF prison through the chain link fence that separated the park from the prison grounds. Knowing Charles Manson was incarcerated there was scary for us kids.

It was inevitable Jim and I would meet. It was predestined that the 'Psycho' and 'Maniac' personalities would develop. As I was running from Mr. Fritch, my science teacher, Jim was creating an international incident as a 7th grader. No wonder we became inseparable.

The tall card shaped like the American flag was a nice gesture from our Golden West School. Each student wrote a note to the hostages taken in the Iranian embassy crisis. They were supposed to be uplifting and give them hope. Everyone wrote kind patriotic words—except a smart-ass 13-year-old from TAFB who would later become my best friend. Among the students Jim became an instant celebrity with his "Be thankful you are being held hostage in Iran. I am being held hostage in Mr. Yrekes' class." He was punished for his written comment, but Golden West didn't have a choice but to send the card with Jim's sentiment anyway.

I knew I owed Jim a lot as I thought about our time together. He introduced me to the game that would change my life. Overnight I went from wrestling and playing baseball to football. It drew me in and I was a natural fit. I never felt that way as a wrestler or baseball player.

Blocking became easy, and running full speed into an opponent was rewarding. The collision didn't hurt. It became pleasant—something I looked forward to feeling. I liked it when my teeth rattled or I saw stars from a stinger. I liked when facemasks collided and I could see into an opponent's eyes. I liked the loud thunder as we crashed into each other. Everything about the game—from a hard forearm rip under an opponent's chin, to using every ounce of strength to bury the guy lined up against me—brought satisfaction.

Being at the bottom of a pile-up or defending our goal line by smashing into the offensive line from my nose guard position made me feel calm. I know that sounds crazy, but it did. All the visuals to my left, right, and in front of me while a play was in motion kept me focused. There was no better feeling than contact being felt from all sides as Big Joe, Jeff, and I bounced off each other as our opponents tried to overrun or overpower us. I knew I was an addict, and I needed my gridiron addiction. As I thought about what Jim gave me with our introduction, I couldn't thank Maniac enough for allowing Psycho to be born.

That Monday after our eighth win, we practiced

and ran hard during our conditioning. We were close to making history at Vanden. We just had to beat our ninth opponent before we could claim it.

The Rio Vista Rams weren't that great of a team but they had a running back who had rushed for a 1100-yard season, and he was very good. He was a hitter and a tough football player. He was their leader and someone to reckon with on the field. I looked forward to meeting him, I thought to myself. Soon we would share the same grass. I couldn't wait.

Friday morning during our church service I prayed hard for a victory. I also thought about family and football and how they were related. My parents didn't attend my games anymore, but I knew that did not mean they didn't love me. Life happened in our lives. I had been raised right by my parents, and they taught me well. After they divorced, though, football took over the reins of my parenting. It was giving me guidance and structure. It was teaching me to be a listener and a leader. It was showing me the strength of friendships and how they flourish through adversity. The game was teaching me to be humble, and the gridiron was teaching me to never quit. I loved my family and football—I needed them both.

Wearing our jerseys that day was a high. We were on the verge of doing something all the other varsity football players before us at Vanden hadn't accomplished: a perfect regular season. The closest any Viking squad had come to that pinnacle was the 1975 team, when they went 8-1. All day long I was asked if would we beat the Rams and go undefeated. Of course we would, I replied more times than I could count. Losing wasn't an option.

Vikings make bid for historic win

Getting thrown into the showers is fine with Vanden's Beverly

"They're excited," said Beverly of his Vikings. "They know the task ahead of them and they know they've got a chance to do something that's never been done in the history of the school.

The above images are from midweek articles courtesy of the Daily Republic. Used with permission. The photo shows Sherman Pruitt, one of the three starting sophomores to play against Rio Vista.

> "We said all along this should be our year. We saw these kids win the SCAL title as sophomores and they stuck around."
>
> "You can't really develop continuity at an Air Force Base because you lose so many people. This year we've been blessed with people who have stayed with the program."

The above image is from a midweek article courtesy of the Reporter.

Being our last game of the regular season, it was Senior Parent Night. The game was to honor all the seniors who were playing their final season at Vanden. A parent of each teammate would be wearing their away game jersey, and at halftime an event was scheduled. My mom had to work and my dad wasn't there, so I had no one in my family who would be wearing my white football jersey.

All the players took extra care dressing for Rio Vista. Everything needed to be right, from the pads secured in place, socks taped up, and the uniforms looking sharp. We wanted to make a statement on the field but we also wanted to look good doing it. If we were going to make history by finishing our regular season undefeated, we wanted to look like champions in the process.

The locker room was one of my favorite places in the world. I always felt at home there. It encompassed many frames like on a roll of film. The invasive aroma of previous games and practices lingered. That damp musty smell intertwined with cologne didn't mix well. Conversations soft and loud echoed. Whispers couldn't be hidden over the raucous laughter. Movements of my teammates preparing for battle were varied from cleats on the tile, to sports tape being torn, and metal lockers slamming. Those scenes could not disturb my mental preparation.

I did extra soul searching during our Zen time. I had to find my inner strength and feed it. We couldn't end our regular season like the 1975 squad. We had to win no matter the cost. I saw those same thoughts in the faces of the other guys as we sat alone. Their eyes were easy to read and their mood was telling. I knew Murdock was wearing his lucky shirt under his shoulder pads. I was glad he had it on. It hadn't failed us.

Our Vanden JV team under coaches Hatcher and Ordez beat Rio Vista, winning their 9th game and finishing their season undefeated. It was the second perfect season in three years for Coach Ordez. His knowledge of building good offensive and defensive lines was strengthening the football program.

The coaches came down from their office. They were quiet and walked to the front of the locker room near the chalk board. Coach Bev looked down at his shoes. He took a few steps and turned around, walking back to where he had been. His arms were crossed. He looked up and said only six words. I told myself I would remember them for years to come. The words were, "How bad do you want it?" We all remained quiet as we watched him. I knew coach Bev wanted it badly. He was on the verge of doing something Vanden's first head coach Ed Serpas never accomplished: finishing the regular season without a loss. Like us, Coach Bev wanted to be the first to secure that claim. He had scored the first touchdown for the program as a player and was very close to hitting another milestone as the head coach.

We exited the locker room and all the players pounded the metal partition with their clenched fists. In response it thundered back our battle cry. It was our call to arms.

We lined up and started slapping our thigh pads in unison. The noise thundered. We walked towards the George Gammon Field as one. Thirty-three Vikings each made better by the other. I could see heads turn in our direction as we approached. Our cleats hitting the asphalt and the sound of our thigh pads being slapped were the only noises I could hear. It was as if time stopped. Jeff had joined the captains leading the team.

Stepping onto the field, the feeling of the grass under my feet reassured me. We were old friends. I knew this field well. Throughout my years at Vanden I had probably touched every inch of it while running, hitting, blocking, and tackling. I had a special relationship with it. It left stains on my uniform; been stuck in my facemask and under my nails; and it had softened my falls. I had thrown clumps of it in frustration when the game wasn't going so well. It never failed me though. I understood it and it understood me. I was happy to see it and it greeted me the way it always had—with optimism.

When we yelled, "What time is it?" The team's response "Showtime!" carried. Our movements were choreographed. We took a lot of pride in our pregame entrance and warm-up; a grand presentation that garnered great reviews. It enhanced our reputation. We're the Vikings from Vanden—you'll never forget us—was our mindset.

It was interesting meeting him at mid-field. He stared back without blinking. There was no intimidating their leader. He had rolled up 1100 yards as their running back, and he was their safety. One position a point of the spear, and the other their last defense. His demeanor said he came to play. He carried himself like their captain. I was intrigued. I knew we would have our moment.

We won the coin toss and the Rams kicked off to us. Our first series of plays sputtered, and we had to punt. As David Smith got the snap, two Rio Vista Rams rushed in and blocked his kick and returned it 24 yards for a TD.

It was happening already—the slide a team can get into—and it is hard to recover from. It was too early though, I thought. We had a history of doing it to our fans and coaches. We would make them nervous only to step up and come back. I knew we were a second half team but it was still no way to start a game. Rio Vista had 7 points on the scoreboard in little over one minute of play. The Rams were playing up to us while we were playing flat.

Halfway through the first quarter Chris recovered a fumble at our 49-yard line. We then drove to the Rams' 9-yard line, and Ronnie took the ball in for a touchdown on a quarterback keeper. Our extra point kick missed, and the scoreboard read 7-6 with us down by one.

By halftime the score hadn't changed. I wasn't worried because we were a third and fourth quarter team. I was confused, though. How was our squad was losing to Rio Vista? The coaches had warned us of complacency and it appeared the team didn't listen.

After the buzzer sounded for halftime we assembled on the field in front of the stands. One by one parents were called down to join their son who was playing his last game at Vanden. Most of my senior teammates had a parent there, except David Reyes and J-p Smith. Both their dads had passed away the year before. As my other teammates were honored, David and J-p wandered off to our end zone, away from the gathering. I watched them. I knew they were hurting and it was an emotional time. They hugged each other not caring who saw their pain. It was a solemn moment and heartbreaking to watch. For the first time in my five years of football my eyes welled up with tears. I was sad for my friends, and for that one moment I was part of their suffering. I wanted to go hug them, but I didn't. They needed that time alone.

After the parents honored their sons and the ceremony ended, we jogged off the field to the locker room.

We were caught in that web: the harder you tried, the worse you would play. We needed to turn it around. Coach Bev basically told us it was our game to win or lose, and he said those six words again. "How bad do you want it?" I hoped it resonated more the second time.

After halftime we kicked off to Rio Vista, and they marched 80 yards in just four plays for another touchdown. Their PAT was good and we were down 13-6. That score was the last time Rio Vista would put points on the board for the rest of the game. We finally awoke. On the ensuing kickoff to us, we took the ball 67 yards for a score in just four plays ourselves. We attempted a two-point conversion but the pass was dropped. We were down 13-12.

After we kicked the ball back to the Rams and I was heading to the huddle to play nose guard, Coach Noos motioned me over to the sidelines where he was standing. He grabbed my facemask and pulled me in close. His glare was commanding. He told me we needed to stop their tailback. I already knew that, I thought. Noos looked at me and said "Stop him." I could see the seriousness in his eyes. They said, "Get it done."

I thought about that as I went back onto the field. His words rang in my ears. My coach, jogging partner, work detail warden, and friend was counting on me. I knew I couldn't let him down. I lined up across from their center and zeroed in on the tailback because Noos was watching. I wasn't sure how I was going to stop him but I had to figure out a way, and quickly. He was faster than me and had better coordination; but that didn't matter.

When the ball was hiked I penetrated into the backfield and hit my target hard in the numbers, tackling him solo. Facemask to facemask I growled at their tailback. Staring him in the eyes I used foul language taunting him. It was no Boy Scout Sunday School Altar Boy speech. My parents wouldn't have been proud of the profanity and context, and neither would my priest. He immediately reacted and began to punch and kick me. I welcomed his attack and lay there playing the victim knowing his actions would draw a penalty. Out of the corner of my eye I saw a referee a few yards away. The ref pulled his yellow flag and threw it in the air. I knew what was coming next. Their captain and my target was removed from the game for unsportsmanlike conduct—even though I was the instigator. My action went undetected by the referee. My plan had worked, and I accomplished what was asked of me in one play. It couldn't have been scripted better.

I was motioned over to the sidelines and pulled from the game for a few plays. Coaches Noos, Kiefer, and Bev all slapped my helmet. It was their way of telling me good job. They didn't know what I had said in my personal attack to cause the ejection. Thankfully, neither did Maurice's dad, or I would've been in confession on Sunday. Noos had asked me to step up for him and the team, and I did. I did it 'Psycho's' way.

It was ironic I chose to use inflammatory language to incite him to react. I wasn't a fan of such measures but knew it would work. During our undefeated season on the JV team two years earlier, a teammate on our squad kept using derogatory language about my mom one day during practice. The kid wasn't a friend of mine, hadn't been a Redskin, and wasn't a starter. His behavior caught my attention, and quickly. I told him there would be consequences. As soon as practice concluded and the coaches left, the team gathered around. It didn't take long for me to unleash my anger and deliver swift punishment. One punch to the face and it was over. He dropped to the ground hard and learned a valuable lesson. He never talked about my mom again.

The ejection resulted in a personal foul penalty that pushed the ball back to their 4-yard line. On the next play the Rams fumbled from a hit and Chuck recovered the ball on the 3. On our first play from scrimmage, Ronnie scored on a quarterback keeper, then passed to Sherman for a two-point conversion. We took the lead at 20-13 and never looked back. The mood on the field switched, and we got into our groove like we had all season long during the second half.

I couldn't believe what I was seeing. It was a first for me—but it didn't surprise me—coming from Baro. I learned with him to expect the unexpected, but I didn't expect him to start his own huddle as Jeff went to call his. There was Mark, though, five yards from Jeff with his arm in the air yelling "HUDDLE" too. (It was Baro in all his glory for everyone to see.) It upset Jeff and he began yelling "HUDDLE" even louder. It was a crazy sight.

I wanted to laugh but couldn't because Jeff's role as our center had to be respected. It was hard not to laugh, though. Some of my teammates even went to Baro for his huddle, while Ronnie and I went to Jeff's. Time was running out in between plays so Ronnie started yelling at Mark to knock if off, and he waved him towards us.

Like a mischievous child, Baro ignored him. I knew Baro well. He was a mix of Albert Einstein, Loki (the mythical Norse trickster), and the Tasmanian Devil. Drop them in a blender, turn it on, and you had Mark. He only listened to the coaches and me, so I stepped in and yelled, "That's enough, Baro! Get your ass over here!" That's all it took: Mark and his half huddle disbanded. He was chuckling when he joined us. His tilt and glare look at me brought a wide smile while I shook my head. We were having fun and on our way to a new school record.

Just like what happened to me two seasons earlier on the JV squad, one of Glenn's contacts fell out and he had to play most of the second half struggling to see. His vision was blurred, so Murdock, from the nose guard or defensive tackle position worked with Glenn by yelling where the ball was going.

The rest of the game was all us. We went on to score two more touchdowns, winning 33-13. We scored 27 unanswered points. We started slow but ended well in the fashion we had all season. Our squad was definitely a second-half and fourth-quarter team. I was sure our coaches would've preferred that we not wait so late in games to overcome our opponents. It was just our style.

After the game, as we went to shake hands with the Rio Vista players, I expected their tailback to be upset with me. I anticipated the possibility he would take a swing, so I was prepared. After all, I said explicit lewd comments directly in his face. I knew he must've taken it personally. It was his last game of his senior season, so I knew he would remember that game and me for the rest of his life—I ended his high school football career.

As we approached each other he looked directly into my eyes. He reached out his hand and shook mine. No punches were thrown. He earned my respect for his composure and play on the gridiron. He was an old-school name taker I knew one when I saw one. Yes I tricked him to react, but that was football. It was like a game of chess versus checkers, with lots of violence involved. In the end, all that mattered was, we won.

Against the Rams Bryan rushed for 107 yards and a touchdown. Maurice added 63 more yards gained. In the second half, our defense forced six fumbles through hard hits, and had three interceptions. Darren caught three passes for 46 yards.

We made history that night for the Vanden varsity football program by finishing our regular season undefeated at 9-0. It felt good to be the first. We did something twenty Vanden squads before us weren't able to do. It didn't surprise me though, because my friends honored the game with their effort. The gridiron noticed their character, heart, and perseverance, and in return it continued to give us victories.

The mood in the locker room was celebratory. The coaches and guys were enjoying the record we just reached. Coach Kiefer's hearty laugh could be heard echoing throughout and Bev's Fu Manchu mustache highlighted his wide smile. I glanced at Coach Noos, and he gave me a wink of approval. We were enjoying glorious times and everyone felt it. Our trip home down Vanden Road included stuntmen rides. We needed those as much as football.

We were heading into the playoffs with a perfect record. Now we would find out how good we really were as a team. The time was coming to face players who had defeated many opponents, like we had, in their quest to be the best. Bev showed he wasn't that 1-5-3 coach. We proved we could win again as teammates and friends, and I was learning that the game still needed me.

Struggling for sleep that night I remembered how it felt to be a Redskin. We were going for another championship and hopefully the result would be different from 1980. Greatness was inching closer.

Beverly relishes unbeaten SCAL record

Vanden High School completed its regular season Friday night with a 33-13 win over visiting Rio Vista.

With the win, the Vikings now have the distinction of being the first Vanden tean to finish the regular season without a loss.

Now the Vikings, ranked No. 3 in the state by Cal Hi Sports, will begin a new season — the playoffs.

The above images are from an article courtesy of the Reporter. The photo shows Bryan running the ball during the Rio Vista game.

After Vanden kicked off to Rio Vista, the Rams began play at their 18. But on first down, Rio Vista incurred a personal foul penalty, followed by an unsportsmanlike conduct call that resulted in the ejection of Anderson. Now facing a first down and 24 at their own 4, the Rams fumbled the ball away on the next play, with the Vikes recovering at the Rio Vista 3.

The above image is from a scanned article courtesy of the Daily Republic. Used with permission.

The above photo, left, shows one of the many banners that were hung throughout the school after our 9th victory. Photo courtesy of Travis Unified School District and Vanden High School. The above photo, right, shows one of the football decorations the cheerleaders would put on our lockers before games. Photo courtesy of Mark 'Baro' Baranowski #64.

Our first of three obstacles to being champions was formidable. We began preparation for our first-round playoff game for the Sac-Joaquin Section title against the Oak Ridge Trojans. We faced them during the first round in 1983. We lost to their squad at their field 27-12 with an injury-riddled team. I remembered watching the game from the sidelines. Things would be different this year. Everyone was healthy, except for Paul. We also had the home-field advantage. We would battle on our field in front of our fans. Both pluses in our favor.

Oak Ridge had an advantage too, which would be hard to overcome. They were a big squad and would outweigh us in the trenches on average 25 pounds per player. Jeff was going to be tested as our lightest lineman. He would need to utilize everything he learned in ten years playing center. I knew Jeff well. He was prepared for that challenge. His heart was much bigger than his body.

The lower left two photos show Jeff Martin #52, our center. The photo on the left shows him in his early days, learning the position. Photo courtesy of Jeff Martin. The photo on the right shows him as we prepared to face the Trojans. Photo courtesy of Travis Unified School District and Vanden High School.

The above two photos show the George Gammon Field. The top is the view as we entered and the bottom view is under the Vanden scoreboard. Photos taken by and provided by Timothy O'Donnell #69 co-captain of the 1984 undefeated Vanden JV 9-0 team.

Our team was a small squad compared to the Trojans. We had only Maurice who broke the 200-pound threshold at 5'9", 204 lbs. Big Joe was the second-largest player on the team at 6'4", 195. What we lacked in size with our bodies we had to overcome with the strength of our resolve. I always believed size didn't matter. Aggression, determination, conditioning, and hustling were the traits that did. We had all those. Oak Ridge would soon discover why we were 9-0.

The above photo shows Maurice running the ball during the Justin game. Courtesy of the Daily Republic. Used with permission.

The photo to the right shows 'Big Joe' #56 during our Saturday game against Justin. He had grit. He didn't let his penny-flattened finger prevent him from burying opponents all season. Photo courtesy of Travis Unified School District and Vanden High School.

I knew I didn't have what they had, as I surveyed the trench crew in our huddle. Jeff was molded from a younger age to be a center. A decade of training. He went to summer camps, and he was a technician. Our best technician. I knew it was very difficult to hike the ball, then control a larger defensive lineman, open holes, and protect Ronnie. I couldn't do what he could do as our anchor. Big Joe had size and grit to his advantage. He made me look small standing next to him. His strength was formidable. Baro had height on me, too—and speed. I just couldn't match it. I was quick; but he was fast and powerful. His leveling skills were impressive. Chris had the athleticism I wished I did. He knew the game and his natural abilities made him stand out. I was different from all of them. I had a few similarities to each, and I mixed in my own style. I knew my strengths and weaknesses. I was aggressive. I also knew I liked the brutality of the sport, and enjoyed the pain that accompanied it. The Oak Ridge Trojans would soon meet our trench crew, and we wanted them to remember that encounter.

    I gained strength under those lights. Looking from the field to the stands and seeing all those faces staring at us in anticipation made me feel like a dog with a bone. I could never adequately describe how it felt to be out there—except it was surreal. I knew the Trojans thought they would walk over us because of their size. I also knew they would be wrong. After all, we were Titans.

    For eleven years I had been a student in the Travis Unified School District as an Air Force brat. From first grade to this, my senior year. I went to Center Elementary (where in music class I learned to dance 'The Hustle' and the words to the songs 'Jive Talkin'' and 'Fame'), Travis Elementary, Golden West, and now Vanden. It was giving me opportunities that were changing my life for the better, and I was grateful for them.

    Everyone wanted to play. I knew that, and I felt for the players who saw little action. We were a small squad but deep in talent at different positions, so some players had to wait to be rotated in. Murdock and Maurice could've started for any school at nose guard but they shared duties with me. Chuck wanted more action on offense, but Big Joe and Chris were great at their positions. He had to wait until they needed a breather or were injured. Dave Smith was Jeff Martin's backup at center. Cliff wanted to run the ball but unless Bryan was out he wouldn't often get the chance. Bryan never left the field, except for injury. (Bryan and Ronnie were our most potent weapons.) David wanted more action as a cornerback and so did Louis Adams. They were competing with Ronnie, Cliff, DeWayne, Felix, and each other. I knew Derrick and Eugene wanted to play guards, but Baro and I never left the field on offense. Dave Haupt played backup quarterback to Ronnie yet he could've been a starter at any school. J-p, Big E, Dave, and Jeff had to share defensive end duties. There were other great players just aching to get on the field: Purnell Jones and Reginald Stover. They were receivers competing against a large stable that included Darren, Big E, Sherman Pruitt, DeWayne, and Felix.

    I also knew Darren—or Red, as Jim would call him—wanted the opportunity to catch more passes. We had played four years together, and he was a very good receiver. He could've started at any school. Our stable of receivers limited his time on the field.

    Louis Adams had a little brother who was a starter on the JV squad. I'm not sure how the difference in their playing times affected their relationship. Louis was a really good player but his minutes on the field were affected by the crew he had to compete against. I could see something in him maybe he couldn't. He was charting a course that would take him down wrong paths. I knew the strength of his character would one day right it.

    I knew it was frustrating because each guy on our squad had talent. I trusted them and knew they could perform well. The coaches had to decide what was in the best interest of the team during a game, and as players we may not have always agreed with their choices. It was their duty to direct and ours to follow.

I always read his articles but two of them he wrote about our 1984 team hit home. I agreed with Jim McKay's assessments in his column "Against the Ropes."

One article titled "Doing it with class" said, *"But there is something about this Vanden team that doesn't show up on a scoreboard or stat sheet....class. The team has class. And this is a reflection on the coaching staff."*

In an article titled "No frills here" he wrote, *"You don't see Vanden players jumping all over the place as they prepare for a game. And you don't see them going crazy after a win either. That's what I like about Vanden. This professional-like attitude."*

His words reflected our squad. All our coaches at Vanden, from my freshman year to this one, had trained us well. They molded us to be better football players and even better men. Football wasn't going to last forever. We had to think past our time on the gridiron; they were teaching us that. Coach Bev taught us discipline and respect. He ran a strict program and he expected much from us. How we acted was a reflection on him, the football program, and our school.

The above image shows the article "Doing it with class." Courtesy of the Daily Republic. Used with permission.

We needed to continue having perfect practices. How we performed while preparing for a game would reflect how we played against an opponent. Coach Bev continued to stress perfection to us. Even after winning nine games he would have us redo the same play over and over again until we got it right. It was having a positive effect because we were still winning.

The timing between our backfield was like a well-oiled machine. Ronnie, Bryan, and Maurice were equal parts to our engine and it fired on eight cylinders. All three were dangerous to defenses. They weren't your run-of-the-mill players. They were thinkers who adapted in the middle of the action. They were a big reason we were having the success we were.

Coach Bev decided we were going to run a 'no huddle' offense against Oak Ridge during our first series. He handpicked ten plays we would run back to back. He thought it would push the Trojans back on their heels and catch them off guard. It was a good plan. We went over those plays all week. The timing and the execution had to be exact.

It wasn't what Coaches Bev, Noos, Kiefer had envisioned when they said we needed perfect practices. Big Joe and I looked like we were on roller skates on wet ice. It was a poor performance by us and a great one by Derrick Davis. Derrick was one of the two juniors in our trench crew and he had just embarrassed us in front of the entire team. During a pass protection play Derrick rushed in and pushed us both back—and it wasn't pretty.

Coach Bev stopped the practice, and he and Coach Kiefer lit into us. They were more than mad. If we couldn't handle Derrick, how could we handle Oak Ridge's much larger players, they barked.

"Run the play again," Coach Bev said with disgust. We must've done something really wrong because karma came visiting again. It was a repeat performance as the first, with Derrick besting us once more. Coach Bev took off his cap and threw it on the ground. He stormed to us as Coach Kiefer arrived. There Big Joe and I stood with our facemasks in their grips. Their barking got louder. "Get it together!" Kiefer yelled at us.

The third time was the charm for us. Derrick rushed in as we stepped backwards on the pass play and we buried him hard, face in the grass. For the rest of the practice we made sure he had a very long day in the trenches. Derrick, Eugene, Chuck, and Murdock were as good as any defensive lineman in our league. They kept us on our toes, and for those two plays Derrick taught us a valuable lesson. Be ready for the Oak Ridge Trojans because they were coming—and it was going to be a knock-down drag-out fight.

I struggled with sleep all week due to insomnia combined with the worry for the coming game. We were three teams away from capturing that elusive championship. The game would be packed on both sides with fans and spectators, and I didn't want to embarrass myself like I had in practice against Derrick. The Trojans were bigger, so they would be unrelenting. They wanted the title and to be the best. We had other plans for them.

I took my role as the captain of the trench crew seriously and wanted to make a statement. I had just three games left in my career as a football player, and the thought of it ending weighed on me. I still didn't like the limelight. Yet, as I lay in my dark room I knew I wanted to be remembered for my style of play. My mindset still remained simple—be smart; impacting; and the most resolute name taker on the gridiron. No football player ever loved the game more.

The odds were noticing us. We were much closer to that .0089 percent chance of being the best. History had moved to the front of the room to get a better view. It took out its paper and pen to document the end to our journey. We wanted it to write great words.

Vikes await big Trojans

"If we get a dry field and some decent weather, we'll be able to use our speed to good advantage," said Vanden coach Ron Beverly, whose charges will take a perfect 9-0 overall record into the contest.

"But if it rains and we have to try to outmuscle these guys, we could be in trouble."

The above images are from a midweek article. Courtesy of the Daily Republic. Used with permission.

Though we were a small offensive line (averaging 186 pounds per player), Coach Kiefer expressed his pride in us often, and that gave us confidence that we could accomplish anything together as a unit.

Vanden line: size is of little concern

Chris (RT), 'Baro' (RG), Jeff (C), 'Big Joe' (LT), me (LG), and Chuck

The current Vanden line consists of tackles Joe Leonard and Chris Stiltner, guards Mark Baranowski and Jeff Rooney and center Jeff Martin. Chuck Coates, a senior transfer student from Germany, also sees plenty of action at either of the tackle spots.

"The line we had in 1975 (the season Vanden won the Sac-Joaquin Section Class A championship) was big, but this line is quick and aggressive," Kiefer said. "Each line is great in its own way. I was just lucky enough to coach both."

"We know Oak Ridge is big, but I think our kids enjoy the challenge," offered Kiefer. "Our line's a throwback to the 50's. This is a macho group. They are aggressive."

Martin indicated the linemen have put in extra hours because they know they are small. According to the senior center, they realize they have to work a little harder.

"We know we don't have the weight, but we try to compensate for it by lifting weights," explained Martin. "We're also a smart group. If we can't out-muscle our opponents, we out-think them."

The above image and images to the left are from an article courtesy of the Reporter.

Friday came fast. We had prepared the best we could to face our much larger foe in Oak Ridge. We knew it would be a hard-fought game, and the team that wanted it the most would prevail.

Revenge: Vikes get second shot against Trojans tonight

The above image is from an article title courtesy of the Reporter.

Vanden begins its quest for section crown tonight

The above image is from an article title. Courtesy of the Daily Republic. Used with permission.

There was no JV contest before us, so we went to the locker room early to get ready for the game. When Oak Ridge arrived and parked in front of the Shubin Sports Building we walked outside to size them up. What we heard about them was true. They were big. As they exited their bus it looked like 15-plus players were over the 200-pound mark.

Not sure what the guys were thinking when we went back inside, but I was all over the map in my thoughts. The locker room was quiet but that wasn't always the case. During halftime breaks the coaches would yell sometimes with cuss words flying left and right. That was okay though, because that was football. We weren't ballerinas, we weren't fragile, and we didn't need to be coddled. We were football players who engaged in violence. We were tough, and we needed the verbal smackdown from time to time. It made us play harder and get our heads on straight. Football wasn't for the weak of heart, and that's why we played the game. If our coaches wouldn't curse or yell I would've been disappointed.

The quiet in the locker room gave me time to think. In my mind I could see all my coaches as players suited before their big games. I wished I could've met them. As coaches they still carried the remnants of their younger selves, and I could sense those young men honored the game like we did. They had paid it respect through big hits, hard tackles, and taking names. I wondered what words they would tell me or what advice they would give. I was pretty sure they would tell me to play each play like it was my last. They probably would tell me to enjoy these years because the decades will pass fast. It would've been nice to meet those young men and share a few minutes together. I knew I could use their strength before we stepped onto the field to battle the Trojans.

Murdock walked around hitting shoulder pads. As I sat back down I looked over at Chris, the only junior on our starting offensive line. He was tapping his feet. I knew he wasn't nervous though, because he was mature for his age. He played like a senior, and was equally good on either side of the ball. It was my third year of playing in the trenches with him, and I knew his skills. He was damn good. I was glad I didn't have to line up against him.

Tuck brought me my helmet and I put it on. It felt good. Murdock walked over and head-butted me. It was his thing. A nice mental wake-up before the contact on the field. I was glad he, too, was on our team. Though he shared nose guard with Maurice and me, he was very fast off the ball. I wasn't sure who was faster into the backfield, him or Maurice. They were both devastating pass rushers. I didn't have their speed. We played differently. I was more designed to plug the center and stop the run.

Coaches Bev, Noos, and Kiefer came down from their office. Bev went over the ten plays we would run with no huddle. Noos and Kiefer laid out their thoughts. They are big, so take the battle to them! they said. Dig in and fight! they continued. Never quit! Coach Bev added.

As usual the partition was pounded as we left. It growled back telling us "Be ready." Maurice joined us, taking the team out. After finishing warm-ups, that familiar sour taste visited, and I spit it out.

When we walked to the center of our field for the coin toss I didn't smile. We weren't there to make friends. I wanted the Oak Ridge Trojans to remember our game for years to come, because we would. I wanted them to know they might play football as a sport but it was the game that my friends and I grew up playing together. Football was our bond and it defined us. No matter what happened on the field the last second on the scoreboard would show us victorious. They would be our tenth speed bump on the road to being champions.

We won the toss and Oak Ridge kicked off to us. As if they had our playbook they shut down our no-huddle offensive plan. Their front defensive linemen were big and strong. Halfway through the first quarter, Oak Ridge drove 85 yards in 13 plays for a touchdown. They were on the board first at 7-0. As we battled in the trenches I dug my back right foot into the turf to gain extra leverage. The weight advantage they had was showing early. The battle was tough, and we were being tested to our limits. The strength of our perseverance was being challenged.

On our first play after receiving the kickoff Ronnie threw an interception. The Trojans took over on our 18-yard line. Three plays later they rushed for a 17-yard touchdown. Their extra point was good, and just like that, we were down 14-0.

We had been behind early before by good teams in the first quarter. Hogan had us down by 13 and Justin had the early lead. It was like the play on the field had been scripted by the same writer. Our coaches and fans must've felt they were watching a bad rerun.

With little over 9 minutes left in the second quarter, we drove 60 yards and scored our first touchdown, when Ronnie went up the middle from one yard out. Dave Haupt kicked the extra point and we narrowed the lead to 14-7. We next swapped touchdowns with Oak Ridge, throwing for a 17-yard score and us going 65 yards, then scoring our own on a 23-yard pass from Ronnie to Eric.

We went into halftime losing 21-14. Coach Bev was animated in the locker room and said we were giving the game away. His frustration showed.

His 'wake up' speech worked because we returned in the third quarter to score 21 unanswered points. We were a second-half team and owned it. The Trojans were learning that the hard way. We scored on 34- and 44-yard runs, by Ronnie following Mark and me on traps, and a 5-yard pass from Ronnie to Eric.

Late in the fourth quarter with 2:26 left in the game, we fumbled on our 47-yard line. Oak Ridge recovered. They used our turnover to drive the field and score a touchdown. During their score we were penalized for unsportsmanlike conduct, so after their two-point conversion attempt failed, they kicked off from our 45-yard line.

Hoping to recover it they attempted an onside kick, but Darren Rysden jumped on the ball at the 32. He saved us. We ran out the clock and secured our tenth victory. We won 35-27. It was a hard-fought game. My teammates had let their character outweigh the Trojans' size. Another notch for our helmets. Ten had challenged us and lost. The title was close.

Ronnie proved his value to our team with the defeat of Oak Ridge. He ran for three touchdowns and threw for two others. Eric proved he was a great tight end by catching two TD scores. Ronnie rushed for 102 yards and threw for 82 more, while Bryan led all rushers with 136 yards on 21 carries.

In the locker room we were banged up but excited. The mood couldn't have been happier. Dirt and sweat covered us and bruises were plenty. More than a few players were limping. I was exhausted as I sat at my locker taking off my gear. My pads had blood on them. Some was mine and some wasn't. It was a tough game. We won though, so we relished in the pain that came with our victory.

That night against a much larger opponent my friends showed how much heart they really had, and the strength of their resolve, and they prevailed.

Beverly leads Vikes past Trojans

But Vanden's Darren Rysden recovered the kick at the Vanden 32, thus thwarting Oak Ridge's last shot to tie the game and send the contest into overtime. The Vikings then ran out the last 49 seconds to secure the win.

The above two images are from an article courtesy of the Daily Republic. Used with permission.

Vanden rallies for playoff victory over Oak Ridge

Vikes win wild one, 35-27

Above two images are from an article courtesy of the Reporter. Photo shows (left to right) sophomore Chris DeForge, who was promoted for the playoffs from the JV squad; Eric 'Big E' Barnes our tight end; and me. Bryan can be seen circling out of the end zone in the back.

Everyone impressed me during our defeat of Oak Ridge. I saw some plays I knew would stay with me. I went to David Reyes, my teammate of four seasons, and gave him a hug in the locker room. He had a defining moment during the game that drew claps and high-fives from the squad. Oak Ridge had a giant of a tight end. He was bigger than anyone on our team. In the fourth quarter he had attempted to catch a pass and David stuck him as the ball reached his hands. He didn't catch the ball, and David buried the mammoth player into the turf. David bounced up, but the Oak Ridge giant struggled to his feet, limping off the field. The tight end was a foot taller than David and a hundred pounds heavier. That is the type of play my friends and teammates had within themselves. When they needed to reach deep inside, they could, no matter what we were facing.

There were two teams left to play and our next opponent was going to be our toughest: Folsom Bulldogs. Like us they were undefeated at 10-0 and ranked in the top 5 in the state of California. Our contest wouldn't only test us as players, it would test the coaches. Our battle would be their battle.

The above photo shows (left to right) teammates Mark 'Baro' Baranowski #64, right guard and defensive tackle, and Jeff Martin #52, center and defensive end, right before the start of our Oak Ridge game. We beat them 35-27 in the first round for the Sac-Joaquin Section playoffs on our gridiron, the George Gammon Field at Vanden. Photo provided by Jeff Martin #52 and used with permission.

The above two photos show us on offense getting ready to pass, with Oak Ridge getting ready to defend. The top photo shows a wide-field view and the bottom photo shows a close-up. Photos were provided by teammate Jeff Martin #52 and used with permission.

The above two photos show us on offense as the ball was hiked, and Oak Ridge about to defend. The top photo shows a wide-field view and the bottom photo shows a close-up. Photos were provided by teammate Jeff Martin #52 and used with permission.

The above two photos show us on offense running the ball, and Oak Ridge preparing to defend. The top photo shows a wide-field view and the bottom photo shows a close-up. Photos were provided by teammate Jeff Martin #52 and used with permission.

The above game photo was provided by Jeff Martin #52 for use.

> Both teams are unbeaten and ranked in the state. The Vikings currently hold down the No. 3 spot, while Folsom is the No. 5-ranked team according to CAL-HI Sports.

The above image is from the Vacaville Reporter, Nov. 13, 1984. Courtesy of the Reporter.

> But if you ask the only two coaches of teams that have played both the Vikings, ranked second in the state by Cal-Hi Sports, and the third-rated Bulldogs, there is no debate. Vanden should come away the winner Friday.

The above image is from the Daily Republic Nov. 15, 1984. Courtesy of the Daily Republic. Used with permission.

Though Defensive Coach Noos was proud of how the defense had played all year, he especially praised his linebacker crew. He nicknamed them 'The Orient Express.' They were led by my five-year teammate Glenn. They were one of the best linebacker units in the state. Below (L to R): Sherman, Danny, and Glenn.

THE ORIENT EXPRESS

Vanden's trio of linebackers earn their keep

"For starters, each kid is part Oriental," Newsome said. "It was only appropriate to call them 'The Express' since we blitz a great deal. We are always moving. We never stay in the same defense. We don't give the offense any tendencies."

In fact, Newsome went to the extent of having "Orient Express" T-shirts made. He didn't just hand them out to his backers, however. Each shirt had to be earned.

The above three images are from an article courtesy of the Reporter.

During our game against Oak Ridge, Bryan became the all-time leading varsity rusher for Vanden in a single season, with 1241 yards. He ran into the record book surpassing the 1979 mark set by Mark Funderburk.

Batchan storms for a new record

"It feels great," said Batchan after the game upon learning he had set the new record. "The line wanted to go out and show everybody they were the best in the league, and they made it all possible for me."

The above three images courtesy of the Daily Republic. Used with permission.

My heart stopped when I saw the hood on fire. Within seconds the entire car was engulfed in flames. It was a terrible end to an evening that should've been a great time. We were at Lake Berryessa celebrating our latest win over the Oak Ridge Trojans. It was Saturday night and John, Baro, Big Joe, Jeff, David, and Pete Watts had joined my brother Tim and me at 'The Point.'

Tim yelled out, "Race you back to Vacaville" and he and John jumped in Tim's old grandma car he had just purchased from Mr. Axehelm, a teacher from Golden West. The car made Glenn's grandmother vehicle look like a Porsche. It was ugly. Only two things were missing: a 'Cat on Board' sign and a quilted blanket across the back seat.

They took off before us and probably had a mile lead before the rest of us left. We sped around the corner by the dam, and there was Tim's car crashed into the side of the mountain with the hood on fire. John was pulling Tim from the driver's seat and dragging him across the road when the car went up in flames. John had just seconds to save Tim before he would've burned to death.

We jumped from our vehicles as John sat Tim down on the curb. Tim was unconscious and John was bleeding heavily from a deep gash to his forehead. An ambulance and fire trucks arrived a short time later and extinguished the fire, and transported Tim to the hospital.

I owed John a lot for saving Tim and it brought us closer. Murdock was a hero in my eyes and a great football player. A better and more loyal friend couldn't be found. A 'race you back' challenge had now caused two serious accidents. We learned our lesson the hard way.

Tim didn't have any serious injuries, and was released from the hospital and recovered quickly. John needed a dozen stitches to close his wound. He practiced all week with a bandage covering the sutures. He was a tough kid. The nickname Murdock fit him.

I wanted them to know what was coming before the snap of the ball. I wanted to build a connection. Not of friendship; but of aggression, violence, and pain that was about to be unleashed. I wanted them to remember me. The unflinching stare that looked through them was meant to be intimidating. It became one of the things my opponents learned from me. I could see the color of their eyes and the size of their pupils. I could count the sweat beads dripping down their face. I never blinked. Was it my stare, watching for the ball movement, or the blood on my uniform (that wasn't mine) that made them look away? I didn't know; but it gave me the upper hand.

Get some sleep, I told myself. I knew against Folsom, Maniac's old partner Psycho had to step up and perform. I closed my eyes, but the Sandman refused to visit.

I was thinking about her mom calling me. Her mom was mad and her voice got louder as she said her daughter was crying because I cancelled our date. I wanted to tell her mom why I cancelled; but I thought better. If she knew why—she would've understood.

I knew her daughter from track and she liked one of the guys on the team, but he was too nervous to ask her out. I taunted him (jokingly) that if he didn't make his move, I was going to kiss her. He didn't believe me. After school I followed her to her locker and kissed her. I probably shouldn't have done that.

She was one year younger than me and innocent. She looked like the girl next door. She asked me to take her out—but not a traditional date. She had other plans. She wanted to lose her virginity on the 50-yard line of our football field. I was stunned. The day of our date I cancelled that afternoon. I couldn't do it. I just didn't feel right. She was a virgin and I couldn't take her innocence because I wasn't really interested in her. The kiss meant something to her, but to me it was supposed to be a harmless gesture. So, when her mom was yelling at me I thought about telling her the truth but didn't. I wanted to take back that kiss, as I counted that one lace and eight stitches on a football over and over until sleep finally found me.

When the alarm went off I jumped from my bed quickly. I had much to do. I ate, showered, and put on my beloved #55 jersey. It was my armor. I knew that evening was make or break. We were about to meet a clone of our squad. They were undefeated; but they weren't us.

Every teacher came up to me at school, and they got my scripted response. We would win. No doubt.

It was quiet in the locker room and movements were slow. I didn't have to ask Tuck to come and get my helmet; he took it off the bench next to me to air it. When he returned he told me he'd checked it twice.

Vikes hope to get a jump on Folsom

Above title from an article courtesy of the Daily Republic. Used with permission.

When the coaches came down to talk to us I hoped to draw strength from their words. Coach Bev had taught us well and after ten games he knew we wouldn't quit on him. The look in their eyes and the tone of their voices said they wanted to battle alongside us. The game had never left them. They were still football players.

Folsom is tough but you're better. Believe in yourselves and each other. Fight to that last whistle, and play as one. It's your game. Take it, they told us. Those few words were revealing and strengthening. They were exactly what we needed to hear.

As we bowed our heads for prayer I felt a brotherhood with the 32 Vikings suited around me. They were my teammates and had been my friends for years. It was only fitting to fight our toughest battle together.

As we exited the locker room door and pounded the partition with our clenched fists, the echoing of the metal warned Folsom we were headed their way.

Our 66 cleats and 66 hands worked in unison thundering as we moved towards the George Gammon Field. There wasn't much light along our path as we moved. It made us appear like a giant shadow devouring its way to the stadium.

We hit the grass jogging to warm up. Our voices barked our movements. We wanted the Bulldogs to hear us. It was our gridiron they were standing on, and we wanted to remind them of that fact.

As we broke off into our groups, I expected the butterflies and adrenalin to collide in my throat. I jogged towards the visitor end zone to do our scrambling. Coach Kiefer was waiting on us.

Familiar faces caught my eye, and I looked towards the four-foot chain-link fence that surrounded the football field and track. There stood my brothers Sean, Tim, and Craig, and most of their friends. My buddy Pete Watts was there with some of our classmates.

It caught me off guard. I could see us four brothers as little boys opening presents on Christmas morning, and when we went to the Grand Canyon as a family. I remembered wiping sweat from Craig's forehead when he was young, as he slept with fever. I remembered looking up to Sean and Tim and wanting to be like them. We were close growing up and along the way we grew apart after dad left. I wasn't sure how many football games they and their friends had gone to during our season. I never noticed. They were here now, as my teammates and I faced our toughest test. They knew Folsom was undefeated and ranked third in the state.

For the second time in five seasons of football and twice in three games, tears welled up. They streamed down the side of my face and my throat choked. Not from that sour taste that was all too common but from pride. My brothers were there to support my friends and me. I told myself I wouldn't let them down. I realized I was from the perfect broken family. Their presence said it.

As we walked to the center of the field for the coin toss, Bulldogs approached us. Their helmets showed their skills. They were covered in stickers. So were ours. It was an intense first encounter. Our looks warned them we came to play and there was a reason we were 10-0. They would soon understand how we honored the game.

The grass on the field was wet from rainstorms. It

was going to be a slippery muddy game. In five seasons my friends and I had played in every type of weather. We were ready for anything Mother Nature would pull.

Both Folsom and us punted back and forth a few times, and in the second quarter we got on the board first. A 14-yard catch by Darren and then a 29-yard diving catch by Eric brought us within one yard of Folsom's end zone. Ronnie took the ball up the middle for the score, and Dave Haupt's extra point gave us a 7-0 lead.

We broke for halftime still leading. Coach Bev told us to keep playing our game. Jeff, Baro, Big Joe, Chris, and I talked about our shock of seeing a full beard on the Folsom nose guard. He was one of the toughest Jeff had faced all year, and Jeff would give him a fight. Folsom's defensive and offensive lines were tenacious. The battle in the trenches was what we expected: challenging.

The field was less slippery in the second half but more muddy. One play during pass protection they blitzed their middle linebacker. As I went to pick him up I glanced over at Big Joe. He had just knocked the defensive tackle down and turned and leveled their defensive end. He manhandled them both. After the play was over I had to tell him I saw what he did, and I slapped him on his helmet. Big Joe's moxie was highlighted with that one play. Two on one and he prevailed.

In the fourth quarter we got on the scoreboard again with 10:44 left in the game, when we intercepted a Folsom pass and then drove 49 yards. Bryan took the ball in for paydirt from five yards out. We extended our lead to 14-0.

During the drive I took a helmet in the groin. I was

not wearing a cup. As I lay on the ground trying to catch my breath the team had begun to huddle. I heard that voice I knew all too well yell, "Get up you pussy!" It was Baro—and his voiced seemed to carry. As I stood it was quiet in the stands. I knew everyone had heard Mark's outburst. That was our trench crew: Man up, or you would hear about it. Mark made sure I heard about it in a very loud public fashion.

Mark and I were called upon to pull and trap often. The call came for Mark to trap on the defensive tackle lined up against Joe and me. When the ball was hiked, I went for their middle linebacker, Joe took the defensive end, and the tackle was let free to penetrate in the backfield. Mark came along the line fast and hit him hard, knocking him down. The hit was so loud it seemed to echo in the open stadium. It was impossible not to hear the collision, as Mark buried Folsom's star defensive lineman.

Bryan scored another touchdown in the fourth quarter only to have it called back on a holding penalty by me. (I felt like I let him down.) When the clock ticked down ending the game we held our lead and won 14-0.

Our defense spearheaded by Glenn, Danny, and Sherman—our Orient Express—stepped up and shut down Folsom. It was the first time all season that the Bulldogs hadn't put points on the scoreboard. Our defense held their offense to 77 total yards with only 36 on the ground. We had 281 total yards, with 189 on the ground. Bryan rushed for 136 yards against the Bulldogs.

We scored 16 first downs to Folsom's 6, and they only penetrated into our territory four times. The closest they got to our end zone was our 26-yard line.

That Friday, Nov. 16th 1984, we faced one of the best football teams in California—and in the country—holding them scoreless and giving up only 77 yards.

When we walked off the gridiron that night we were one opponent away from the championship title, and one game from another undefeated season. Thankfully we were injury-free. We broke another Vanden football record, winning the most games in a season, 11.

The team and coaches were ecstatic. We were wet and covered in mud but we didn't care. That was football and it was why we played the game. In the locker room it was a madhouse. Mud covered the tile on the floor and it was so loud you needed ear plugs. Players were thrown in the showers with their uniforms on.

The ride home to Vacaville included a cold roof trip. We were Vikings, we were name takers, and we were stuntmen.

Unbeaten Vanden blanks Folsom

Vanden defense had flawless outing

Vikes need 1 more win for crown

The above images are from articles courtesy of the Daily Republic. Used with permission.

The above images are from articles courtesy of the Daily Republic. Used with permission. The top photo shows Big Joe, Darren, Murdock, and Derrick; the bottom shows Stephen (canoli) after our victory.

"The defensive line was a big factor," the senior explained. "The ends were coming in hard pushing to the inside and the defensive backs and linebackers were able to slide in."

Bulldog quarterback James Murdock decided to crank up a long pass.

That turned out to be the mistake of the contest.

Vanden defensive lineman John McClellan came crashing through to belt Murdock as he got his pass away

One in particular was late in the fourth period when Murdock scrambled out of the pocket only to meet Vanden's Glenn Kelly and Cliff Roberts head-on in a ferocious hit that sent the crowd buzzing for minutes afterwards.

"Hitting had a lot to do with it," Kelly said of Vanden's tough defense. "We started shooting different holes in the second half, switching from a 5-2 to a 5-3 (alignments)."

The above three images are from articles courtesy of the Daily Republic. Used with permission.

Vanden yardstick

Folsom	0	0	0	0—0
Vanden	0	7	0	7—14

V — Beverly 1 run (Haupt kick)
V — Batchan 6 run (Haupt kick)

	F	V
First downs	6	16
Rushes-yards	26-36	51-189
Passing yards	41	92
Return yards	73	24
Passes	5-17-1	6-12-0
Punts	5-32	3-21
Fumbles-lost	4-4	4-4
Penalties-yards	2-20	4-30

INDIVIDUAL STATISTICS

RUSHING — Folsom-Staley 6-15, Theis 5-12, Duffy 2-7, Murdock 3-2. Vanden-Beverly 20-24, Gwinn 7-29, Batchan 24-136.

PASSING — Folsom-Murdock 5-17-1—41. Vanden-Beverly 6-12-0—92.

RECEIVING — Folsom-Briscoe 2-28, Oreno 2-18, Staley 1-(-5). Vanden-Pruitt 2-22, Rysden 1-14, Barnes 1-29, DeForge 1-14, Gwinn 1-13.

The above two images are from articles courtesy of the Daily Republic. Used with permission. The photo shows J-p #68 and Danny #63, left, stopping Folsom's run.

The above two images are from articles courtesy of the Daily Republic. Used with permission. The top photo shows DeWayne Quinn #28 and Dave Haupt #17 making a tackle against a Folsom player. The bottom photo shows us on offense with Ronnie about to pass. (L to R) Ronnie, Joe, me (losing my balance), Maurice, Mark, and Chris are shown.

Vikings stretch record to 11-0

The above image is from an article title courtesy of the Reporter.

The above photo shows Maurice and Ronnie celebrating our 11th win from an article courtesy of the Reporter.

The above hand-drawn image of Glenn is courtesy of the Daily Republic. Used with permission.

It was five years in the making for us and twenty-one years for Coach Bev. We grew up together from ages 13 to 18 through junior high and high school. We had seen good times and bad. We had been chased by cops for no reason, and defeated many opponents on the football field. Some of us had nicknames, and we were the best of friends.

Coach Bev started his journey as a senior at Vanden when it first opened and he returned a few years later to start his coaching career. He coached on the JV level, and then became only the second skipper in the school's history to lead the varsity football program.

We worked hard as friends to learn the game and along the way we became unstoppable as teammates. We were taught to be relentless and to sacrifice our bodies to stop our opponents' forward progress. We listened well and earned a reputation as 'No Names.' No one really knew who we were because we were from an Air Force school with about 600 students.

No city claimed us, so we didn't get the sports coverage the Fairfield Falcons, the Armijo Indians, or the Vacaville Bulldogs received. Yet none of their programs were 11-0 or had seen perfect seasons in decades—or ever. After we entered the playoffs undefeated and their seasons ended, we started receiving extra coverage. We were still No Names and that was okay with us. We weren't looking for the limelight. We wanted a championship and the memories that would come with capturing it.

All the coaches worked as hard as we did. Every coach each season poured his heart into the squads. They made us into the football players we became. We followed their direction and became mirrors of them.

Coach Bev got up early and worked hard to change the program in three short years. He braved the heat, winds, cold, and rain with us. As we were sweating, coaches Bev, Noos, and Kiefer were sweating. When we got wet from rains, they got wet, too. We were in it together. Each hard hit they felt and each block they assisted. They ran the ball in for a TD or caught the pass for a score. Their eyes saw the view through our facemasks.

We were shades of green and gold. We were vegetable soup and Air Force brats. Our 1984 team was a lot like the 1980 Redskins. We both were unique and made better by new additions. Guys like Danny Miller and Cliff Roberts made our roster, and they were standouts. Danny came onto the squad and earned the middle linebacker position. That was no easy task. It took a tough kid to shut down the run up the gut and punish opponents ruthlessly. Danny did that job well. In our opening game against Galt, Cliff single-handily helped us prevail. He made a kickoff runback look like a beautiful painting, not on a canvas but on a field of grass. Cliff not only could run well with the ball he could deliver crushing hits. We were better because of them.

I didn't blame the game for my injury. I knew it was an unfortunate accident. I had been involved with 50 games during my career and had watched easily 50 more at Vanden. I followed all the local schools' play and watched professional and college football. I never saw or don't remember seeing or hearing of a football player being knocked unconscious as long as I had been. I didn't blame the Dixon player who leveled me. I knew that hit, that one moment in time, had shortened my football career and altered my life. What happened to me was rare. I also knew things happened for a reason. I was just thankful to have these twelve games with my buddies. I knew one day as an old man the memories of this season would still bring a smile and a longing to do it again. Who could ask for more? I couldn't.

Just one game left, four quarters and only 48 minutes of play, and we would see the end to our journey. Our last chapter would be written on the gridiron in Hilmar, California. By bus it would take us about 2.5 hours, the longest we had traveled since our trip down south for the Redskins in 1980. Like Oak Ridge and Folsom, Hilmar was going to be a hard-fought game. They stood at 10-1, winning ten straight after losing their season opener. They had outscored their opponents 283 to 77. We were coming into the contest outscoring ours 281-117. Hilmar was also ranked #8 in the state.

I didn't know much about the Hilmar Yellowjackets—except they were our last roadblock. I had never heard of their town and really didn't know where it was located. That didn't matter much, though. I knew they had kids like me looking back on their football careers and thirsting for the title. They wanted to be the top team in the Sac-Joaquin Section. Only one of us could claim it.

All week felt like waiting for high noon to arrive. There was no escaping the confrontation Friday night. We were forced into a showdown, but it was one we had been wanting for a long time. We wanted to see who the best was. We knew the answer but we wanted history to record it. Those .0089 odds were about to be beaten.

All my teammates were born to be football players. The game was successful because of guys like them. They were entertainers who awed and wooed the crowds. Football wasn't an easy sport. It took guts, a little bit of craziness, and a lot of heart. It was a bone-crushing game where injuries would happen and lifelong friendships were made. It tested emotions and brought happiness or heartache. Not everyone could win but everyone could play like winners. Life lessons were taught and teenagers were molded into men.

When I finally saw the movie Porky's I realized we were those characters. We did the same type of high jinks not knowing they were doing them on screen. We didn't have criminal intent, just wild mischievous personalities that had to flourish. We were good kids with good hearts. We didn't know life had plans for us. It picked our small group and said we were destined to take names on the gridiron. We heard its plan and followed its blueprints.

How I went from an Altar Boy and Boy Scout to this personality on the football field I really didn't know. I knew when I shelved my shoulder pads and helmet for the last time, Psycho was going to be buried. There was no place for him outside the gridiron. He was created there and would stay there. As my feet left the grass for the last time he and I would part ways.

I was feeling the itch for our final battle. I was sure my buddies and coaches were feeling the same. I knew Coach Bev wanted to see how our time together would end, and he wanted it to be glorious. He had been a football player once. Every kid who ever wore shoulder pads wanted what we were about to achieve.

Vikes one game away from perfect season

Beverly keeps the champagne on ice

"A big part of our success this season can be correlated to that jayvee team two years ago," he said. "I could see the nucleus of a good varsity team forming."

One game away from perfection...

Above three images from a midweek article courtesy of the Reporter.

Vikes battle Hilmar Friday

Perfect season on line as Vanden travels to Hilmar

Friday's game will also feature a pair of rugged defenses. Hilmar allows an average of seven points per game, Vanden 10.6. Hilmar will be trying to slow down a Viking offense that is averaging 25.5 points per contest.

Above three images from articles courtesy of the Daily Republic. Used with permission.

Vanden's Kelly is a hitter

J.P. SMITH, Vanden football — The senior defensive right end had three solo tackles and three assists against the Bulldogs, and "he turned their offense the other way," according to Beverly. "They started out the game running to his side, but he made them go to the other side."

DANNY MILLER, Vanden football — The senior middle linebacker had three solo tackles and seven assists in the Folsom game. "He was just everywhere on defense," said Beverly.

Can Vikes beat 'Oak Ridge' again?
TVL champ Hilmar bears certain resemblance to earlier Viking foe

Vikes suit up for section title game

Above four images from articles courtesy of the Daily Republic. Used with permission.

Both teams can definitely put points on the scoreboard — Hilmar has scored 283 in 11 games, Vanden 281. Hilmar has the better numbers on defense, allowing just 77 points to Vanden's 117.

Above image is from an article courtesy of the Daily Republic. Used with permission.

Vikes go after section title tonight

"This type of season only comes along once in a lifetime," said Vanden Head Coach Ron Beverly. "Nobody remembers the second place team, so we're going to see if we can't go out and do it."

"We've been lucky to have no serious injuries this season. Being lucky and good sort of works together," Beverly said. There is no doubt we're good, but we're a little lucky too."

The above three images are from an article courtesy of the Reporter.

The above photo shows Danny Miller #63 making the tackle with Glenn Kelly #33 about to assist. Baro is seen in the background moving in to help. Photo from an article courtesy of the Reporter.

There was an allure towards them, and the atmosphere was unlike anything I had experienced prior to playing football. Those huddles with my teammates before a play drew me in. They reinforced why I needed the game. The aura in those few seconds between plays was like preparing to face an enemy in battle. It was a war without guns, and we were the weapons. We weren't fighting for a country decided by diplomats; but fighting over a pigskin between schools. Each play made us more hardened and battle-tested.

    Breaking the huddle and going to the line of scrimmage and seeing all the visuals in front of me and peripherally—of our opponents and my teammates wearing helmets and shoulder pads—was intense. It was an adrenaline rush each time I got in my three-point or four-point stance on offense or defense. My fingers in the grass, feet ready to push off, while my heart pounded away waiting for the snap of the ball. Sometimes it came within a few seconds and others it seemed like hours. When the ball moved there would be hard collisions of raw brute force slamming together. Arms pushing and legs driving forward; jarring head slaps and forearm rips. Noises and grunts filling the air. That feeling and experience was worth its weight in gold. It's why the game had a hold on me. Maybe it is why I became a different personality on the field also. As I thought about those images, I knew I couldn't wait for those huddles against Hilmar.

When I awoke that Friday morning I wondered what that night would bring. Would we win or lose? I didn't know. I knew for certain, though, it was the last day I would play football with my friends, and the last time I would suit up to step on the gridiron. I was determined to do my best that evening because those memories would stay with me. I still remembered my brother Sean's regret. I knew I didn't want to feel his pain of wishing for a do-over or another chance.

The team and cheerleaders were going to travel on our bus, with two more carrying support staff, students, and some fans. Parents and other classmates were going to follow us there. As we loaded our equipment under the bus that afternoon, and I saw all the cars preparing to follow us, it mirrored our trip with the Redskins to play for the California State Championship.

As we left Vanden, Coach Kiefer joined us trenchers sitting in the back of the bus. Talk was little most of the way. Not sure why. Maybe nerves, maybe mental preparation, maybe no one wanted to jinx us. I still believed in those jinxes, and we were facing a hard game as it was, without being branded with some bad luck before the opening kickoff.

The prolonged bus ride gave me time to prepare and reminisce. I had become David Smith. I fell for Baro's taunt and it didn't end well for me. "Screw that! Just head to Joe's! Take a left instead of a U-turn. They won't follow us," he said. But Mark was wrong. We were headed to the gym the previous Sunday, and I left my military dependent ID card at home. The guard at the front gate wouldn't let us through. I was instructed to drive forward and turnaround and exit the base. Listening to Mark I took a left and sped to Big Joe's. I drove as fast as I could hoping the base police didn't see us and wouldn't pursue.

I parked at Joe's house and we hid in his backyard. There we stood peering through the fence as a patrol unit stopped in front. Oh crap! I thought. We were caught. Baro was let go because he was the passenger, but I was taken back to the front gate. My dad was contacted and told what happened.

It took him three years and three tries. Our Wile E. Coyote and Road Runner chase was finally over. Cathy's dad had caught me. He won and I lost.

"How long were you going to workout at the gym?" I was asked by one of the guards. I told him three hours. I was then cuffed with my hands behind my back and stood at the front gate on display for all the incoming cars and their occupants to see. For three hours I stood there. Then I was let go. I had learned my lesson never to fall for one of Mark's taunts again or run from the base police.

We finally arrived at Hilmar. As we exited the bus I looked around. This is where it would all end. The

Yellowjackets had a nice school. In some ways it reminded me of Vanden.

As I walked with my teammates and coaches into the locker room to dress, I knew I couldn't have a better group of friends to battle alongside.

I knew I wouldn't put pads on again, so I wanted to take my time doing it. As I sat there I wondered what had happened to my black-padded gloves that I wanted so badly and bought at the end of my freshman year. I loved those gloves, and they worked their magic—we went undefeated and unscored-upon.

Tuck took my helmet to air it and when he handed it back to me, I took my mouthpiece in my hand. There would be no more boiling and molding a new one to fit my teeth. I looked around at my friends. Tomorrow this all would be no more. I glanced over at Chris. He would have to play without us next season. Chris, Ronnie, Eugene, Derrick, Louis, DeWayne, Sherman Pruitt, Stephen, Rob, and Scott Sherman would be on their own. We would be a memory. Let's make it a good memory then, Psycho whispered to me.

I was surprised I wasn't nervous. The butterflies left me alone, and I felt content, like after eating a full meal. We had fun these past eleven games and during Hell Week. I saw my friends do some amazing things during the season and it was the best time of my life. I couldn't have felt more content; except now I was ready for dessert and the Yellowjackets would do.

Coaches Bev, Noos, and Kiefer walked to the front of the room. Twenty-one years after graduating from Vanden and achieving a milestone for the varsity football program, Coach Bev still looked like he could play on the gridiron. Noos kept the weight off and looked lean. Losing that extra baggage had given him so much energy. Coach Kiefer looked like a large statue when he stood, because he stood so straight all the time. He was sporting a freshly cut flat top and looked like a trencher coach.

Coach Bev's eyes carried the great speech and his words said everything we had waited five years to hear. He believed in us. "You're the team of destiny. You have the opportunity to show how good you are and history will remember this game and how you fought here as friends. Make it glorious and grab greatness. It's yours. Take it!" He then looked at each one of us and said, "Make it memorable so no one ever forgets Vanden or its Vikings." Coach Bev's words couldn't have sounded more uplifting and true. They galvanized the squad's soul. Those impassioned words reflected what our battle against Hilmar truly meant. It was much more than a contest of which team was better. It was about being remembered for never quitting; for trusting in each other; and playing like each play was our last. It was about honoring the game. We then took a knee for our final prayer as a team and stood strengthened.

We left the locker room and didn't pound on the partition. It wasn't ours. The sound of our pads being slapped and our cleats told them we were coming. It was getting cold out, and the field looked ready for our battle. Bryan stated he thought he could run well on it. I hoped he was right. We needed his best. When Bryan delivered, we couldn't be stopped.

I could see many of our fans had traveled the long

distance to support us. Our cheerleaders were there like a shadow following its host. They didn't walk behind us, though. They led with their spirit. They were the best, and we were lucky to have them because they made us look good and play better.

I saw Jeff's, Chris's, and Bryan's parents, and many more. Broyce was there, along with my brothers and some of their friends. My pride swelled. Coaches Hatcher and Ordez from the JV team were on the sidelines. Ten of their best players from their undefeated squad were brought up to bolster our team for the playoffs. They were there to give us depth in case of injuries. The Hilmar Yellowjackets had to face our combined 20-0 winning squads.

Unlike us, most of the Hilmar players taped their arms and hands without wearing pad protection. It was an old-school look. We looked different. We had taken precautions and padded up. Those pads had kept us healthy throughout the season and brought us face to face that evening. It was obvious they had their own hitters by the stickers on their helmets. We would have to play our best to win. The demeanor of the Orient Express warned the Yellowjackets not to test their resolve.

It was a high noon showdown at center field. It didn't disappoint. Stares and glares from both sides cautioned of the violence that was coming. Pain would be abundant. The coin toss was thick with testosterone.

After the kickoff, in the first quarter Glenn intercepted a Yellowjacket pass. Our offense capitalized and drove 33 yards and scoring our first points from a 22-yard TD pass from Ronnie to Eric. Our extra point missed and we led 6-0. As hard as they tried they were unsuccessful. We stopped Hilmar on offense and forced punts. We maintained our lead through the first period. In the second quarter we scored again with 11:03 left in the half, when Maurice bounced off players and rambled 40 yards into the end zone. Ronnie passed to Eric for a two-point conversion and we widened our lead to 14-0.

Periodically I would glance over at the sidelines. If he wasn't in on defense Murdock was playing his character to the hilt. Spectators from both sides were given a show. He would flap his arms like he was going to fly onto the field, or he could be heard yelling at the Yellowjackets that he was coming soon and they better be prepared. Murdock's style was different than mine but I had to smile at his antics. He made our final game together memorable. We had been Redskins and Vikings together. He saved my brother Tim's life. I owed John a lot and knew it. He was one hell of a football player and a better friend.

John playing his 'Murdock' character to the hilt during the Hilmar game. Both images taken from the 1985 Vanden yearbook. Photo courtesy of Travis Unified School District and Vanden High School.

Every attempt by Hilmar to move the ball successfully, our defense stepped up and shut them down. They had few third down conversions. We went into the locker room at halftime with our two TD advantage.

Continue to play your game, Coach Bev told us. Coach Kiefer commended the trench crew for taking the fight to Hilmar, and Coach Noos was happy with the big hitting by our defensive squad.

In the third quarter DeWayne recorded an interception. After forcing another Hilmar punt late in the third period we took the ball 31 yards. Bryan ran in for our third score from 11 yards out, with 1:31 left in the period. Ronnie attempted a two-point conversion pass but it was knocked down. The scoreboard read 20-0.

We continued to maintain our lead over halfway through the fourth period. For 90 minutes we had played flawless football against two of the best football teams in California, Folsom and Hilmar, holding them scoreless.

Then it happened: Ronnie was stripped of the ball on a quarterback option by Hilmar, and they recovered it on our 17-yard line. Five plays later they scored on a one-yard run. They tried to run for a two-point conversion but we buried their running back before he could score. They had closed the gap to 20-6.

Hilmar kicked off to us and on our fourth play from scrimmage Bryan fumbled a pitch out from Ronnie, and Hilmar players jumped on it. They took over on our 37-yard line. The game was turning quickly on our two costly mistakes. On the very next play, Hilmar burst through the line and ran 37 yards for their second score, with 4:25 left in the game. Their two-point conversion pass was good.

They moved within six points of us at 20-14.

We were always a second-half team, so our dominance most of the game had caused us to let down our guard. Hilmar exploited it, and we were starting to panic. In the offensive huddle Ronnie and I told the guys to take a deep breath. We would be alright. We were Vikings.

All game, our defense had made big hits and big plays. Our offense had powered over the Yellowjackets, and the contest between the two of us was ours to lose. We weren't going to let that happen.

I knew my football career was coming to an end. As we huddled and went to the line of scrimmage, my five years on the gridiron with my friends as a Viking and Redskin flashed before my eyes. All those wind sprints and gassers, hitting the sled, three-a-day practices during Hell Week, the sweat, the vomit, the pain, the cages, my time with 'Maniac' and our championship game with the Redskins played out. Those scenes gave me strength and conviction.

Chris, Baro, Jeff, Big Joe, and I had played our hearts out. We had been hitting and blocking Hilmar's defense aggressively and moving downfield to chase their linebackers and cornerbacks. That wasn't going to stop.

During our first two plays we moved the ball some. On the third play, on Jeff's snap, I fired off and hit their middle linebacker. He was a tough kid. His arms and hands were protected only by tape. Mine were padded. I wore a special helmet. He didn't. We locked horns and battled. His years of experience on the gridiron were being tested against mine. We both were determined to best the other. He spun right, then tried left. All I could think of were those dreaded sleds with driving your legs, and the name Coach Hatcher gave me as a freshman: 'Psycho.' I pushed and he spun, and we fought until the whistle blew.

    I broke off left from the linebacker towards our sidelines to head back to the huddle. I saw him as my head turned. Kiefer was staring at me. He had followed on the sidelines as I pushed the linebacker back about 12 yards. Our eyes locked just momentarily, and he nodded his head a little and smiled. He didn't say anything, and I went to the huddle. I knew in that moment words weren't necessary. I had fought to the last whistle and his nod said it all. I had heard Coach Kiefer say a thousand times, "To the last whistle!" And I honored that.

    We came up short on that play and had to punt. After the kick I was pulled from the game. I stood on the sidelines next to Coach Kiefer as my friends battled the last few minutes. I was given one last opportunity to watch them, and they looked like champions. I knew I couldn't hide it anymore—I was their biggest fan.

    Hilmar attempted a pass and it was intercepted by us. Less than a minute was left in the game. We huddled on offense sweating, covered in dirt and grass and smiling. All those perfect practices had brought us here. Coach Bev was right. They would make us champions. We knew we were seconds away from the title we had chased for so long. Forty-eight minutes of bruising battle and one play left. Just one. Five seasons of chasing a dream and it all came down to this last moment. All sorts of emotions were spinning inside of me. My stomach felt like it was in a blender. Excitement, sadness, and fear for what came after the last second ticked off the clock.

There were no more challengers we would face. No more victories to win. I was anything but calm.

I looked around at my friends in the huddle. They were seasoned but worn. There was Baro's tilt and glare staring back at me. I had to chuckle a little. He still looked cool. Big Joe put his arm around me. He was tired, too. I felt small standing next to him. Chris looked like he could go four more quarters. He probably could. I knew Jeff had one last huddle in his voice. Bryan still had that piercing look in his eyes. It was intimidating. Maurice had that beaming look like his dad at our Sunday sermons. Big E gave me his gratuitous nod. I needed it. Ronnie looked like our leader preparing for that final whistle. We clasped hands for our final play. Eleven friends holding hands like an iron chain—yet we were stronger. We broke the huddle, went to the line of scrimmage, and Ronnie took a knee at the whistle. We ran out the clock and won 20-14.

Our last chapter was written, and its end brought happiness with our long-awaited victory and championship and sadness, because I would never play with my friends again. Teammates, coaches, fans, and family spilled onto the field. It was a grand sight and a fitting picture to end our journey. We did it again as Vikings. I had been given one final time to play with my friends, and we had one last chance to win that title and secure another undefeated season. We met those goals together.

I lingered on the field by myself. I was one of the last to leave because I knew I was going to miss the feel of that grass under my feet. I needed that moment. I was leaving an ally, a mentor, and a confidant. I had bonded with the gridiron. I made a promise to my mom I had to keep. I knew I would never again put on shoulder pads or see that view through a facemask. The game would always be a part of me, but it was time to say goodbye. I was leaving my first love, and I was losing my identity. I felt empty.

The bond I built with my teammates and coaches was going to last a lifetime. We had accomplished something special together, which few football players get to experience: an undefeated season. Not once but three times. I would never again see Bryan run over and drag defenders. I would never witness Glenn crush running backs, and I would never battle in the trenches with Jeff, Baro, Big Joe, Chris, Murdock, and the others. I was going to miss battling alongside them. I wore the trench scars proudly. During those five years I saw the most amazing things on the field and off. We shared many laughs and emotional times together. We were teammates but we became much more. We became brothers. We were a family. There was a saying at Vanden, "Once a Vike, always a Vike." As I walked off the gridiron for the very last time, I told myself, we would always be Vikes, teammates, and brothers. The sound of my cleats against the asphalt consoled me as I walked alone.

When I entered the locker room, cases of sparkling cider awaited, while 'We are the Champions' by Queen blared loudly on a looped tape, echoing throughout the room. There were my Viking and Redskin teammates, there was our Triple Threat Backfield, there were our Orient Express linebackers, there was my close-knit trench crew, and there were my friends and coaches celebrating. They were standing on the benches and singing in unison. It was intoxicating.

Coaches Bev, Noos, and Kiefer looked like they were standing in the maternity ward viewing their sons for the first time. Their smiles were a mile wide. Coach Bev's vision for the program was perfect. He turned the worst record in Vanden's varsity football history to the best in three years. He would be remembered not for that 1-5-3 record but for leading our 1984 team to a 12-0 undefeated season and the Sac-Joaquin Section championship. He proved he was the coach to beat. He was Mr. Football, and I owed him a debt of gratitude. He gave me a gift—one more season with my friends.

I knew I was going to miss that moment and those guys. I wanted to hit the pause button and stop time so that feeling would never end. I knew soon it would only be a memory. As I walked through the locker room an older brother came up and handed me a bottle of champagne. He had about a dozen bottles and handed them out to the trench crew, Glenn, Bryan, Maurice, and Ronnie.

I walked to the showers and turned on one to warm water. I took off my air helmet Coach Bev and Vanden had purchased for me, and I placed it at my feet. I stepped under the shower in uniform, wearing everything but the helmet, and I opened that bottle of champagne shooting the cork into the air. I was toasting those odds. We beat them and we were the best. My friends' smiles, laughter, and joy mixing with the music, drowned me in emotions. It was hard to keep it together. I almost lost it. As I tipped that bottle straight into the air I closed my eyes. The water poured over my head, down my back and under my shoulder pads. It calmed me.

Conclusion

My eyes started to focus on the Vanden scoreboard. I saw movement to my left and glanced over. The Vikings were warming up on the gridiron. They looked like name takers.

My eyes scanned them. Where was Bryan? I didn't see Glenn, David, Big Joe, Baro, Ronnie, Murdock, or Chris. That wasn't Jeff snapping the ball. I turned to the sidelines. Where was Coach Bev? That wasn't Kiefer or Noos either.

A somber mood came over me. That wasn't us on the field.

David and Mrs. Valmore were still talking. I didn't turn my head towards them. Mrs. Valmore stated she and the old teachers missed us kids from the 1980's. It was a good era, she continued.

I agreed with her. I missed it too, I thought to myself. Those were amazing days.

At some point every person wishes they could go back to when they were younger. As I stood there silently, I realized I just had. It brought a smile and a tear. I could still see that long-ago era. It was the time of Vikings, friends, and family.

Vikes cap perfect season with 20-14 victory over Hilmar

"The dream has been fulfilled. I am speechless for the first time," said Beverly who led Vanden to its first section crown since 1975.

The Vikings played flawless ball in the first three quarters, rolling to a 20-0 lead, but two fourth-quarter fumbles brought the Yellowjackets new life.

The above two images are from an article courtesy of the Reporter.

Section title for Vanden

Vikes stiffen when Hilmar comes back

The above two titles are from articles courtesy of the Daily Republic. Used with permission.

"We knew two years ago with could win this thing," said senior lineman Jeff Rooney. "We went undefeated as sophomores and we knew that we had a chance to win it all this year."

The above image is from an article courtesy of the Daily Republic. Used with permission.

The wait is over

Vanden's miracle season will certainly be remembered

The above two images are from an article courtesy of the Reporter. Bryan is shown running over one Hilmar player, while he drags another. The photo shows the 'piercing look' in Bryan's eyes.

The above photo is from an article courtesy of the Reporter. The team is shown celebrating our Hilmar win. In the photo Sherman Pruitt #84, David Reyes #24, Dave Haupt, and Paul Holes (not in uniform) are shown with some of the ten JV players brought up from their 9-0 undefeated squad, to give us depth in case of injuries.

"It's a once-in-a-lifetime thing," said senior fullback Maurice Gwinn Friday night after the Vikings' 20-14 victory over Hilmar in the section championship game. "We worked hard all season, and it really paid off.

The above image of Maurice's quote is from an article courtesy of the Daily Republic. Used with permission.

The above photo shows the team celebrating our Hilmar win. Mark 'Baro' Baranowski #64 is seen upper left, Derrick Davis #71 center, John 'Murdock' McClellan #65 top center, David Smith #60 right, with some of the ten JV players who were brought up from their 9-0 undefeated squad, to give us depth in case of injuries. Below, Coach Bev is shown right after our Sac-Joaquin Championship victory. Both photos courtesy of Travis Unified School District and Vanden High School.

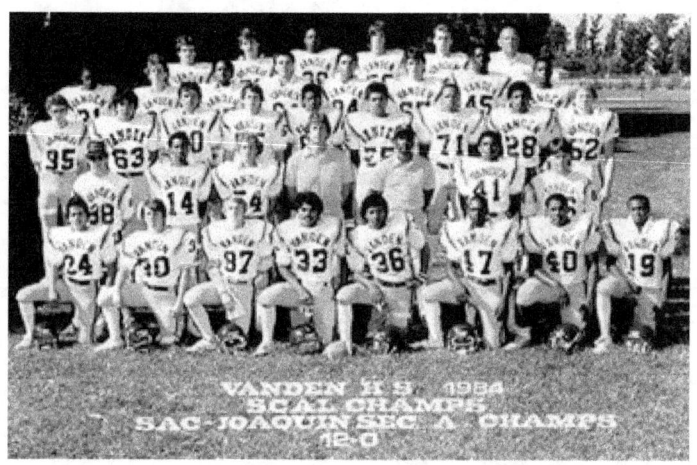

The 1984 Vanden Viking championship team consisted of 33 players, 3 coaches, and 3 captains. The Viking squad of name takers went 12-0 winning their Sac-Joaquin Section and SCAL league, and were ranked #2 in the state of California by Cal-Hi Sports. The linebacker trio known as 'The Orient Express' led the charge to hold opposing teams to 132 total points between them during the 12-game season. The trench crew averaged 186 lbs. The heaviest player on the 1984 Vanden football team was the fullback at 204 lbs.

1/28/2014: Coach Bev's assessment of '84—Great season! Outstanding student leadership and athletes, team unity, desire to win, skilled athletes at the right positions, not big linemen but tenacious competitors, a coaching staff that realized early on what this team was capable of, a strong supporting staff of stat girls and cheerleaders, a student body, parents, and an administration that supported this amazing team.

Above photos taken and provided by Timothy O'Donnell #69, co-captain of the 1984 undefeated Vanden JV 9-0 team. Use courtesy of Vanden High School.

COACHES

Ronald 'Bev' Beverly
Head and Offense

Tom 'Noos' Newsom
Defense

Tom 'Kief' Kiefer
Trench Crew

CAPTAINS

Ron Beverly, Jr. #10
Offense

Glenn (Kelly) Barretto #33
Defense

Jeff Rooney #55
Trench Crew

TTB—TRIPLE THREAT BACKFIELD

Ron Beverly, Jr. #10
Quarterback
1760 total yards:
1100 passing—13 TDs
660 rushing—10 TDs

Maurice Gwinn #40
Fullback
734 total yards:
640 rushing —7 TDs
94 receiving

Bryan Batchan #47
Tailback
1759 total yards:
1539 rushing—13 TDs
220 receiving—3 TDs

'ORIENT EXPRESS' LINEBACKERS

Glenn (Kelly) Barretto #33
Leader, Left side

Danny Miller #63
Middle

Sherman Pruitt #84
Right side

TRENCH CREW

[Head Coach and Offensive Coach]

Ronald 'Bev' Beverly

(Coach Spotlight) - Ronald 'Bev' Beverly

Coach Bev was in his third year of leading the Vanden varsity squad in 1984. He was an alumnus of Vanden and a former standout athlete there. Coach Bev played on Vanden's very first football team in 1964, and he scored the very first touchdown for the school. His son, Ron Beverly, Jr., was our starting quarterback on the undefeated championship team. From a player's perspective, Coach Bev was Mr. Football. He was a student of the game and a master of developing a football team. Coach Bev was our mentor who taught the players values that mattered off the field. Coach Bev stressed hustling, aggression, and playing from whistle to whistle. He wanted us to be perfect. Conditioning and perfection were two values he stressed. Under his guidance the 1984 Vanden 12-0 football team was more prepared physically and mentally than any team we faced. That was as a direct result of Coach Bev pushing us. Coach Bev was admired by his players because, though he was firm, he was always fair. In 1984, we couldn't have had a better coach to lead, guide, and mold us into football players, into an undefeated championship team, and into men. He was patient with us when we struggled to learn his offensive scheme even though he demanded perfection. Sometimes we would keep redoing one offensive play a dozen times in a row or more, until we got it perfect. During Hell Week, Coach Bev had us do three-a-day practices versus the two other teams were doing, so we could learn his new offensive and defensive changes. Coach Bev was right: conditioning and perfect practices would make champions. During games he was a steady leader on the sidelines and knew the right interaction with the players to gain the best performance from the team and from each individual player. Coach Bev was Mr. Football and a great skipper. Thanks for the memories, Coach. You took names.

[Defensive Coach]

Tom 'Noos' Newsom - (RIP)

(Coach Spotlight) - Tom 'Noos' Newsom, RIP

I met Coach Noos in 1981. He was part of the track program and oversaw the pole vault, shot, discus, and high jump. I joined the track team because they needed bodies and it sounded like fun. I took an instant liking to Noos. He asked me to start jogging with him, and over a 4-year period throughout the summers and school year, I would jog with him periodically because he struggled with weight issues. Noos was a former standout college football player and had hurt his back. In 1984, he was in his third year of coaching the varsity football team, and he was the defensive coach. He took a fancy to his hard-hitting linebackers. He called them the 'Orient Express,' and they were led by Glenn Barretto. Under the guidance of Noos the defense held the opposing teams to 132 points total during the twelve-game season. During Hell Week, Noos loved standing on the 8-man sled and tormenting us as we pushed it. I think through his snarls I saw a smile as we grunted. We pushed that sled a lot with Noos barking at us. During the 9th game of the 1984 season we were losing at half time. They had a stud of a running back and safety. As we went out after half time and kickoff, Noos motioned me over to the sidelines and told me we needed to stop their tailback. I already knew that, I thought, and Noos looked at me and said, "Stop him." I thought about that as I went back onto the field. His words rang in my ears. I lined up as a nose guard and zeroed in on the tailback because Noos was watching. I hit the tailback and tackled him in the backfield solo. Facemask to facemask I incited him with gridiron talk. He reacted to my words and was removed from the game for unsportsmanlike conduct. We went on to win. That is the relationship I had with Noos. He was my coach and friend. Sadly, we have lost Noos. Thanks for the memories, Coach. You took names.

[Trench Crew Coach]

Tom 'Kief' Kiefer - (RIP)

(Coach Spotlight) - Tom 'Kief' Kiefer, RIP

Kiefer was our trencher coach, the offensive and defensive lines, and our history teacher. He would tease us all the time and had Mark Baranowski, 'Baro,' the starting right guard on the team, fill his two water jugs every day in class because Kiefer was a diabetic and needed to drink lots of fluids. Kiefer liked to razz Baro because they shared a connection—they both had the same birthday. In 1984, Kiefer came out of retirement to coach the trenches. He had previously coached the 1975 Vanden Football Team Section Champions as their line coach, and coached the trenches at Vanden from 1964–1976. Kiefer was a master at what it took to make a good lineman, as he was a trencher during his football career. Coach Kiefer came up with the unusual idea to have the offensive linemen yell out movie-character names as we went to the line of scrimmage and point at the defensive players, as a reminder when we would hike the ball and to confuse the defense, right as the ball was hiked. It gave us an edge. One time out of 10, though, it meant something. We might point at the middle linebacker and all yell the same movie-character name, then we ran right up the gut at him. I doubt it was ever used before or since. Coach Kiefer was a big man but had a bigger heart with his trench crew. He always sat with the trenchers in the back on the bus going to and coming from games. Kiefer coached 2 of the 3 Vanden Section Championship lines. He was our coach, our teacher, mentor, and friend. We lost Kiefer about 15 years ago, sadly. Thanks for the memories, Coach. You took names. Tom Kiefer was an alumnus of the University of San Francisco, where he was the starting right guard and defensive tackle on the football team. The same positions Baro played. At his request, Coach Kiefer's ashes were spread on the 50-yard line of the football field at Vanden when it was still grass.

[Quarterback and Offense Captain]

Ron Beverly, Jr. #10

(Player Spotlight) - Ron Beverly, Jr. #10 - [Offense Captain] - Quarterback, Defensive Back and Specialty Teams. *3-Year Varsity Starter. *Ironman Player. *Two-way Starter. *Leader of the TTB—Triple Threat Backfield

Ronnie was our starting quarterback in 1984 and a captain on the team. His dad, Ronald Beverly, was our Head Coach. Ronnie was a three-year starting varsity quarterback at Vanden. I started playing football with Ronnie in 1982 when he was our freshman quarterback on the undefeated 9-0 and unscored-upon JV football team at Vanden. Ronnie was the all-around best athlete on the team in 1984 because he could throw, run, catch, and stick you so you felt it the next day. Ronnie was fast, and could juke linebackers and defensive backs easily, and he was a nightmare for quarterbacks when playing cornerback. Being a quarterback himself Ronnie could read what an opposing passer might do. In three years (83–85) as the starting varsity quarterback, Ronnie threw for 3476 yards. He is still the 3rd all-time passer at Vanden, in over 50 years of records. Ronnie is also 4th on the list for total yards gained (83–85)—4079—and he is the 3rd for 36 passing touchdowns (83–85). He also holds the 8th and 9th records for single-season passing yards—1205 and 1171—in 83 and 85. In 1984, Ronnie threw for 1100 yards (only because Bryan our tailback and Maurice our fullback were busy eating up the ground game), his lowest of the three seasons he started, and he rushed for 660 yards, combining for 1760 total yards himself. Our final year together Ronnie threw for 13 touchdowns, rushed for another 10 TDs and threw only five interceptions. I once saw Ronnie get hit by three opposing players on their goal line, spin through the air like a helicopter, land straight on his head and twist his neck, then bounce up and trot back to the huddle. Tough as nails. That was Ronnie. Thanks for the memories, Ronnie. You took names.

[Outside Linebacker and Defense Captain]

Glenn (Kelly) Barretto #33

(Player Spotlight) - Glenn Barretto #33 - [Defense Captain] - Outside Linebacker, Specialty Teams, and Place Kick Holder. *Leader of the Orient Express

Glenn was our defensive captain and starting outside linebacker in 1984. His command of the defense held the twelve opposing teams we faced to a total 132 points between them. Glenn could read offenses masterfully and rarely got beat on the gridiron. He was one of best pass defenders we had. Old-school tough name taker. I played football with Glenn for five seasons. Every year Glenn was a starter and a solid leader. He anchored three undefeated football teams in 1980 with the Travis Redskins, 1982 undefeated and unscored-upon JV team and the 1984 12-0 Section Champs. The teams Glenn led went 45-4-2. Glenn was 5'9" and 170 lbs. but his size did not dictate his play. He was fierce and unstoppable, and he hit like a brick wall. As a linebacker Glenn never failed. When he stuck opposing players their dentists were happy for the work. He was a teeth rattler. The linebacker crew Glenn led was known as the 'The Orient Express.' They were punishers. He was the defensive equivalent of Bryan Batchan, in that he took names, plenty of names, and stored them in a very large warehouse. Those who tested Glenn on the field quickly learned the gridiron was his conquest. Off the field Glenn's temperament was 180 degrees different. On the field he was an animal; off the field, he was the nicest guy. Glenn had sure hands, so he was also our place kicker holder. The 1984 Vanden Viking defense squad under Glenn was one of the best in California. On the Travis Redskins in 1980, Glenn rushed for 2458 yards and 33 touchdowns up the gut and over linebackers as our fullback. On our 1984 squad as the anchor of our defense, he devastated running backs. If Glenn hit you, you remembered it the next day. Thanks for the memories, Glenn. You took names.

[Left Guard and Trench Crew Captain]

Jeff Rooney #55

(Player Spotlight) - Jeff Rooney #55, Nickname - 'Psycho' - [Trench Crew Captain] - Left Guard, Defensive Line, and Specialty Teams. *Ironman Player. *Two-way Starter

I was the starting left guard on the 1984 team. I was a captain and the leader of the trench crew, the offensive and defensive lines. I was the second-smallest guy on the offensive line at 5'10", 185 lbs. I started on both sides of the ball and on defense played nose guard and defensive tackle. I began playing football in 1980 on the Travis Redskins, and we went undefeated and played for the CA state championship. I was a starting running back for the Redskins and played defensive end. I played on the 1982 undefeated and unscored-upon Vikings JV team as the right tackle and middle linebacker, and I was blessed to play on the 1984 Vanden Section Champs. The teams, my friends and I played on in 5 years went 45-4-2. My junior season I was the starting left guard and a middle linebacker. Three games into that season, I was seriously injured at Dixon on a blitz from my middle linebacker position. I was knocked unconscious with a head injury and was unable to play again that year. The medical doctors did not want to clear me for my senior season and the school was worried about me incurring another head injury. Vanden and Coach Bev were kind enough to purchase me an 'air helmet' so I could play. It was the first of its kind at Vanden. I will always remember the memories we made in 1984, the friendships, the team, and the play on the gridiron. I was honored and humbled to lead my friends and teammates of the 1984 12-0 Sac-Joaquin Section Champions, ranked #2 in California by Cal-Hi Sports. We took names. My nickname 'Psycho' was given to me in 1981, my freshman year, by the JV Football Coach for my play on the gridiron, and the nickname followed me throughout my years playing football.

[Tailback]

Bryan Batchan #47

(Player Spotlight) - Bryan Batchan #47 - Tailback and Specialty Teams. *Member of the TTB—Triple Threat Backfield

Bryan was one of my favorite players on the gridiron. I played with him for five years, and I always knew that when he was in the backfield and about to get the ball, things would be alright. Our senior year in 1984, Bryan rushed for 1539 yards, 13 touchdowns and had 10 100-plus-yard games. He caught an additional 220 yards in passes and 3 touchdowns, for a total of 1759 combined yards and 16 TDs. During Bryan's career at Vanden he averaged 7.1 yards a carry. In 1984, Bryan was one of the top running backs in California and in the nation. One thing I really liked about Bryan and respected him for is that he wasn't a trash talker on the field. He let his play speak for itself. Bryan would run around defenders, and through defenders, but mostly over them, carrying them as he went. At 5'9", 165 lbs. in 1984 Bryan was a sight to see. He ran a 4.3-second 40-yard dash. He was fast and very hard to take down. Running backs are normally hunted by defensive players but not Bryan. He became the hunter and the 11 guys on defense were the hunted. He was unstoppable. As opposing players went to tackle Bryan he would either stiff arm them or lower his head, causing his helmet to hit their facemask, knocking them on their back, as he literally ran them over. Bryan couldn't be taken down by one player. He played on three undefeated football teams in 5 years with a record of 45-4-2. During each of the three undefeated seasons in 1980, 1982, and 1984, Bryan rushed for over 1000 yards each year. In the five years I was blessed to play football I never saw a more explosive player. Teams would set their defensive strategies to stop him and they usually failed. If not for injuries, Bryan would have had 12 100-plus-yard games in 1984. Thanks for the memories, Bryan. You took names.

[Fullback]

Maurice Gwinn #40

(Player Spotlight) - Maurice Gwinn #40 - Fullback, Nose Guard, and Specialty Teams. *Ironman Player. *Member of the TTB—Triple Threat Backfield

Maurice was our starting fullback in 1984. He was 5'10" and 204 lbs. He was the heaviest player on the team. As our starting fullback Maurice ran up the gut like a bull. He was fast, had quick moves, and was hard to take down. Maurice was one of the best fullbacks in California. He could do it all on the gridiron. When opposing teams concentrated on stopping Ron Beverly, Jr.—our quarterback—or Bryan Batchan—our tailback—Maurice quickly made a name for himself as the third offensive threat. During the season he rushed for 640 yards and 7 touchdowns. He caught an additional 94 yards in passes, combining for a total of 734 yards. In Game 7 against St. Patrick's when the Pats were busy trying to shut down Ronnie and Bryan, Maurice stepped up and rushed for 130 yards on 10 carries for two touchdowns. Maurice was a jovial player and a brute of a fullback. On Friday mornings before a game the entire 1984 team and coaches would meet on Travis AFB at church for a morning service. That service was led by Maurice's dad. I enjoyed those times, and it was during those services that I noticed Maurice got his outgoing personality from his father. In 1984, Maurice made a name for himself running up the gut and over linebackers. He ran fast, explosive, and powerfully. When not running the ball Maurice was a bulldozer as a blocker. He was the very best at what he did. Maurice did what the team needed him to do, open up a hole blocking for our tailback or quarterback, or move the ball upfield by powering over defenders. He did both extremely well. Maurice was also a nose guard on defense, a devastating pass rusher, and an anvil at shutting down the run up the middle. Thanks for the memories, Maurice. You took names.

[Center]

Jeff Martin #52

(Player Spotlight) - Jeff Martin #52 - Center, Defensive End, and Specialty Teams. *Ironman Player. *Two-way Starter

Jeff was our starting center and defensive end. He was a two-way player who rarely left the field. He was the smallest trencher on the offensive line at 5'9", 170 lbs. but his size did not dictate his play. He was a tenacious competitor. I played football with Jeff for five years, and he played on three undefeated teams. The teams Jeff played on went 45-4-2. He was a very good center and played his heart out on the gridiron. The center is not an easy position, as you have to line up, hike the ball, and defend at the same time. Jeff was our best technical lineman in 1984. He was skilled and aggressive and stood his ground against much larger nose guards, linebackers, and defensive linemen, and he knew the tricks to use against them to gain an upper hand. Jeff was an important member of our undefeated team. He was a proud Viking who never let up on the gridiron, even when he was hurt. If Jeff got beat on a play he dug in and worked harder so it didn't happen again. Whether it was opening a hole, containing a defender, pass protection, or forcing the run inward on defense, Jeff rarely failed. Because he was a small trencher Jeff lifted weights regularly to compensate for his size. If Jeff faced a stronger or more athletic opponent, he used his gridiron experience to outthink them. In the summer of 1984 prior to our senior year, Jeff joined a group of us doing drills and running wind sprints to get in shape for the upcoming season. Jeff was my compadre, and I am proud he was a member of the trench crew. If we could play football again Jeff would be my choice for center because no one played with more grit. He was willing to give it his all every play. Jeff played football for ten seasons, in the trenches, as the center. He was as good as they came. Thanks for the memories, Jeff. You took names.

[Right Guard]

Mark 'Baro' Baranowski #64

(Player Spotlight) - Mark Baranowski #64, Nickname - 'Baro' - Right Guard, Defensive Tackle, and Specialty Teams. *Ironman Player. *Two-way Starter

Mark was our starting right guard and starting defensive tackle. He was 6'1" and 190 lbs. He was a two-way player who rarely left the field. I played football with Mark for five years, and he played on three undefeated football teams, amassing a 45-4-2 winning record. In 1984, Baro was used as a pulling and trapping guard, and would hammer opponents relentlessly. He was the fastest offensive lineman we had. That season Baro was one of the best offensive/defensive combo players in Northern California. When Mark was not tormenting opposing teams he was our team rebel and prankster. I am very grateful he was a Viking and not an opponent, because in 1984 he was as good as they came. Mark was my compadre. He was a master at taking names and couldn't be intimidated on the gridiron. In game #11 against Folsom, the second round of the playoffs for the Sac-Joaquin Section title, Mark pulled left on a trap and hit their star defensive lineman. The hit was so hard and brutal it echoed in the open stadium at Vanden's George Gammon Field. The following Monday when we watched game film, that hit was replayed over and over. When Baro hit an opposing player on a pull or trap it became a very bad day for them. I think his look in this photo says it all, he was a tough trencher, and those who tested him usually came out on the losing end. Prior to the 1984 season Mark worked out for a full year and spent the summer before Hell Week doing drills and running to get into shape with a group of us. That season in 1984 there is no one else in the state or country I would have wanted pulling right or left with me on a sweep, because I trusted Mark, and I knew the damage he was going to unleash on opposing players. Thanks for the memories, Baro. You took names.

[Left Tackle]

Joe 'Big Joe' Leonard #56

(Player Spotlight) - Joe Leonard #56, Nickname - 'Big Joe'- Left Tackle and Specialty Teams

Joe was our Alaska boy. He came down from the cold state before the 1983 season. He wore his Alaskan roots well with his thick hair. He was our starting left tackle on the 1984 team. Joe was a big 6'4" and weighed 195 lbs. He was the second-heaviest player on the team, and he spent many hours at the gym working out. Joe spent a full year in the gym before the 1984 season. In the summer of 1984, Joe worked out with a group of us doing drills and running to get in shape for the upcoming season. It paid off well for him. Joe could not be intimidated on the gridiron, and did his job well, without failing. Joe was rarely beat by an opposing player, and together many times we buried opposing defensive tackles in the turf. He was a rock. When times got rough during a game Big Joe stepped up and never failed. Great heart. In the second round of the playoffs against Folsom, we were doing pass protection one play, and they blitzed their middle linebacker. As I went to pick him up, I saw Joe knock the defensive tackle on his rear, then turn and do the exact same to their defensive end. Big Joe manhandled them both—and those were tough players—as Folsom was undefeated at the time and ranked #3 in the state of California. That was the type of performance that made us champions in 1984, because my teammates played like champions. In the fall of 1983, we were at the gym at Travis AFB working out when Joe smashed his right index finger flat as a penny, as he was putting down some weights. We immediately took him to the hospital for medical treatment, as his finger was severely injured. The very next day Joe was back in the gym lifting weights. He had a truckload of grit, and that is why I am glad he lined up next to me. Thanks for the memories, Big Joe. You took names.

[Right Tackle]

Chris Stiltner #70

(Player Spotlight) - Chris Stiltner #70, - Right Tackle, Defensive Tackle, and Specialty Teams. *3 Year Varsity Player. *Ironman Player. *Two-way Starter

Chris was the only junior on the starting line in 1984. He was our right tackle, and anchored the right side of the line with Mark Baranowski. They worked very well together. Chris was 6'0" and 190 lbs. He had started on the varsity level as a sophomore also and spent three years in the trenches anchoring the offense and defense. Chris was a two-way starter and rarely left the field. He was on all specialty teams. Chris was a natural athlete and the most all-around athletic trencher on both sides of the line, and as durable as they came. He was an all-star catcher on Vanden's varsity baseball team, and he incorporated those skills on the gridiron. Chris joined us throughout the summer of 1984, doing drills and wind sprints in preparation for the upcoming season. Chris was quick off the ball, aggressive, and very tough to beat one on one. He was one of the best at what he did, and he was a big reason why we went undefeated that season. Chris was probably the steadiest player we had on the line. He kept his emotions more in check than the rest of us. We needed that. Chris played like a senior when he was still a sophomore. He matured before his time. If Chris got beat on a play, which was rare, he did a gut check and made sure the opposing player paid the price on the next snap. On goal line defense, Chris was an unmovable rock and plugged his hole, making it impossible to penetrate for paydirt on his side of the line. Chris was my compadre in 1984, and I am thankful he was a member of our close-knit trench crew. I never played with or against a more natural offensive or defensive tackle than Chris. He was extremely fierce in the trenches, and his endurance level was untouchable. Thanks for the memories, Chris. You took names.

[Nose Guard]

John 'Murdock' McClellan #65

(Player Spotlight) - John McClellan #65, Nickname - 'Murdock'- Nose Guard, Center on Punts, and Specialty Teams

John started playing football with us in 1980 on the 11-0 undefeated Travis Redskins. He played on three undefeated teams in a five-year period, including the 1982 JV 9-0 unscored-upon team and the 1984 12-0 Section Champs. The teams John played on went 45-4-2. John was a defensive lineman and nose guard and at 6', 185 lbs., he was dynamite off the ball. Murdock quickly earned the reputation as being the fastest defensive lineman when the ball was hiked. He was our roadrunner. John penetrated into the backfield often and easily, disrupting plays, making tackles, or sacking the quarterback. In 1984, he made sacks look easy. John was zany and unpredictable when he played, so early on we nicknamed him 'Murdock' after a 1980's quirky sitcom character. He joined Baro as being one of our pranksters. John had a lucky shirt he wore under his shoulder pads for every game. It read, "I am not crazy, I just act it." Murdock was an old-school football stud and a one-man wrecking crew. Many times he would penetrate into the backfield before the other trenchers. Murdock made a big impact on the gridiron. Murdock was also a center on punts because he had perfected the long hike. One day when we trot onto the gridiron again to play ball with Coaches Tom Kiefer (RIP), Tom Newsom (RIP), and Chuck Coates (RIP), John will be in the lineup as our nose guard. He saved my brother Tim's life when his car caught fire. John pulled Tim from the wrecked vehicle as it erupted in flames. John had a deep gash to his forehead and Tim was unconscious, yet he dragged Tim to safety by himself. I have never forgotten that moment. It bonded us for life as brothers. Thanks for the memories, Murdock. You took names.

[Cornerback]

David Reyes #24

(Player Spotlight) - David Reyes #24 - Cornerback and Specialty Teams

David played football with us for four years, starting in 1980. He missed only his junior season. David played on three undefeated teams starting with the Travis Redskins in 1980 at 11-0, the 1982 9-0 and unscored-upon JV team, and the 1984 12-0 Section Champs. The teams David played on went 39-0-2, since he missed our junior year. David was a smaller football player but that did not dictate his impact on the field. He would drive through a defender with a ruthless stick and bury him in the turf. David was 'Mr. Hustle.' He hustled and played 110% each play. David played cornerback, and made passes in his territory hard to catch. He was like his older brother Frank Reyes, just a little smaller. One play I remember when David made a big impact was a hit he delivered on a much larger opponent. I saw him deliver a devastating hit against a tight end who was about 12 inches taller and 100 lbs. heavier than he was. David stuck the tight end, as he attempted to catch a pass but dropped it. The tight end hit the turf hard and when he got up he limped off the field. That was the type of play from my teammates back then. They dug down deep and stepped up to every challenge they faced on the gridiron. David liked the challenge of taking it to bigger players, and those who underestimated him paid for it. Seventeen years after the 1984 season, David and I went to Vanden to watch a football game. We ran into a teacher from when we were in school there, Birdie Valmore. She recognized us. In talking with her she said she missed us kids from the 1980's. She said it was a good time. As I listened to her and David talk, I reminisced about those days. They were good. They really were the time of Vikings, friends, and family. Thanks for the memories, David. You took names.

[Trencher]

Chuck Coates #72 - (RIP)

(Player Spotlight) - Chuck Coates #72 - Trencher - OT, DT, and Specialty Teams. *Ironman Player, RIP

Chuck was 6'3" and 185 lbs. He was a member of our close-knit trench crew. Though he was large in stature his personality was even larger. Chuck stood out on the 1984 team not just for his play but for his personality. The most likeable guy I ever played alongside on the gridiron. He was one of the few players who could always draw a laugh from you, even when we were playing a tough game, the play on the field was brutal, and you were tired and physically hurting. Chuck could still make you smile, and everyone on the team relied on him to lighten the mood when we needed it. Sadly, we lost Chuck about 6 years ago. Looking back almost 30 years later the perfect nickname for Chuck would be 'Jolly' because he was a giant trencher who was always in a good mood. I do not think I ever saw him get upset on the field. Chuck was our sixth trencher on offense, in that he swapped out playing left or right offensive tackle when Joe Leonard or Christopher Stiltner needed a break or were injured. Chuck filled the void perfectly. He never missed a beat or a block. Chuck also saw plenty of action on the defensive line as a trencher. He hustled and never backed down. When the gridiron play was merciless, Chuck dug in deeper and hit harder. I am honored I shared the field with him because he made the game fun. We will play football together again one day, and I look forward to battling alongside you. Thanks for the memories, Chuck. You took names.

[Tight End]

Eric 'Big E' Barnes #88

(Player Spotlight) - Eric Barnes #88, Nickname - 'Big E' - Tight End, Defensive End, and Specialty Teams. *Ironman Player

Eric was our tight end, and he was big at 6'4" and 185 lbs. He could run a route that was text book, and Ronnie, our quarterback, connected with him often. When we needed big clutch catches, Eric would deliver, even if he had to dive to pull them in. During the 1984 season, Eric caught 24 receptions for 394 yards, averaging 16.4 yards per catch and 7 touchdowns. He was a hard hitter, had great hands, and could move the ball upfield well after catching it. As a defensive end, Eric kept the play inside and knocked down many passes because he had an amazing leap, making it virtually impossible to complete a pass if Eric was in the way. Though he seemed like he was flash, and a talker, Eric really wasn't on the field. He was business when we needed him. Eric rarely missed a catch, a block, or a tackle, and he was a big part of our success in 1984. I always liked to see him in the huddle because he would give me a nod. 'Big E' was what I called him. Eric made the 1984 season memorable because he was a big-impact player. He always had a cool story to tell and with me he had an audience. Thanks for the big plays, laughs, and stories, Big E. We couldn't have done it without you. On the field and off, Eric was liked by anyone who met him. Looking back three decades later, I can still see him in uniform running a route and making a big catch. You made the game fun, and I am glad I had the opportunity to share the gridiron with you. Thanks for the memories, Eric. You took names.

[Kicker]

Dave Haupt #17

(Player Spotlight) - Dave Haupt #17 - Kicker, Defensive End, Backup Quarterback, and Specialty Teams. *Ironman Player

Dave was our kicker, our backup quarterback, and our starting right defensive end. He kicked off, kicked field goals, and made extra points. Dave was exactly like this picture depicts, a nice guy. It was guys like Dave and Chuck Coates that made the game fun because we had our share of chest thumpers, me included, and we needed some levity from time to time. Dave easily stepped in the void when Ron Beverly, Jr. got injured, and he led us. Dave could have started for any team in our league because he was a very good QB. During game #4 against Dixon, our starting quarterback Ronnie was injured, and left at the end of the first half in an ambulance with a concussion. Dave stepped in at the helm, and stepped up and directed the winning touchdown. We won that game 19-14. Dave was an excellent kicker, too, and rarely missed the uprights. He was capable of kicking long field goals also, as he made a 55-yarder in practice. As a defensive end, he contained the outside, forcing the play inward. Those teams that tested Dave, usually came up short when running to his side. Dave took his athletic skills he learned being a great skateboarder and utilized them on the gridiron. Dave was an important member of the 1984 squad because he did his job well, scored points, and made us laugh when we needed it. Dave's smiling photo is in Hilmar, California when we won 20-14, securing our 12-0 record and winning the Sac-Joaquin Section championship. Thanks for the memories, Dave. You took names.

[Wide Receiver]

Darren Rysden #83

(Player Spotlight) - Darren Rysden #83 - Wide Receiver and Specialty Teams

Darren was our redhead wide receiver. In 1984, he was in his 4th year of football and seasoned on the gridiron. He made big catches and big plays when we needed them. Darren had great hands and agility as a receiver. He never dropped the ball. He was always in the game and in the mix, keeping our opponents scrambling. Darren would deliver stinging hits and blocks to opposing players, putting them on notice. He started playing football with a group of us back in 1980. Darren played four seasons of football with us and played on three undefeated teams, including the 1980 Travis Redskins Pop Warner undefeated 11-0 squad, the 1982 unscored-upon 9-0 JV team, and the 1984 12-0 Section Champs. Darren played on teams that recorded a record of 38-4. I enjoyed my time on the gridiron with Darren because I knew when he was on the field, he would get the job done. When opposing linebackers or cornerbacks tested him, Darren usually came out on top. When he was going for what appeared to be an uncatchable pass, many times he pulled it in for a reception, giving us the yardage we needed. He was one of the guys on the team who was lighthearted, and that made the game fun and memorable. Darren could make us all laugh with his quick wit, and he always had something funny to say. Thanks for those great memories, Darren. You took names.

[Middle Linebacker]

Danny Miller #63

(Player Spotlight) - Danny Miller #63 - Middle Linebacker and Specialty Teams

Danny was our middle linebacker and a member of the 'Orient Express' headed by Glenn Barretto—and Coach Tom Newsom's famed defensive unit. Danny was a fierce-hitting quiet middle linebacker. He let his play speak for him. Danny was a hard-charger, and could shut down the run up the gut. Tough kid. He mixed it up often and never complained of an injury. An old-school hard-nosed sticking machine. I liked that in him. He took a beating and kept on sticking. Danny was a huge part of holding the opposing offenses all year to just 132 points combined. When times got tough on the field, and they did often, Danny never faltered. He stood his ground and never backed down when players were much larger than we were. He was the right player for the middle linebacker position. He plugged the center of the field and made it difficult for offenses trying to move the ball up the gut. I only played one season of football with Danny, in 1984. During those four months we shared on the gridiron he made an huge impact. Thirty years later, I can still see his resolve in shutting down the opposing offenses we faced. I am thankful I shared the field with him. He was something to see during those 12 games. The middle linebacker has to be tough to shut down the run up the gut. Danny fit that mold perfectly. He was a bone crusher. Thanks for the memories, Danny. You took names.

[Outside Linebacker]

Sherman Pruitt #84

(Player Spotlight) - Sherman Pruitt #84 - Outside Linebacker, Flanker, Tight End, and Specialty Teams. *Ironman Player

Sherman was a member of our linebacker crew known as the 'Orient Express,' which Glenn Barretto led. It was Coach Tom Newsom's famed defensive unit. Sherman played outside linebacker, and was a crushing hitter. He could sting you and leave you feeling it. Hard hitter, hard-nosed football player. Sherman was a vital member of the 1984 team that held the twelve opponent offensive teams we faced to just 132 points combined. Sherman could stuff the run or shut down the outside passing game. Sherman was also our flanker and backup tight end, and he had great hands, and he could deliver a text book block. In 1984, Sherman was a big play maker and always in the mix, causing havoc for our opponents. He was a powerful runner and could drag opponents across the goal line. As only a sophomore, Sherman stood out on our 1984 championship team. Our success that season was a direct result of the performance and dedication from players like Sherman. When we needed him to prevail, Sherman always stepped up and played with heart. I respected his guts and fortitude. In every game we played, Sherman made his presence known with big plays. He was equally good on offense and defense. Thanks for the memories, Sherman. You took names.

[Cornerback]

Clifton Roberts #36

(Player Spotlight) - Clifton Roberts #36 - Cornerback, Kickoff Returns, Backup Tailback, and Specialty Teams. *Ironman Player

Cliff was a senior transfer student in 1984 from Okinawa, Japan where he had spent most of his life. Coming onto our Viking football team he quickly cemented a reputation as a great player. He earned a starting position as a cornerback, kickoff returnee, and a backup to our tailback, Bryan Batchan. Football teams have all sort of players, some rough-looking like the trench crew, and others who just look good when they play well. That was Cliff. He was fast, had quick moves, could stick like a freight train, and still look good doing it. We needed some pizzazz on our squad, and that was Cliff. Many opposing players, though, underestimated him and paid for it. Cliff was another jovial teammate who could make me smile when the play on the gridiron was getting trying. A calming force when you needed him most. Those are the players I appreciated, because it was easy to lose it on the field and let aggression become the dominating factor. Cliff was level-headed and always did what we needed him to do—move the ball upfield on kickoffs or shut down passing games. He did both extremely well. Against Galt, a school bigger than ours with more players suited, Cliff ran back a kickoff for a touchdown, and he looked good doing it. He caught the ball running, zigging and zagging, breaking tackles, and dodging opponents, and scampered 82 yards for the touchdown. Cliff did it with style and pizzazz. His run secured our first win. Cliff was new to Vanden our senior season but he made our team more formidable, and he gave it class. I was blessed to have shared the gridiron with him. Thanks for the memories, Cliff. You took names.

[Defensive End]

J-p Smith #27

(Player Spotlight) - J-p Smith #27 - Defensive End and Specialty Teams

J-p was a transfer student to Vanden in 1984. From the first time I met him, I liked him. Coach Bev would drive J-p to school each day, as they both lived in the same town. During Hell Week he earned a reputation as a hard-hitting machine, and won a starting position as a defensive end. A true nice guy with guts and grit on the gridiron. J-p was an old-school-style player—he would stick you, stick you, and stick you. He never lost his cool like some of us; he just performed—and performed extremely well. J-p played defensive end and slot-back, and he was on all the specialty teams. When we needed to contain the outside, shut down the run or air defense, J-p was there making his presence known. Our opponents came to know him well. He never failed and was always making a huge impact every play. J-p was probably one of the more well-rounded players on the team. He could catch, run, lay out opposing players, and intercept passes. J-p had the size and demeanor to play linebacker or fullback. He had the tenacity to take on opposing players much larger for four quarters. There wasn't much J-p could not do in 1984. To put it plainly, I am thankful he was a teammate and not an opponent. When I look back on those days 30 years later, J-p is at the top of the list of players I enjoyed battling alongside. He made the Vanden Viking football program proud. Thanks for those great memories, J-p. You took names.

[Punter]

David Smith #60

(Player Spotlight) - David Smith #60 - Punter, Backup Center, Defensive Line. *Ironman Player

David was a member of the trench crew, where he was our backup center and defensive tackle, and he also was our starting punter. He was very good at punting, and could send them 50+ yards deep and extremely high. His accuracy at punting was amazing, as he often gave us great field position with his well-placed kicks. David had only one punt blocked. He was a quick thinker on the field and could adapt to any situation. He also was our backup center—and that is a difficult position to play in the trenches. It takes technical skills and aggression. David had them both. He wasn't afraid to take on players much larger than himself, and he stood his ground as a ferocious Viking. David was my compadre, and I can still see his smile through his facemask. I am proud David was a member of our close-knit trench crew, but I would never let him watch my contacts again. Thanks, but no thanks. David would go to the gym with us regularly to lift weights, and away from school, we spent much time together. He was a good friend, along with a great teammate. He served the Vanden Vikings' tradition proud on the gridiron in 1984. David was also a member of the Vanden band, so there were a few times he was in his football uniform playing his instrument. Thanks for the memories, David. You took names.

[Trencher]

Eugene (Burton) van Eikenhorst #75

(Player Spotlight) - Eugene van Eikenhorst #75 - Trencher - OL, DT, and Specialty Teams. *Ironman Player

Eugene was a junior on the 1984 team. He was a trencher and played on either side of the line. He lined up against the starting offensive line in practice, and was a very worthy challenge for us. Eugene was a hard-nosed tough kid who fit perfectly in the trenches. He took it to the bigger opponents he faced and never gave an inch. He set the tone. Eugene was very durable, and if you hurt him, he would come back at you harder the next play. I liked Eugene back in those days and so did everyone. Just a great guy to be around. Eugene would battle anyone on the gridiron. It was guys like Eugene and Derrick Davis who made us champions, because they challenged us in practice and were tough opponents every play. Practice makes champions and Eugene made sure we didn't slack during ours. He was a gutsy and gritty trencher who could battle you all day long. He was as good as most starters we faced. Opposing teams that tested Eugene quickly learned, he was going to take it to them, and he did. Eugene was a battering ram and a sticking machine. I am glad he was a member of our close-knit trench crew. In the next life I want him on my squad. The following season in 1985 Eugene wore the #55 as a Viking and a Titan. I know he honored my old jersey with big sticks and big plays. Thanks for the memories, Eugene. You took names.

[Trencher]

Derrick Davis #71

(Player Spotlight) - Derrick Davis #71 - Trencher - OL, DT, and Specialty Teams. *Ironman Player

Derrick was a junior on the 1984 Vanden Vikings undefeated championship team and a member of the trench crew. Derrick played on either side of the line in the trenches. He battled regularly against the starting offensive line in practice and held his own. In fact, one practice Derrick was lined up as defensive tackle against Joe Leonard and myself. He beat us badly on a play knocking both Big Joe and me backwards. Coach Bev stopped the practice and laid into Joe and me, as he should have. Next play, Derrick did the same thing again. Joe and I got beat twice badly by Derrick in front of everyone. Needless to say, after that, we made sure Derrick had a very long practice. Derrick was quiet back in those days but stepped up and got the job done well. He was as good as most of the starters in our league. Derrick was a hard-nosed Viking. He made the Vanden tradition proud because when he was on the gridiron he gave it his all, every snap. I respected that quality in him. Derrick never backed down from larger opponents and held his own, many times besting them, like Joe and me. He was one tough kid back in 1984 and you couldn't intimidate him on the gridiron. I know I am glad he was a member of our close-knit trench crew. I want to play with him again one day. I know his heart and his tenacity. Thanks for the memories, Derrick. You took names.

[Cornerback / Safety]

DeWayne Quinn #28

(Player Spotlight) - DeWayne Quinn #28 - Cornerback, Safety, Kickoff Returns, Receiver, and Specialty Teams. *Ironman Player

DeWayne played with us in 1984 on the varsity squad as a sophomore. He lived in the same housing development as my family, and he was at our home often while we were growing up. DeWayne was liked by everyone in those days because he was always positive and smiled often. On the gridiron, though, a different persona emerged. He was a tremendous competitor. He would run back kickoffs or punts, and played as a defensive back or receiver. There wasn't one thing DeWayne couldn't do on the football field that season. He was very fast with quick moves, he hit hard, took punishment well, and was a ferocious tackler. He was a resilient kid who never complained but got the job done. He did exactly what the team needed him to do—perform flawlessly. Dewayne was a multi-talented player. If we needed a tailback, he could handle that job, too. Short of the trenches because he didn't have the weight, DeWayne could play anywhere on the team, on either side of the ball. One thing I see 30 years later is that he was a good kid who loved the game of football. We were blessed to have shared the gridiron with him, and he was an important member of the 1984 undefeated Vanden Vikings SCAL and Sac-Joaquin Section championship team. Thanks for the memories, DeWayne. You took names.

[Cornerback]

Louis Adams #19

(Player Spotlight) - Louis Adams #19 - Cornerback and Specialty Teams

Louis was one of our cornerbacks in 1984. He was skilled in pass protection and defending our secondary. As a smaller player Louis worked extra hard to prevent receivers from exploiting his size and catching passes in his area of responsibility. Louis took pride in sticking and hustling. He was gregarious, and an important part of the 1984 Vanden championship football team. Louis had great hands and a no-fear attitude to hammer an opponent and run through him on the tackle. He worked hard to make his presence known every down. If an opposing player bested Louis, he made sure they paid a penalty for it on the next snap. Louis also played on specialty teams and was always ready to jump in the action. He loved mixing it up. When his cleats stepped on the field, Louis became a wrench in our foe's game plan. It took everyone to do their best all the time to win, and Louis fulfilled his obligation to our undefeated squad. I was honored to share the gridiron with him in 1984, and though we only played one season together we had fun during those four months. Thanks for the memories, Louis. You took names.

[Multi-position / Linebacker]

Paul Holes #54

(Player Spotlight) - Paul Holes #54 - Trencher, Linebacker, Defensive End, and Specialty Teams

Paul was a multi-talented player in 1984. He was a trencher, a member of the offensive and defensive lines, a defensive end, and linebacker, and also played on specialty teams. Paul could fill in where we needed him and get the job done well. He was a good hitter and took punishment like a rock. He could not be intimidated on the gridiron. Paul never complained and was a quiet player, but one of the nicest guys on the team. He was always ready to jump in the fray on the field and take on any opposing player. He had guts and grit, and I respected that. Paul would go regularly to the gym with Mark Baranowski, Joe Leonard, Jeff Martin, and me to lift weights to put on mass and increase his strength. Paul was my compadre, and I am glad he was a teammate on our championship team because he made the game fun. Thanks for the memories, Paul. You took names.

[Receiver]

Felix Davis #14

(Player Spotlight) - Felix Davis #14 - Receiver, Cornerback, and Specialty Teams

Felix was a wide receiver and cornerback in 1984. He also saw time on the specialty teams. Felix was a talented player with great hands that could deliver a ruthless stick or make a good tackle in open field. He had quick moves and great speed when running a route. Felix was liked by everyone in 1984 because he was one of the more cordial players on the team. When he was on the gridiron, though, he was a force to reckon with because he hustled and gave it his all to the last whistle. Felix stepped up every time the team needed him, and he performed exceptionally well. Thanks for the memories, Felix. You took names.

[Multi-position]

Reginald 'Reggie' Stover #21

(Player Spotlight) - Reginald Stover #21, Nickname - 'Reggie' - Cornerback, Receiver, and Specialty Teams

Reggie was a hard-hitting Viking teammate in 1984. He loved getting on the gridiron often and tangling with opposing players in games or with us in practice. I liked Reggie and so did everyone. He was quiet but amicable, and pulled his weight on the squad, doing what the coaches asked and whatever the team needed to prevail. He could catch, run, and hit with the best. Reggie was a hard-nosed kid and a durable player who could perform relentlessly for four quarters, without faltering. I trusted and applauded him as a teammate. As a friend, I valued him. It was players like Reggie who made us champions in 1984, because he performed to the best of his capabilities every single play. I respected his moxie, and his dedication to our team was paramount. That fall in 1984, we shared amazing times as teammates and had a lot fun. I just wish we could do it again; but only if Reggie was there on the gridiron with us kicking ass. Decades later, I can still see him smiling behind his facemask. Thanks for those great memories, Reggie. You took names.

[Multi-position]

Scot Sherman #30

(Player Spotlight) - Scot Sherman #30 - Multi-Position

Scot was a multi-position player in 1984. Those were the type of players we needed to help us win the championship. He could play cornerback, receiver, and running back, and also on the specialty teams. He was always there when we needed him and stepped up and took on the challenge. He performed extremely well. Scot was a reserved kid back in those days, yet he hustled all the time. Thirty years later, Scot's hustle still lingers in my mind. He was a dependable teammate who could deliver a savage hit and make an impressive open-field tackle. We were lucky to have players who could step up like Scot. I will always remember his perseverance. Thanks for being part of the team and the memories, Scot. You took names.

[Receiver]

Kye Purnell Jones #80

(Player Spotlight) - Kye Purnell Jones #80 - Receiver

I was blessed to share the gridiron with Kye for two seasons. He was a member of our 1982 9-0 undefeated and unscored-upon squad and our 1984 12-0 championship team. The Viking teams he played on went 21-0. Kye never saw a losing game during his time on the gridiron at Vanden. He was a receiver with great hands and great speed. He could take punishment well, or deliver crushing sticks. He was very dependable as a teammate—he never let us down. As a competitor he was a tough kid; a hard-hitting football player. I respected, trusted, and liked him. He was my friend. It was teammates like Kye that were our mortar. Our squad was better because of him. Kye was sociable but reserved. His style on the gridiron didn't match his personality. He was an aggressive player and never gave up. Kye was another guy who kept the team balanced from the emotional players like myself. He was a Viking through and through. Kye was always ready to take on any task asked of him on the field or off. Who could ask for more? We couldn't. He gave everything for our undefeated Vanden squad in 1984. Thank you for the memories, Kye. You took names.

[Multi-position]

Stephen Harrison #87

(Player Spotlight) - Stephen Harrison #87 - Multi-Position

Stephen was a multi-position player in 1984. He could play cornerback, and receiver, and also on the specialty teams. Stephen was always ready to jump into the fray on the gridiron. He loved mixing it up. Though a smaller player, his demeanor showed the heart of a lion. Stephen hustled all the time and gave 110%. It took everyone on the team to play to their fullest potential every down for us to win the championship in 1984 and go undefeated. Stephen fulfilled his role admirably on our Viking squad. He had a great sense of humor back in 1984, and he was one of the players who made the game fun. During Hell Week his outgoing personality led to him spending time as a cannoli. Thanks for being part of the team and the memories, Stephen. You took names.

[Receiver]

Rob Cantley #85

(Player Spotlight) - Rob Cantley #85 - Receiver

Rob was a member of our 1984 12-0 championship Vanden team. He was a smaller player who showed conviction and great heart. Rob was always ready to get on the field, and when did, he made the Vanden football program proud. Rob was a receiver, and he could run a good route. He had strong hands and a will to perform to the best of his capabilities. He also could deliver a text book hit and tackle. Rob gave his all every down. He hustled non-stop and never quit. As a smaller player I respected his guts. I am glad he was a member of our undefeated squad. Thanks for the memories, Rob. You took names.

[Multi-position]

Kenny Spencer #41

(Player Spotlight) - Kenny Spencer #41 - Multi-Position

Kenny was a resilient player in 1984, and he worked hard to beat our opponents. Kenny was a back-up running back, and he could run the ball equally well as a tailback or fullback. He wore his Vanden pride openly, and I am grateful he was a member of our team. Kenny performed well when on the gridiron. He ran fearlessly, blocked skillfully, and tackled with passion, always making his presence known. A tough kid and a great teammate. We were blessed to have him on our squad. Kenny was athletic and also played on Vanden's baseball team. Thanks for the memories, Kenny. You took names.

[Safety]

Steve Crittenden #45

- No photo -

Steve was our starting safety on the 1984 12-0 team. He caught the final interception against Hilmar in the Sac-Joaquin Section championship game, which gave us the ball back to run out the clock and secure the win.

Steve was a junior on our squad. Besides playing safety, he also played on special teams. He never played offense.

Two years after our championship season Steve was playing football at Chico State in California. He was accused of and arrested for the double homicide of a prominent Chico couple. Dr. William Chiappella, 67, and his wife Katherine, 66, were found murdered in their home. They were bound, gagged, stabbed, and beaten.

Steve was tried for their murders in Placer County California after a venue change from Butte County. A jury from Auburn found him guilty. On June 13, 1989 Steve was sentenced to death. He has been incarcerated on San Quentin's death row since his conviction.

The absence of a photo was intentional. What my friends and coaches accomplished is what should be remembered from our story.

[Team Equipment Manager]

James 'Tuck' Tucker

(Equipment Manager Spotlight) - James 'Tuck' Tucker

Tuck was the equipment manager for our 1984 Vanden Viking championship team. He was always 'Johnny on the Spot.' He made sure we had what we needed—from equipment, tape, Icy Hot, water, ice, or Gatorade. If we wanted it, he would get it. Tuck worked well with the team, coaches, and players, and we could not have had a better or more enthusiastic manager. Tuck was present at all team functions and never missed a practice or game. He was very loyal to Vanden and wore his pride well, as shown in the patch photos supplied by Tuck from his letterman jacket. It takes everyone to win a championship because football is a team effort. Tuck was part of that team. I'm sorry we left you in Dixon after the game. I'm glad you got home safely before those cowboys took you apart. We appreciate and recognize what you did for the squad and how hard you worked to help us win the Sac-Joaquin Section championship. We couldn't have done it without you. Thanks for the memories, Tuck. You took names.

[Assistant Equipment Manager]

Eddie Hopkinson

(Asst. Equipment Manager Spotlight) - Eddie Hopkinson

Eddie was the team's manager assistant. He helped get the equipment ready, and always had ice, water, or Gatorade, tape, and Icy Hot for the players. He was a vital member of the Vanden football team, and he stepped up when we needed him. Eddie was present at all team functions, practices, and games. He was a quiet kid who wore his Viking pride. Thank you, Eddie, for the memories and for all that you did for the squad. We recognize your assistance in helping us win the Sac-Joaquin Section title in 1984. We couldn't have done it without you. You took names.

The following season in 1985, coaches Bev, Noos, and Kiefer directed the Vikings to a 8-2 record. Ronnie, Chris, and the other Vikes lost to Hogan. They entered the Sac-Joaquin Section playoffs facing Folsom in the first round. They lost a tough-fought contest to the Bulldogs, 21-20.

In 1986, the Vikings again went 8-2 under the direction of coaches Bev, Noos, and Kiefer. It was their final year at Vanden coaching the football program.

In 1987, Coach Bev followed Ronnie to UOP where he was playing football. Coach Noos took a hiatus from the game, and Kiefer retired for a second and final time from the gridiron. My former Redskin coach, Mike Kelly, joined the Viking varsity staff during the 1987 season. He remained with the program a few more years.

During Coach Bev's five-year tenure leading the Vanden varsity football program, the Vikings saw a winning 35-13-3 record. In 1964 he scored the first TD at our school, and in 1984 he recorded the first perfect season.

I kept the promise I made to my mom for allowing me to play my senior year. I never played football again.

According to the website Maxpreps.com there are 1187 high school football teams in California. In 2012, only 3 football teams in that state ended their season undefeated: Citrus Hill, De La Salle, and Wasco. According to the website Cnsnews.com there were 14,048 high school football teams in the U.S. Only 125 went undefeated.

Less than 1 percent of football teams see an undefeated season. My friends and I were blessed to have 3 in a 5-year period—from Pop Warner in 1980, to JV in 1982, to our final varsity season in 1984. We recorded 45 wins, 4 losses, and 2 ties during our time together on the gridiron.

Our coaches drew the best from us. We trusted them, we respected them, and we listened to them. They taught us to take names. Our conditioning programs were unrivaled. Our fortitude was unmatched.

All four of my head coaches had undefeated seasons during our time on the gridiron. Coach Mike Kelly in 1980, Coach Lou Moore in 1982, and coaches Gerald Hatcher and Ron Beverly in 1984. Our squads were mirror images of them. They made us champions.

As teammates we shared a closeness most players will never develop. We became brothers, and that bond has lasted a lifetime. We didn't see skin color, and race was never an issue. We only saw red and white as Redskins, and green and gold as Vikings. We loved football and we were unstoppable as friends. As my Travis Redskin Coach Mike Kelly described us, we were 'No Names.'

Coach Bev had a comeback season in 1984. His vision for the Vanden football program was right. Our final year together my friends had a dream to win that championship and record another undefeated season. They made it happen. I wanted to play with them again and enjoy the gridiron one last time. And I did.

1985 Season Photos

Above (L-R): My Viking coaches shown together. Coaches Hatcher, Kiefer, Bev, Newsom, and Moore. All five led us to undefeated seasons during my years at Vanden. They worked their magic. Photo courtesy of Travis Unified School District and Vanden High School.

Below: The 1985 8-2 Vanden Viking football team is shown on the flight line at TAFB. It represents the close bond between the two. Photo courtesy of Travis Unified School District and Vanden High School.

Mr. Ronald A. Harden
Assistant Principal

Above: Coach Harden is shown. He retired from coaching football to join the school administrative staff at Vanden. Photo courtesy of Travis Unified School District and Vanden High School.

Below: Ronnie and Chris with two teachers showing their Viking pride. (L-R) - Ronnie, Mrs. Valmore, Mrs. Rich, and Chris. Photo courtesy of Travis Unified School District and Vanden High School.

Above: Father and son together for one last season as Vikings. (L-R) - Coach Bev at practice stepping in at quarterback to direct a play, and Ronnie behind the facemask. Photos courtesy of Travis Unified School District and Vanden High School.

Below: Coach Newsom directing some mock plays on the George Gammon Field. The Vanden scoreboard is shown behind them in the distance. Photo courtesy of Travis Unified School District and Vanden High School.

Above (L-R): Eugene (Burton) van Eikenhorst wore the #55 the next season as a Viking and a Titan; Sherman Pruitt (former member of the Orient Express) shown at practice; and Derrick Davis in the school quad. All three were vital to the 1985 8-2 Vanden Viking SCAL champion football team. Photos courtesy of Travis Unified School District and Vanden High School.

Below: The Vanden Viking band leading the procession during the football parade as it went around Travis AFB. Photo courtesy of Travis Unified School District and Vanden High School.

30th Reunion - July 19, 2014
The players and coaches return to Vanden

Sports
Vanden 1984 title team holding reunion
By Paul Farmer   From page B7 | July 18, 2014

The above and below images are from an article courtesy of the Daily Republic. Used with permission. Below three images are excerpts.

FAIRFIELD — Fresh off a 1-5-3 campaign in 1982, his first year as Vanden High football coach – after having replaced Ed Serpas, the only coach in school history to that point and his coach with the Vikings nearly two decades earlier – Ron Beverly had some doubts.

But only a few. He knew a solid group of underclassmen was in the pipeline, a set of players who would gel quickly and go undefeated to capture the school's second Sac-Joaquin Section championship in 1984.

Beverly and most of the players from that SJS title team will renew old memories at a reunion in the back quad of the Vanden campus on Saturday at noon.

"It was just a matter then of coming up to varsity and not messing it up," said Beverly, recalling that as freshmen and sophomores, they were undefeated. "The talent was there as they were coming up."

Surveying the scene in the postgame locker room that night, Beverly said, " I'm really going to miss this group."

"I haven't seen probably 80 percent of them since they graduated from Vanden High School," Beverly said. "They left as young men, 17 or 18 yearsold. Now they're 48, 49 years old. It's like looking in a mirror, there's a transition. They're fathers and some are grandfathers.

Former Vanden High School football player organizes reunion to remember perfect 1984 season

By By Tim Roe

The above title is from an article courtesy of the Reporter.

Thirty years after our undefeated season in 1984, we had our first reunion at Vanden High School. On July 19th, 2014 we came back for the first time as grown men, fathers, and grandfathers. Many of us hadn't seen each other in three decades. Coaches Bev, Moore, and Hatcher joined us, along with Coach Larry Hogue, and Levon Haynes, the 2014 Vanden head football coach.

I organized the reunion at the request of Coach Bev. I couldn't have pulled it off without the help of my friends and former teammates David Reyes #24 and John 'Murdock' McClellan #65. My brothers Sean and Craig, and their wives Kim and Erica, along with my dad, worked hard to make the reunion memorable. I would also like to thank my mom and stepdad Chet, may you rest in peace, for their assistance in making it all happen.

At the reunion I supplied my former teammates with a signed copy of the first edition of this book titled, "We Took Names: The Time of Vikings and Friends." Teammates and coaches joined us from all over. Some flew in from out of state.

We took photos, shared old stories, reminisced, and ate together. David and Lisa Reyes's son Daniel barbecued while their daughter Gabby checked in guests and provided name tags.

On that hot windy July afternoon as I spoke to my former teammates, coaches, and friends, I could see the love for the game in their eyes. They hadn't forgotten the times we shared. For one day we lived that journey again.

We were given a tour of our old locker room and the new gridiron, which is now artificial turf. It is still called the George Gammon Field.

I would like to thank Coach Bev for suggesting the reunion, coaches Moore and Hatcher for joining us, and Coach Hogue and Coach Haynes for giving us a tour. I would like to thank Jackielyn Barretto and the Texas Roadhouse for supplying the large barbecues. I would like to thank Richard 'Breeze' Quinn and Food Maxx for providing us with a gift card to purchase some food for the reunion; and Wendy Murray and Sweet Occasions from Vacaville for making us 350 custom cupcakes. I would like to thank Vanden High School and the Travis Unified School District for allowing us to use the school grounds. I would like to thank Bozo's Bandwagon and Elaine and Ralph McClellan (Murdock's parents) for hosting our after-reunion party. Finally, I would like to thank my former teammates, friends, and their families for attending. It was great seeing you all. We'll always be brothers and Vikings. We shared the gridiron, battled to the final whistle, and won. We were the best.

30th Reunion - Photos

Four of our former Vanden coaches joined us, with 18 players and our 1984 team manager, 'Tuck.' My former five-year teammates, Jeff Martin, Glenn (Kelly) Barretto, John 'Murdock' McClellan and Bryan Batchan attended. All three captains from the 1984 team were present.

In the above photo (bottom L to R): David Reyes #24, Frank Reyes #54 (1983), Coach Hatcher, Jeff Martin #52, Glenn (Kelly) Barretto #33, Cliff Roberts #36, Head Coach Beverly, Pervis Alexander. (2nd Row L to R): Bryan Batchan #47, Ronnie Beverly, Jr. #10, J-P Smith #27, John McClellan #65, Dave Haupt #17, Alan Casner. (3rd Row L to R): Coach Hogue, James Tucker, Jeff Rooney #55, Louis Adams #19, Kye Purnell Jones #80, (top L to R): Eric Barnes #88, Alvin Baldwin #28 (1983), Joe Leonard #56. These are the men in this book.

Above: My dad, me, Sean, and Craig at the reunion. I couldn't have made the reunion happen without their assistance.

Above: Coach Bev speaks to the guests reliving our 1984 undefeated championship season. Below: Coaches Hatcher and Moore are shown. Three of my four head coaches attended.

Above (L-R): Alvin Baldwin, me, Bryan Batchan, Jon Martin, Coach Moore, Richard 'Breeze' Quinn, Ronnie Beverly, Jr., David Reyes, and John 'Murdock' McClellan.

The banner welcoming the players and coaches back. Below: guests arriving. Dave Haupt is shown left, with Coach Moore. Center: Cliff Roberts and Big Joe. Right: Jeff Martin.

Above: Coach Hatcher (JV) and Coach Bev (varsity). They combined for a 21-0 undefeated record for Vanden's football program in 1984.

Above (L-R): Alvin Baldwin, Bryan Batchan, J-p Smith and Glenn Barretto. Below (L-R): Eric Barnes, Purnell Jones, and 'Big Joe' Leonard.

Above (L-R): John McClellan and Ron Beverly, Jr. Below (L-R): Todd Noble, David Reyes, and Frank Reyes.

Below: James 'Tuck' Tucker, our team manager, and his mom, who looked for him when we left him at the Dixon football game in 1984.

Above (L-R): Glenn (Kelly) Barretto and Cliff Roberts shown 30 years apart. Top at the reunion and bottom during our season in 1984. Bottom photo (L-R): John 'Murdock' McClellan and David Reyes.

Above (L-R): Jeff Martin and David Reyes. Below (L-R): Louis Adams, Eric Barnes, and J-p Smith.

Below (L-R): Our cheerleader Michelle Paisley (Reed) and me.

Above (L-R): Pervis Alexander, and Lisa and 'Big Joe' Leonard.

Above (L-R): Current Vanden Coach Larry Hogue, Coach Bev, and former Vanden Head Coach LeVon Haynes. Below (L-R): Ron 'Ronnie' Beverly, Jr. and Alan Casner.

Above (L-R): Jon Martin, Richard 'Breeze' Quinn, Greg Coleman, and Bryan Batchan.

Above (L-R): Sean, Tacia Ponce Taylor, Richard Quinn, and Alvin Baldwin. Below one of the 350 custom cupcakes made for the reunion by Sweet Occasions and Wendy Murray of Vacaville, California.

Above (L-R): Coach Hatcher, Mrs. Beverly, Coach Bev, and Jeff Martin.

Above: Coaches Hogue and Haynes with the Beverly family. Below (L-R): Ronnie Bev, Jr., Bryan Batchan, Cliff Roberts, and Dave Haupt

Above (L-R): Glenn (Kelly) Barretto, Frank Reyes, and James Tucker.

Above (L-R): Cliff Roberts, Dave Haupt, and Alvin Baldwin. Below: John 'Murdock' McClellan sits alone.

Above: Coach Bev and his son Ronnie hugging. The coaches and each teammate were called up on stage, and I gave them each a copy of the first edition of this book.

Below: Coach Bev hugging Eric 'Big E' Barnes his stepson. David Reyes and Jeff Martin are seen to the right. I am pictured center.

Above: I am shown hugging Glenn. Ronnie is seen on the left.

Below: Joe 'Big Joe' Leonard and I are shown again. We anchored the left side of the line in 1984.

Above (L-R): Jeff Martin our center, 'Big Joe' Leonard, Ronnie Bev, Jr., Coach Bev, and me.

Below (L-R): Bryan Batchan our tailback, 'Big Joe,' and John 'Murdock' McClellan hugging Coach Bev.

Above (L-R): 'Big Joe,' 'Murdock,' Dave Haupt, Cliff Roberts, and J-p Smith.

Above (L-R): Ronnie, Bryan, me hugging Frank Reyes, John, Dave, and Cliff. Below: Coach Bev speaks to those that attended.

Above (L-R): me, John and Jeff. Below (L-R): Frank Reyes, Julie Ponce Bradley, and Alvin Baldwin. Frank and Alvin were captains on the 1983 6-4 Viking team.

It was a family event, and some children of teammates assisted. Above: Daniel Reyes, son of David and Lisa Reyes, and a friend barbecued.

Below (L-R): Gabrielle Reyes, daughter of David and Lisa Reyes, and Melanie McClellan, daughter of John and Kris McClellan, checked in guests.

Above: The Wall of Fame wasn't present during our time at Vanden. All the walls in the locker room are now covered in memorabilia. It is a testament to the great players and teams that have called Vanden home. (L-R) Lisa Reyes, married to my teammate David Reyes, Lisa Leonard, married to my teammate 'Big Joe,' Kris McClellan, married to my teammate 'Murdock,' me, and Kim Stone Capp. All four women attended Vanden during our playing years.

Left page top to bottom: The George Gammon Field at Vanden. It has changed much since our time. It was grass during our playing years and it's now artificial turf. The stands are the same and haven't changed since I watched the Vanden Vikings play as a 13-year-old on the Travis Redskins. Center: Our old locker room is shown. It has changed some since our playing days. My locker was the third one from the left in the center group.

Left page top to bottom: Glenn and Bryan. I played five seasons of football with them from the Travis Redskins in 1980 to our undefeated 12-0 Vanden Viking team in 1984. Some of the ladies who used to watch us play. (L-R): Kim Stone Capp, Lisa Reyes, Katora Bacon, and Lisa Leonard enjoying the after-party. The first edition book is shown on a table at Bozo's Bandwagon. A free copy was given to each player and coach that attended the reunion. I autographed all their copies.

Our reunion attracted other football players, too. My friend Anthony Poulos—shown above with me, and when he played semi-professional football in 1974. He was 6'5" and 297 pounds. It was important to him to meet my teammates and coaches. He had heard their stories of greatness, and he wanted to meet the champions. He never had an undefeated season.

Quotes from Teammates

Jim 'Maniac' Wallace—Jeff, the book was great. It really took me back to a simpler time. Though hard to believe, the shenanigans were just as I remember. I just wished that I could have finished my football years with all you guys. It helped shape us into the men we are today. I wish you all the success on your book.

Jeff Martin #52 Center—I look back fondly on these years with the players and coaches. I believe that my sense of camaraderie, teamwork, and commitment were shaped by my experiences playing football. I know that my adult life has been positively impacted by the challenges, sacrifices, and successes of being a Vanden Viking. Thank you, Jeff Rooney, for pulling together the reunion and writing the book.

Mark 'Baro' Baranowski #64 Right Guard—High school football was a wonderful episode of true camaraderie; bonding relationships forged in the weight room, locker room, and on the field—united for a shared purpose and indelible on the soul.

Bryan Batchan #47 Tailback—Man, those were the days. Wish we could do it again.

David Reyes #24 Cornerback—The memories of the 1984 team and all the friends that I've made will be forever etched in my mind. Thank you all. We had a great time during our football years. It was nice seeing everyone at the reunion. What time is it? Showtime!

Joe 'Big Joe' Leonard #56 Left Tackle—"Those that work hard in life get something...Those that work twice as hard...get everything." Coach Tom Kiefer drilled that statement into my head in 1984. His words have remained with me in every aspect of my life for the last 30 years...high school, on the field playing football, marriage, parenthood, and 20 years serving as a United States Marine. Thank you, Tom Kiefer. Forever grateful. I will pass on your words to my own son. - Joe Leonard #56 GySgt USMC Ret.

John 'Murdock' McClellan #65 Nose Guard—To me my friends were my family. I would do anything for them. The football team was another way to fill the voids in my life with something other than anger and wrongdoing. I wasn't the best kid I could have been, but my friends and football, along with wrestling and baseball are what got me through my school years. Coach Kelly was the first to check my grades once a week to make sure I was on track. Coach Bev was the next one to keep an eye on me and my grades. If not for all of you, I wouldn't be who or where I am today. To all my gridiron brothers: To battle we have gone and conquered those that opposed us. The gridiron and life that we have experienced together has made better people out of all of us. I am indebted to you all for what you have given me. Without you I would have been a lost soul in this world and never found my way. Bonds have been made that can't be broken. I am proud to have played football with all of you and I am honored to call you my friends. Thank you all for a time that will not be forgotten. It truly was a time of Vikings and friends. Go Vikings!

Ron Beverly, Jr. #10 Quarterback—Thanks for doing this. It brings back so many memories.

J-p Smith #27 Defensive End—Coach Bev, the best coach I ever played for. Being a part of the 84 Vanden Vikes was a memory I will never forget, and playing with some guys that had the will to win!

Louis Adams #19 Cornerback—I began school at Vanden in the fall of 1983. My brother (Antonio Adams) and I were the new kids on the block. Along with the adjustment of school schedule and making new friends the two of us started playing sports immediately. We started off playing Junior Varsity football. We knew a couple of kids that were playing (Chris DeForge, Jerold Roundtree) that had played Pop Warner football in Vacaville with us. We all continued playing basketball and baseball together as well. As we spent more time in the school, we got to know everyone. Our school only consisted of about 600 students in all, so it wasn't hard to at least know a face. The teams from 1984–1986 were so competitive and seemed to win in every sport. That was reflected on the walls of the gym, where all the SCAL champion banners were hung. Trust me; nobody had the success that the Vanden Vikings had year after year. We were a collaboration of Air Force brats and a handful of locals. We were a talented, competitive, and very blessed high school. We would even go to church on Travis AFB every Friday before a game. I hadn't been back to the school since 1986 in which I graduated. When one of the teammates decided it was time to let the world know about the Vikes, we had a 30-year anniversary for the 1984 Champions.

Louis Adams cont.—It was my first time back and it was nice to see everyone again. Currently I am very close to receiving my Bachelor of Science in Religion and plan to be a Christian Counselor with the blessings of God. I have a couple more years I want to do with the Army then retire. And I am married to a cheerleader (Stephanie Chaloux, now Stephanie Adams) from high school. It's amazing how the Lord and Savior lines us up for success. But with success comes some bumpy roads. Trust me, I have had mine as well. In conclusion, I would like to leave this scripture with you all, "Two are better than one because they have a good return for their labor. For if either of them falls, the one will lift up his companion. But woe to the one who falls when there is not another to lift him up." Ecclesiastes 4:9–10

Mike 'Spartacus' Holovach Kicker 1983 team—I had moved to California from England where I was the goalkeeper for our soccer team. That is where I got my strong foot. We played lots of football in my backyard on Travis AFB. I remember mud games in the rain long before Pop Warner football. Pop Warner was great. When we went down south I was one of the kids staying with another player from the other team. That night for dinner I saw guacamole for the first time. It was a very weird experience that you would never see happen today. Letting your kid stay the night with a strange family in a new city. I remember the game as well. It was just like you said. I remember the guy I was lined up against had a mustache. When I moved to Georgia it wasn't the same. I didn't fit in and was a fish out of water. The coach found my record and sought me out when he saw how successful

Mike Holovach cont.—we were. They asked me to play but it was nothing like Vanden. It was too business and not fun. At Vanden we played because we enjoyed the game and it was a great time with our friends. It was a job in Georgia.

Darrick Peterkin Tight End and Linebacker 1983 team—My time spent at Vanden was so brief but in only one season of playing football I have gained a lifetime of memories and friends that I will cherish the rest of my days. What makes my time at Vanden so sweet is that even though the 83 team didn't win the Sac-Joaquin Section title, the 84 team took care of our unfinished business! Go Vikes!

Vanden High School Logo

Where Are They Now?

The characters are listed chronologically as they appear in the book and by chapter. Some aren't listed because I haven't been able to locate them or don't know their current status.

David Reyes married a classmate from Vanden, Lisa Shaw, and they have two children. He still lives in Vacaville and works in the dairy industry.

Carlos Ponce still lives in Vacaville.

Jim 'Maniac' Wallace lives in Arlington, Texas and he is married with three daughters. He is a truck driver.

My dad retired from the medical field and lives in Northern California.

My mom retired from nursing and remarried. She lives in the Pacific Northwest and is widowed.

My brother Sean is married and has three adult children. He became a probation officer in Northern California.

My brother Tim was killed in an auto accident Nov. 14th, 1996 in Northern Oregon. He was running late to work and speeding in the rain. The accident was his fault and no one else was injured. He was only 31. He was divorced and didn't have any children. Tim's life sadly went full circle. From driving our family van through our garage door when he had his learner's permit, to crashing his vehicle at the dam at Lake Berryessa where John pulled

(Tim cont.) him from the car as it was engulfed in flames. Tim's driving habits never improved and ultimately cost him his life. He has been missed by us dearly. (RIP)

My brother Craig retired from law enforcement with a disability. He has since returned to a career in the same field in Northern California. He is married and has five kids.

The 'Beast' was retired after my 1980 season on the Travis Redskins. The frame got bent from too many crashes because it didn't have brakes.

Vanden Road hasn't changed much in the last 30-plus years. It still looks almost the same as when we tempted fate playing stuntmen riding on top of speeding cars.

'Black Bridge' was removed some years back. Where it once crossed Vanden Road is still visible if you know where to look.

Jeff Martin is in network planning for telecommunications and lives in Denver, Colorado. He is married with two daughters.

Glenn (Kelly) Barretto is in law enforcement in Northern California. Considering I thought he looked and acted like the 'Ponch' character from the series 'CHiPs,' his career may have been predestined.

Coach Kelly retired from coaching football and lives in Northern California.

John 'Murdock' McClellan works for the department of corrections. He is married with three daughters.

Mark 'Baro' Baranowski works with computers in instructional design. He lives in Texas and has two children.

Bryan Batchan went on to play college football and still lives in Solano County.

Mike 'Spartacus' Holovach became a golf professional and lives in Florida. He is married.

Pat Woods still plays the guitar and lives in Vacaville, California. He is an IT manager. He is married.

Darren Rysden works for the department of corrections.

Greg Kling is married with two sons. He lives in Seattle, Washington.

Bruce Batchan, Sr. passed away. (RIP)

Mr. Elkins passed away after a long illness. (RIP)

Cathy Price is married with two sons and works in San Francisco, California.

Pete Watts works in the grocery business and lives in Northern Oregon.

Coach Hatcher retired from Golden West as a teacher and lives in Tennessee. He is married.

Coach Moore retired from teaching in the Travis Unified School District and still lives in Solano County. He is married.

Coach Cesna retired from teaching and passed away after a long illness. (RIP)

Broyce Batchan went on to play college football and is the CEO of a music company. He lives in Northern California and is married with children.

Frank Reyes works in law enforcement in Northern California. He is married with children.

Erwin Hardy works on the East Coast as a trucker. He has children.

Robert Kulinski works for Union Pacific Railroad and lives in Northern California. He is married with children.

Ed Serpas retired from teaching at Vanden.

Coach 'Bev' is retired and married with children. He still lives in Solano County. He spent 28 years coaching football. He left Vanden for UOP, then went on to Solano Community College as the head coach for 12 seasons. In 2005, he was inducted into the Solano College Athletic Hall of Fame along with Ed Serpas.

Coach Harden retired from the Travis Unified School District.

'Psycho' character and sweatshirt. Psycho was left behind on the gridiron in 1984. The sweatshirt's whereabouts are unknown.

Tami Hatcher lives on the East Coast and is married with children.

Andre and my mom broke up. He still lives in Northern California.

Rob Alexander is in law enforcement in California.

Lesly Barnard is married with children. She lives in Solano County.

Coach Newsom continued working in the Travis Unified District until he passed away suddenly. (RIP)

Kenny Tarver is in law enforcement in California.

Ron 'Ronnie' Beverly, Jr. played football and baseball at UOP. He is a football coach in Solano County and was the coach for Lesly Barnard's son.

Chris Stiltner works for the state of California and has taught baseball at Dixon High School.

Coach Ordez passed away years ago. (RIP)

Dave Haupt is a teacher in Northern California. He is married with children.

Bill Green joined the Air Force. He is married.

Lyent Hogue passed away shortly before the reunion. (RIP)

Larry Hogue is a coach for the varsity football program at Vanden.

Julie Leopold and I reconnected when I was 22 but we lost contact shortly after.

Gem (Nalkiran) Bertone is a general manager of an auto dealership in Texas. He is married with children.

Joe 'Big Joe' Leonard retired from the U.S. Marine Corps after 20 years. He lives in Southern California and is married with a son.

Darrick Peterkin retired from the U.S. Army. He lives on the East Coast and is married.

Alvin Baldwin joined the U.S. Army and he lives on the East Coast.

Maurice Gwinn followed his father's footsteps into religion. He still lives in California.

Michael Farace joined the U.S. Marine Corps and retired after 20 years. He lives on the East Coast and is married with children.

Eric 'Big E' Barnes still lives in Solano County.

Paul Holes became the District Attorney Chief of Forensics Investigator for Costra County in California.

Coach Kiefer passed away some years back. I was able to visit him a few months before his death. (RIP)

Stephen Carpenter lives in San Francisco, California and is married with children.

Chuck Coates worked for the Dixon Police department and passed away several years ago. (RIP)

Danny Miller joined the Air Force and lives in Texas. He is married with children.

Cliff Roberts lives in Northern California and was a candidate for the 2016 Presidency of the United States representing the Humane Party. He has children.

J-p Smith lives in Northern California. He is married with children.

Sherman Pruitt works in law enforcement.

James 'Tuck' Tucker still lives in Vacaville.

Derrick Davis works for Costco and lives in Arizona.

Eugene (Burton) van Eikenhorst lives in the Netherlands. He is married and is a father.

Louis Adams retired from the U.S. Army. He lives in Northern California and is married with children.

Steve Harrison lives in Las Vegas and works in the casino industry.

Steve Crittenden has been housed on death row at San Quentin prison.

Chaplain Gwinn passed away some years ago. (RIP)

Scot Sherman works in home improvement and lives on the East Coast. He is married with children.

Rob Cantley works as a Sr. Communication Engineer and lives on the East Coast. He is married.

Kye Purnell Jones works for the state of California. He is married and has children.

Reginald Stover lives in Alabama. He is married with children.

Alan Casner works for Harley Davidson in Northern California. He is married with children.

I live in the Pacific Northwest, and I'm writing more books.

Eleven years after our undefeated comeback season in 1984, the 1995 Vanden Varsity squad recorded their own perfect record, going 13-0. They were ranked the number-one team in California Division 4 football by Cal-Hi Sports, besting our number-two ranking eleven seasons earlier.

Divisions A, B, and C were replaced at the start of the 1985 season with 1, 2, and 3. Our 1984 squad was the last Vanden football team to play in Division A football.

In five decades of football at Vanden, only two varsity football teams have recorded perfect seasons. We were the first. Only three Vanden football squads have won the Sac-Joaquin Section Title. We were the second.

On September 12, 2014, Vanden High School celebrated 50 years of Viking football. Former players and coaches attended from different years. Vanden's first skipper Ed Serpas attended, along with my former coach Ron Harden from our 1983 squad. John 'Murdock' McClellan #65, Coach Bev, Louis Adams #19, and I represented our 1984 12-0 championship team. We are shown together in the photo below.

Collecting data and putting this book together was a very large project that was made easier because of three of my teammates. I would like to thank Jeff Martin #52 for providing 30-plus-year-old newspaper articles that he had saved. Jeff took the time to scan the articles and email each one to me. I would like to thank Mark 'Baro' Baranowski #64 for taking the time to design the book cover. It was his vision and artistic skills that created it. Finally, I would like to thank David Reyes #24 for making multiple visits to the libraries with me and by himself, checking old newspaper archives on microfilm for data.

I'm very grateful for their assistance and lifelong friendships. I couldn't have done this without them.

Below are photos of my friends and teammates Mark 'Baro' Baranowski #64 and Jeff Martin #52. Mark sporting his 'no sock' look at practice and Jeff as a young trencher with his dad.

From 1980 to 1984 I was blessed to play on the gridiron with the best of friends, teammates, and coaches. They were something to see. Though their jerseys read Vikings and Redskins, they were much more than that. They were giants, and their play was legendary.

In 1984, the Vanden football program was perfect. The varsity and JV squads combined for a 21-0 winning record. The foes we faced, we vanquished as Vikings, friends, and brothers.

We Took Names

| PAGE FOUR | THE VALHALLA | MONDAY, OCTOBER 19, 1964 |

VIKING BATTLEGROUND
Varsity Vikings 1st in SCAL QB Sneak

The Vikings final TD came on Crowe's third scoring pass, this time to flanker Ron Beverly. The first quarter touchdown which enabled Vanden to tie the Rams at the half came after Dixon fumbled a punt and six plays later, fullback John Carson crashed over from the six-inch line.

...Yarsity coach Tom Kiefer kept his promise to his linemen by doing one minute of reaction drills following the Vikings 12-6 win over Winters... Tom Kam, the Vikings' pre-season quarterback before he cracked an ankle bone, is expected to play for the first time Friday verses Benicia

The above image is from Vanden's school newspaper, The Valhalla Vol. 1 No. 1, October 19, 1964. It mentions Coach Bev as a flanker on the football team and Kiefer as the varsity line coach. The newspaper said the squad was 2-0 at the time. The image contains three parts of the Valhalla pieced together to capture all three elements. Courtesy of Vanden High School and alumnus William Marks class of 1973. Used with permission.

In the above photos I am shown during my four years playing football at Vanden High School. The top left photo was during game #10 against Oak Ridge in the first round playoff for the Sac-Joaquin Section title. It was taken from an article courtesy of the Reporter. We won 35-27. That photo shows me on our George Gammon Field. The other three photos were all taken on our practice fields for team photographs.

I'll never forget those trips on the Beast, or the first time I put on shoulder pads. After all these years I can still see that view through my facemask and feel the collision of a hard hit. I remember that 32 Dive. I dove far and held onto the ball. I remember all my coaches and their love for the game. I learned much from them that I still follow today. I remember being a spectator from the sidelines when I was hurt. I remember that 1984 season, and wish I could go back to enjoy it one more time. I remember the jubilation of victory and the sadness of defeat. I remember the sound of those cleats. I can still hear them. I remember those huddles—they felt like home. I miss those moments my friends and I shared. We lived an unforgettable journey, and what we accomplished together, time can never take from us. We needed the game of football, and the gridiron forever bonded us as brothers. I wouldn't change those years for anything. They still bring a smile. It was one incredible ride.

Writing this book about my teammates, coaches, friends, and family was rewarding and emotional. I'm very fortunate I've had the opportunity to share it. I'd like to thank everyone mentioned within these pages. In my eyes you'll always be the best. I hope this story really honors you.

There's a quote from the 2000 football film "The Replacements," which states, "And greatness, no matter how brief, stays with a man."

It does.

Jeff Rooney ("Psycho") #55

Addendum

Oct. 11, 2016, the squad met for our second reunion. Teammates Derrick Davis #71 and Darrick Peterkin (1983) joined us. Neither made our first reunion. July 30, 2017, we held our third reunion. Players from other years joined us. Bill Green (1982—p.97), Juan Martinez (1981), Willie Lipkin, Bob White (1975) represented their squads. Coach Harden from my 1983 team was present.

It was the first time I had seen Bill since high school. We talked about my brother Tim and shared old stories. It brought back many memories. Some I had forgotten from that long ago era. It really was the time of Vikings, friends and family.

Coach Ron Harden still had a love for the game. As we talked, I could see him directing me in the trenches three decades earlier. He taught me much that season in 1983 and made me a better player. He still had the mustache; but was no longer grizzled.

Where are my former Redskin teammates? Mike Lindsey is back living in Fairfield, and he became a football coach. Anthony Gonsalves still lives in California. Kenny Herbert was murdered in 1991 in the Sacramento, California area.

One year after our 30th reunion, I began to suffer motor skill deterioration, which affected my speech and movement. I started having seizures. I've been in neuropathy physical therapy, along with speech therapy. My condition

Addendum—cont.

hasn't been diagnosed. According to the neurologists I don't have Parkinson's, ALS, or MS. We're seeing some success with Parkinson's drugs lessening my symptoms.

I'm told my football years may be responsible, but they don't know at this point. During my time on the gridiron I may have suffered several concussions. The only documented one was during the 1983 season—which was classified a major concussion—because I lost consciousness for three hours.

If it's Chronic Traumatic Encephalopathy (CTE) that has been found in the brains of deceased NFL players and other athletes, I'm told it won't be diagnosed until my brain tissue is checked postmortem. I've informed my family I want my brain donated for an evaluation. CTE is caused by repetitive brain trauma. It's a progressive, degenerative condition with no known treatment.

I never envisioned this ending when I began to write our story. In the ultimate gridiron surprise: the thing that gave me the best times—may be the thing that's bringing me the worst; the thing that taught me camaraderie and relying on others—may have caused me to battle my greatest foe alone. And the thing that gave me the most—might be the thing that takes the most from me. This is just one more opponent I have to face, and I will battle it until the last whistle. Football was worth the risk for me, and I have no regrets. I know that sounds crazy; but I truly needed the game.

www.ingramcontent.com/pod-product-compliance
Lightning Source LLC
Chambersburg PA
CBHW051932290426
44110CB00015B/1949